The Q-Sort
in Character Appraisal

The **Q-Sort**
in Character Appraisal

Encoding Subjective Impressions
of Persons Quantitatively

JACK BLOCK

American Psychological Association
Washington, DC

Published by
American Psychological Association
750 First Street, NE
Washington, DC 20002
www.apa.org

To order
APA Order Department
P.O. Box 92984
Washington, DC 20090-2984
Tel: (800) 374-2721; Direct: (202) 336-5510
Fax: (202) 336-5502; TDD/TTY: (202) 336-6123
Online: www.apa.org/books/
E-mail: order@apa.org

In the U.K., Europe, Africa, and the Middle East, copies may be ordered from
American Psychological Association
3 Henrietta Street
Covent Garden, London
WC2E 8LU England

Typeset in Goudy by Circle Graphics, Inc., Columbia, MD

Printer: Book-mart Press, North Bergen, NJ
Cover Designer: Naylor Design, Washington, DC
Technical/Production Editor: Tiffany L. Klaff

The opinions and statements published are the responsibility of the authors, and such opinions and statements do not necessarily represent the policies of the American Psychological Association.

Library of Congress Cataloging-in-Publication Data

Block, Jack, 1924–
    The Q-sort in character appraisal : encoding subjective impressions of persons quantitatively / Jack Block. — 1st ed.
        p. cm.
    Includes bibiographical references and index.
    ISBN-13: 978-1-4338-0315-4
    ISBN-10: 1-4338-0315-1
    1. Personality assessment. 2. Psychiatry—Research. 3. Psychology—Methodology. I. Title.

    BF698.4.B55 2008
    155.2'8—dc22

                                                                2007033130

British Library Cataloguing-in-Publication Data
A CIP record is available from the British Library.

Printed in the United States of America
First Edition

A philosopher must be very honest to avail himself
of no aid from poetry or rhetoric

—Schopenhauer

CONTENTS

ACKNOWLEDGMENTS

Any work has untraceable links to earlier contributors, to colleagues, and to friends. This effort in its several phases has benefited from many persons at one time or another. I recognize, forlornly, that I have failed to remember a number of names from long, long ago that properly should have been recognized. For this I am sad and sorry.

I have better memory for the help received more recently. Parts of this volume have been critically read by a number of people and have become much the better for having run these friendly gauntlets. Various elliptical, tangential, and circular arguments have been brought closer—if not entirely—to earth and I have been able to correct certain errors before the embarrassment of seeing them in print. I have not accepted all of the offered suggestions for, on certain partisan issues, I have chosen to express my own standpoint. I have been made aware, however, and I trust subsequent pages now reflect this recognition, of the diversity of viewpoints on some of the issues treated in this volume. Of course, for such errors as still remain, I alone am responsible. For their incisive and yet not ego-wounding cognitive help—recently and from other times—I am much indebted to Jeanne H. Block, Lee J. Cronbach, Lew Goldberg, William Grove, Robert E. Harris, Robert R. Holt, and others beyond recall. For computer help in preparing this volume, I am providentially grateful to my offspring, Carol and David. The organizational structure of the chapters has benefited importantly from the suggestions of Emily Leonard.

This work was supported initially by National Institute of Mental Health Research Grants M-1078 and M-1680. The aid afforded by these grants helped immensely in beginning and later extending this effort.

In both her professional and nonprofessional roles, I am indebted, deeply, to my late wife, Jeanne, for her faith and encouragement during the earlier part of this enterprise.

The Q-Sort
in Character Appraisal

INTRODUCTION

In everyday lay life, person evaluations by an observer are of central significance. Person evaluations are usually formed or inferred on an ad hoc, informal basis; they are based almost universally on *subjective impressions* often of great moment. People in everyday life make many such subjective but far-reaching person evaluations quickly, casually, and intuitively. Individuals in certain professions—psychiatrists, clinical psychologists, personality assessors, developmentalists, social workers, psychotherapists, personnel specialists, lawyers and judges, close teachers, and sundry others—are especially dependent on their subjective impressions of a person. These impressions can have fundamental life consequences for the person involved. By and large, the accuracy of these subjective impressions is only rarely evaluated, given the bustle of busy professional lives. However, such judgments are omnipresent in all social situations and acted upon, in effect, as valid.

As a separate endeavor, the study of personality attributions—their accuracy and errors—has compiled a long, complicated history in experimental social and cognitive psychology. Definitionally, persons have *attributes*: Observers or appraisers provide *attributions* in regard to those person attributes. The conjunction of *attributes* with *attributions* results in *allegations*. Efforts to understand attribution largely have focused on the psychological principles underlying attribution, per se. A number of attributional error proclivities have been identified, but there has been remarkable indifference in the accuracy or verisimilitude of allegations about persons. For the purposes in this volume, consideration of these alternatively oriented efforts is largely peripheral and abstruse. The motivated reader may gain useful perspective and insight on this particular body of research from the catholic review by Funder (1995).

In what follows, an individual—lay or professional—involved in person evaluations is termed, interchangeably, an *observer, evaluator, appraiser, judge, assessor,* or *experiencer*. The individual involved may be a highly trained, experienced, credentialed professional who is evaluating a person with a mental disability or an unseasoned college student who is evaluating a prospective roommate or date—both use subjective impressions.

When seriously reflected on, person evaluations have been recognized as often unreliable and as conveying judgments that can be quite amiss. Indeed, in the field of psychiatry a half-century ago, the anomalous evaluative divergences so often manifested by clinicians who are assessing the same person came to be perceived within and beyond the mental health community as intellectually devastating. In response, the American Psychiatric Association catalyzed creation of the *Diagnostic and Statistical Manual of Mental Disorders, Fourth Edition, Text Revision* (2000) to serve as a clarifying, universally applicable compendium for diagnosis of psychiatric disorders. However, despite successive revisions, in practice the *Diagnostic and Statistical Manual of Mental Disorders* has proven to be diagnostically unstable and otherwise controversial (e.g., Kirk, 2004; Kutchins & Kirk, 1997; Widiger & Trull, 2007).[1]

The diagnostic failings of contemporary psychiatric or clinical psychology practice, evidenced in the empirical literature, argue tellingly that different observers who provide person evaluations of the *same* individual must achieve better correspondence if the semantic haze is to be lifted. Evaluation correspondence is no guarantee of the validity of person evaluations, but it remains a precondition. This premise for progress frequently fails to obtain.

For subjective impressions of a person to be respected, a basis for calibrating these impressions must be established. Without the opportunity of evaluating the correspondence existing between various subjective impressions, such evaluations have obscure or uncertain implication. Person evaluations, in which may be imbedded the most perceptive of recognitions or the most deadly of distortions, cannot be granted credence or disallowed given an inability to align and contemplate alternatively proposed understandings. Therefore, practitioners and investigators must ensure that person evaluations are *commensurable* or serve a common standard. Only then can differ-

---

[1]The concerned reader may wish to reference GOOGLE SCHOLAR, questing "*DSM* CRITIQUES."

ently based subjective impressions and opinions be compared so that recognitions and disagreements indisputably can be seen.

It has not been explicitly recognized or emphasized sufficiently that a major reason for discordant mental health or characterological evaluations by appraisers devolves from their differential language usage. Character formulations by different observers in regard to the same person tend to be expressed in disparate terms. If only for such linguistic reasons, the extent of agreement or disagreement in regard to a person's characteristics may not be seriously discernible. Apparent disagreements between observers may seem to exist when only fortuitous differences in phrase making are actually involved; actual agreements may be hidden by different lexical practice.

This treatise reintroduces, with appreciable recasting and elaboration, an evaluative method from 50 years ago that since has demonstrated a good deal of usefulness (Block, 1961). Long out of print in its original form and often unknown even in psychology, it is extensively furthered now by later conceptual, methodological, and research recognitions, extensive and diverse empirical experience, the envisaging of broader contexts of application, and the advent of computer resources to resolve analytical concerns.

The method is the California Q-sort procedure (the CQ procedure). The procedure is specifically implemented through the California Adult Q-set (Revised Adult Set; CAQ) or the California Child Q-set (CCQ), a somewhat modified CAQ more suitable for describing children and preadolescents. The designation, CQ procedure, should be understood as implying use of either the CAQ or the CCQ.

The CQ procedure is intended for use as a descriptive language by intelligent, motivationally sensitive, nonjudgmental, culturally aware observers. It is purposed to capture the character of a person as it is subjectively apprehended by an interested appraiser. By the nature of its development, it is especially suitable for individuals who are working in the mental health domain, but it has proven also to be surprisingly fruitful in a variety of fields in which person assessment by socially intelligent, often nonprofessional observers is involved.

The CQ procedure guarantees *commensurate* person evaluations by providing a standard vocabulary—a comprehensive set of person descriptors—conjoined with a prescribed method of using this vocabulary—what may be called its "syntax." This standard language, laboriously evolved and embodying a good deal of thought and experience, is a way of encoding complex, configural descriptions of persons in a form suitable for communication, for quantitative comparison, and for statistical evaluation. As attested in later chapters in this volume, the CQ procedure is well-supported empirically in diverse studies. The CQ procedure has the large promise of demonstrating the deep usefulness of commensurable observer evaluations in clinical, research, personnel, or other contexts. A most rich informational resource—

the perceptions and knowledge of psychologically perceptive observers—achieves the potential of coming into versatile and fruitful research use. Many psychologists and psychiatrists are likely to find the method especially congruent with their own descriptive and research requirements.

Of special and unique interest, the property of commensurateness permits and encourages the aggregation of differently provided CQ descriptions of the same person. Such composited CQ descriptions have proven unusually productive empirically, dependably bringing out subtle clinical recognitions that have large consequence. Further by-products of the commensurateness property are that it facilitates the referencing of an individual's CQ-person description to psychiatric diagnostic or conceptual CQ prototypes and that it provides appropriate numerical data for a broad variety of statistical analyses.

This compendium is not meant for a quick, casual skim. Besides its immediate purpose of bringing forward the CQ procedure, it serves a larger function as well. Although the CQ procedure has been used in numerous and diverse studies, its principles, rationale, methodological intricacies, and wider possibilities have been insufficiently discussed. Herein, details of the CQ-sort procedure, previously uncollected and unconnected, are brought together, reviewed, and evaluated. Some features and capabilities of the method are made public that until now have been the knowledge, lore, and savvy of relatively few methodologists.

A deliberate effort has been made to discuss procedural details to justify the decisions reached. Consequently, the reader is in a position to agree or to disagree with the course taken rather than being asked to blindly accept fiat or fait accompli. This approach, however, is attended by its own disadvantage: The reader may feel weighed down sometimes with methodological detail, seeming digression, and inordinate reflection as the exposition is carried through. Skimming text may save the reader some time but likely at the cost of CQ understanding.

Beyond this prefatory warning, readers may wish to consult certain chapters again, to refresh their specific understandings. With this likelihood in mind, some principles judged important to remember have been deliberately reconveyed.

I

THE CALIFORNIA Q-SORT PROCEDURE: EXPRESSIVE INTUITIVELY AND EMPIRICALLY

1

A PERSPECTIVE ON SUBJECTIVE PERSON EVALUATIONS

Before speaking for the singular value of having observers use a special, prearranged language, it is in order to indicate why subjective impressions of persons are inevitably influential and how it is proposed to meet the criticism that subjective person evaluations, often very consequential in the real world, earlier have received.

TWO KINDS OF PSYCHOLOGICAL DATA

In the broad study of human beings, a method of person characterization is required. How has this desideratum been sought? What are the potential ways of developing sufficient person information? Two approaches have been emphasized. In assessment psychology, the use of self-report personality questionnaires—what has been called S (for *self*) *data*—has been predominant. S data are data collected directly from individuals in regard to the behavior, attitudes, feelings, and characteristics they acknowledge or inadvertently communicate.

9

In psychiatry, the predominant approach has been on the informal, unsystematic, too often sketchy, subjective impression and evaluation of a person (patient) by a presumably astute, well-grounded, often clinically experienced observer—what has been called O (for *observer*) *data*. However, the lexical divergence invariably characterizing different subjective interpretations of the same person has rendered such O data incommensurable and therefore difficult to integrate.

Self-report inventories are extraordinarily, even seductively convenient to use. In the context of a pressured professional life, they are easy to seize upon, administer, and analyze. Over the years, their range of inquiry has importantly increased and the best of them have attained appreciable validity, as evaluated by various criteria. In some planning for the forthcoming fifth edition of the *Diagnostic and Statistical Manual of Mental Disorders*, it has been suggested that S data may provide a beginning foundation for subsequent psychiatric diagnosis (Widiger & Lowe, 2007; Widiger & Trull, 2007).

However, in disquieting ways, self-report inventories are widely recognized as insufficient in their coverage or penetration and often are distorting. In self-responding to questionnaires or inventories, the reacting person may be deliberately deceptive or unwittingly defensive or may not be sufficiently self-observant and insightful to be authentically revealing. Should one uncritically accept a layperson's response to inventory self-questions about, for example, narcissism, hostility, sexuality, repression, jealousy, and compulsivity? In almost all circumstances, the perfunctory, impersonal administration of self-questionnaires understandably activates a layperson's façade for socially desirable self-presentation. Self-report measures can be helpful, certainly, and are much improved when subtly effective validity scales are also incorporated to identify anomalous respondents. For many involved in person evaluation, however, self-report inventories are reasonably viewed as providing information that cannot be fully or sufficiently relied on.

Because of continuing and likely endless limitations in the realm of S data person assessment, the ancient subjective impression approach— O data—remains paramount among mental health practitioners and therefore still has a presumptive function to serve. A place continues for the complex assessment of persons (patients) by subjective evaluations offered by intelligent, mature, motivated, well-grounded observers. Such assessments, if suitably rendered, can provide a basis for decision in regard to others and various life criteria. The California Q-sort (CQ) procedure, as will be seen, was introduced as a way of transforming an observer's *informal* subjective impression or evaluation of a person into an explicit, quantifiable form that was commensurate with the impressions or evaluations held by other observers and could have a larger implication.

THE INELUCTABLE ROLE OF PERSON EVALUATIONS

A foundational reason for the universal use of subjective impressions of persons is that they offer everyone an arresting, convenient, and most immediate kind of information—they are intuitively compelling. Additionally, such observations are often the only kind of person information available. In particular, the professional and scientific enterprises of psychiatry and personality psychology likely will never be able to escape reliance on informed, considered, but subjective opinion as basic information about persons.

Observer evaluations are so central an aspect of everyday life because of their "face validity." The observer reasons—usually—that the apparent meaning or "surface" behavior of the observed person importantly signifies its psychological meaning. Although the face validity of behavior that is directly observed may be misleading, direct observation begins as—and may remain—an informational resource imperatively impressing the observer. To understand why observer evaluations are so importunate and influential, one must remember the perpetual difficulty confronting appraisers alert to objective, discernible indicators of the person's underlying nature.

Herewith, a brief disquisition on the nature and relevance of observable person indicators or signs: In considering any indicator about the nature of a person, there is the presumption that the indicator is a veritable manifestation from the person of the underlying aspect the observer is interested in evaluating. To the extent this correspondence fails to obtain, the observer evaluation will possess only irrelevant or uncertain meaning.

How is it "known" that an observable indicator believably and sufficiently signifies the person's underlying attribute or concept of interest? The answer, briefly and unhappily, is that it cannot ever be certainly "known." This is in the nature of theory and theory establishing (cf. e.g., Cronbach & Meehl, 1955). Concepts always have "surplus meaning," have implications extending beyond any manifest behavioral indicator. By the same token, any particular observation is an "insufficient translation" of the underlying attribute.

Absence of certainty, however, by no means requires an absence of likelihood. One begins tentatively with the hope that a nomological network of specifically sought empirical relationships will emerge, one coherent with the underlying framework that prompts the search. When this eventuality develops, then—in a kind of reciprocal validation—the empirically supported behavioral indicators give flesh to the appraiser's implicitly projected conceptual skeleton.

The foregoing simply restates some elementary principles in the understandings of science; it also portrays the nature of developmental ontology, of how the infant learns about the world. Its pertinence here is to call attention to the obscurity existing at the beginning of the knowledge-seeking process—

in science and in the infant's cognitive graspings—before the required scientific or child's *nomological net* has developed.

Initially, before a consistent, interlocking collectivity of construct-supporting empirical relationships has been found, particular evaluations of behaviors cannot be justified. Instead, there is recourse only to projected or anticipated connections, not yet corroborated. The congruence between a particular behavioral indicator and a particular presumed interpretation is proposed or inferred by the observer out of personal conviction or observation that it is *appropriate* or *fruitful* to do so. That is, at the outset, the immediate basis of the conviction that a behavioral indicator is related to an underlying facet or attribute is nothing more than and nothing less than the highly personal and tentative inference that it is *reasonable* to do so—the ability to convince oneself of the relevance of the behavioral indicator for the underlying attribute of interest.

Let us presume that an observer is bright, psychologically oriented, value neutral, and has lived in the prevailing cultural social world for a quarter century. Over years of living in an interpersonal and intrapersonal world, the observer will have had manifold learning opportunities to detect and to personally, knowingly improvise behavioral indicators—subtle and obvious—of consequential psychological significance. Socially intelligent, thoughtful lay people—not just professionals—universally develop such experientially reinforced patterns of anticipation, evolving some degree of observational expertise.

By lifelong learning, all socially intelligent individuals become observational "experts" simply by growing up in an interpersonal and intrapersonal world, often holding rather consensual understandings. We come to recognize that a particular behavioral indicator reasonably has a particular psychological meaning. A particular behavioral indicator becomes probabilistically or conditionally tied to a particular psychological meaning. Only after much interlocking and supportive empiricism can a behavioral indicator first proposed only as reasonable take on a more general understanding.

Thus, for example, it is reasonable intuitively, experientially, to consider *heart rate variability*—personally experienced or observed in another—as an indicator of underlying anxiety. It would have been less reasonable—intuitively, experientially—to argue *buttoning speed* is an anxiety indicator. Or to reflect *conservatism*, it is more reasonable to note an individual's political party affiliation than the theatre aisle the individual characteristically takes, left or right. Such proposed reasonable indicators may contribute to the emerging nomological network for person understanding.

To return now to the face validity power of subjective impressions, observer evaluations stand in faithful correspondence with the observer's apperception of and beliefs about where the person (patient, social object) is positioned on attributes of interest. This is not to say that observers are necessarily accurate or possess truth; their degree of veracity remains to be evidenced. The point is more that observers—on the basis of having lived in the social world, intuition, and perhaps augmented by professional training and experience—are likely to have developed some evaluative acumen in discerning a person's important psychological attributes. These subjectively formed understandings, however reported or acted on, are interpreted as implicative of significant but physically intangible psychological attributes.

The dean of a medical school, distressed at the burgeoning of medical selection procedures all of marginal validity, once sharpened the point this way: Given the selection efficacy of contemporary psychological tests, in choosing a mate would one be willing to trust this fundamental selection to available objective measures or would a personal interview be desirable as well?

Certainly, a great saving in time and cost would result from total elimination of observer evaluations. Such elimination is unlikely, however, not simply because their widespread use is already ensconced but because they are powerfully rooted in the observer's life-evolved, complex understanding of the implications of social interactions. It may be more consequential, therefore, to see whether such inevitable subjective evaluations can be used in important, validity improving, and useful ways.

IMPROVING OBSERVER EVALUATIONS

If observer evaluations—O data—are to be used, what can be done to improve this modus operandi?

Two essentially different ways in which observer evaluations have been registered may be distinguished—the *variable-centered approach* and the *person-centered approach*.

Conventional person research has emphasized the variable-centered perspective and has used methods and analyses appropriate to ascertaining the correlations among variables within a specific group of persons. Person evaluations, in this context, exist within a "normative" frame of reference (Cattell, 1944), for example, a person is rated on a particular variable vis-à-vis a specified reference or normative group. A typical instance of normative rating might be the assigning, on a 5-point scale, of degrees of *masculinity, conservatism, warmth,* or *neuroticism* to each of 100 male college students.

Normative ratings have delimited implication because they have reference only to a specific, arbitrarily selected, anchoring sample. Furthermore, normative ratings—each formulated separately—do not reflect the *coherence* of the individual, the particular conjunction of attributes within the person.

The variable-centered, normative way to the specification of a person is frequently used; the psychological, psychiatric, and developmental literature is replete with examples. It provides data in a convenient and quantitative form, and the approach has not been unproductive. For a thoughtful presentation and general discussion of the methodology of normative rating, refer to an old but still admirably explanatory chapter by Guilford (1954, chap. 11). The volume by Nunnally and Bernstein (1994) may also be helpful.

The person-centered approach takes a different tack and may have been first intimated by Stern (1911). The concern here has been with the close characterization of an *individual* person. Person-centered description seeks to convey the individual's crucial characteristics and their intertwining, the appositions and oppositions within the individual, the individual's personality *system,* given the cultural environment. When a particular person is studied intensively and prolongedly, the interrelationships of attributes within that individual—in terms of which the evaluation is expressed—take on system-organized qualities. The observer perceives certain couplings and contingent, contextual dependencies as indicating the functional behavioral or perceptual laws and predilections governing the particular person. Because manifold patterns of covariation and contingency are observed, because different systems of personality functioning exist, it follows that a configurational method of person evaluation that can encompass and then re-issue this kind of information is required. So runs the person-centered argument.

The prime distinction between the variable-centered approach and the person-centered approach has been very aptly expressed analogically: "If the variable-centered approach describes the building blocks of personality, the person-centered approach describes the building" (Scholte, van Lieshout, de Wit, & van Aken, 2005, p. 289).

Although the variable-centered use of ratings has predominated in the mainstream of psychological research, for many and especially in the clinical field, the person-centered orientation has had a fundamental resonance. Traditionally, the person-centered orientation has been manifested through *clinical formulations*—variegated informal portrayals, verbal or written, of an individual. When well done, these can suggest the configurational essence of a person. However, such formulations have tended in clinical practice to be sketchy and, when created by different clinicians or assessors with reference to the same individual, embarrassingly disparate. A major reason for the problem stems from differential, highly variable language usage.

Given a metascientific commitment to the person-centered approach, the problem of differences in language use necessarily requires that subjectively based evaluations be *encoded* in a form subsequently commensurate and therefore comparable. Such subjective encodings, when operationalized, become numerical in form and result in what Cattell (1944) has labeled "ipsative" data, wherein attributes are considered relative to each other with respect to a particular person.

The CQ procedure exemplifies ipsativity, involving a scaling method providing person-centered data. The procedure requires the observer to subjectively arrange the standard set of person descriptors to characterize their *salience*—positive or negative—with regard to the designated individual. Degree of judged salience in regard to the individual is the common principle underlying all subjective decisions by CQ assessors.

For example, the assessor may be asked to judge the relative salience of the Q descriptors, "behaves in a masculine style or manner" and "favors conservative values in a variety of areas," as these qualities apply within the particular person being described. Is the first descriptor a more crucial attribute of the person than the second or is the second more salient than the first in understanding the person? Or are the descriptors undistinguishable as to salience, also an option? Through multiple comparisons and choices among Q descriptors relative to each other, the CQ procedure contributes a special kind of thoughtful observer evaluation, a means of configurationally quantifying the observer's impressions and understandings of the designated person.

However, a number of hurdles must be cleared before subjective evaluations become methodologically viable. A variety of widely unconsidered factors adversely influencing observer evaluations require attention and control. Only if subjective impressions are carefully developed and articulated can they issue trustworthy and impressive evaluative data. The next chapter demonstrates the utility and scientific capability of the method; succeeding chapters are devoted to methodological considerations, illustrations of various research applications, and derivative implications.

2

THE CALIFORNIA Q-SORT
PROCEDURE DESCRIBED
AND DEMONSTRATED

The California Q-sort (CQ) procedure is a method for portraying in a comprehensive, articulated, and commensurate configurational form the subjective evaluation of a person formulated by a competent observer. The CQ procedure consists of a carefully selected and carefully evolved set of person descriptors (i.e., the California Adult Q-set [CAQ] or the California Child Q-set [CCQ]), coupled with a standard way of ordering these descriptor variables. The CQ procedure may be viewed as providing a "Basic English" for anyone—but usually psychologists, psychiatrists, and those in the field of mental health—to use in their descriptive evaluations of individual persons. The CQ character depiction, once developed, subsequently permits quantitative evaluation.

Ideally—and it will never be ideal—the CQ procedure permits the portrayal of any kind of psychopathology and any kind of normality. Despite the constraints the method necessarily imposes, the descriptions possible through the CQ procedure should be perceived by the appraising observer as registering a sufficient and sensitive characterization of the person being described. The claim of a good language for person description can be only that its inexpressibles are infrequent enough that the language remains essentially serviceable.

17

As will be seen in the next chapter, the process by which the CQ language sequentially evolved ensured that it increasingly would grow to express more and more of the aspects of person evaluation competent observers believed to be important. To the extent the procedure fails in this aspiration and to the extent it may be deemed unable to reflect the discriminations and integrations the assessor would wish to report, we would judge the method as deficient.

No claim is made that the CQ procedure represents an ultimate way of portraying the necessary and sufficient facets in terms of which observational understanding can be registered. Rather, the CQ procedure, by virtue of its rationale and developmental evolution, may provide a broadly ranging, widely useful language for person description.

The CQ procedure derives from many years of conceptual effort and empirical usage. About 100 psychologists and psychiatrists have contributed to CAQ and CCQ development and 100 or so studies using the CQ method have entered the psychological literature. The psychometric properties of the method have been found to be substantial and, as will be shown later, the CQ procedure has generated an impressive set of empirical findings.

The person attributes of which the standard language is composed come from no one theoretical conceptualization because no systematic, exhaustive, and fully acceptable view of the person exists; there is no even semiformal personological system that includes the complete array of character attributes observers have come to believe it is important to consider. If it did, the necessary and sufficient language to portray person functioning would be known, and no problem of language choice would arise. In an endlessly imperfect situation, however, some reasonable criteria for constituting a still-expressive person-descriptive vocabulary had to be found. The solution adopted attempts, as will be seen, to respect contemporary informed opinions as to what aspects of character have import. The consequence is that the CQ language has links to a variety of theoretical orientations; it enjoys many of the emphases (but also the deficiencies) of contemporary views and in content is familiar to trained workers in psychiatry, clinical psychology, and personality psychology.

Also, as elucidated in chapter 1, bright appraising adults developmentally have long learned the subtle rules and manifestations of social interplay so that the cognitive task presented by the CQ procedure does not faze them. One does not have to be an experienced clinical practitioner to meaningfully use the CQ procedure.

With this perspective on the reasoning and intentions underlying the CQ procedure, the effort may now be considered in more detail.

THE CQ METHOD DESCRIBED

It will help the reader new to the CQ method and its relevance for encoding observer evaluations of a person if the essentials of the method are first described specifically, and then two engaging applications of the procedure are illustrated. The burden of understanding the Q procedure can be faced with greater resolve if its nature and immediate usefulness are first made apparent.

In the CQ method, the judge or evaluator is given the set of CQ-descriptor statements previously developed and fixed on. For the CAQ, Appendix A lists the 100 CAQ descriptors. In Appendix B are listed the 100 descriptors of the CCQ. These sets of statements constitute, respectively, the entire vocabulary the appraiser is permitted to use to psychologically describe an adult person or a young child.

A language, however, is more than a vocabulary; it requires as well a syntactic structure—the vocabulary must be used in comparable ways. Special features of the CQ method stem from this latter requirement; descriptions in the standard vocabulary must be offered within a standard grammar so that a standard language results. By so doing, psychological descriptions of an individual are both qualitatively informative and quantitatively comparable.

Usually, the CQ descriptors are printed separately on 3 × 5 cards, and the CQ statements—randomly shuffled—are spread on a large table (a logistically simple computer method using MS Word 2003 to physically create the necessary Q-set cards for any Q-set is specified in Appendix G).

This card display is not simply a matter of convention; it permits a first arrangement or sorting of the descriptors by the appraiser, then easy rearrangement as desired, and then—when a satisfying arrangement of the Q descriptors finally is achieved by the Q-sorter—an explicit depiction by the evaluator of the particular person under scrutiny.

The CQ descriptors "are put in an order of representativeness for the individual, those most characteristic of him being given high scores (i.e., values), whilst those least characteristic are scored low" (Stephenson, 1936, p. 357). That is, the CQ descriptors are sorted or arranged according to the appraiser's personal judgment of their relative salience—positive or negative—in regard to the person being evaluated. The sorting procedure effectively involves a compromise between pair comparisons and simultaneous ranking. Because of this feature of descriptor sorting, this general scaling procedure has become known as "the Q-sort method."

Originally, Stephenson devised the Q-sort method to provide, in convenient form, data suitable for his heuristic studies in what was termed Q-factor analysis. The letter, Q, was simply generalized from its initial meaning—as referring to a concern with correlating persons—to apply to a particular, appropriate way of preparing data for the person-correlating approach. Much confusion has been generated by the intimate connection the Q-sort method per se has appeared to have with a special Q-factor analysis orientation. In fact, the Q-sort method stands in its own right as a valuable scaling technique, with no necessary relation to subsequent factor analysis. For a more extensive historical clarification, refer to an old recounting by Mowrer (1953).

The Q-sort method imposes certain technical constraints, to be discussed and justified shortly, in that the evaluator must place the Q descriptors into a designated number of ordered categories and, most important, with an assigned number of descriptors being placed into each category. For the CQ-set, nine dimensionalized categories are conventionally used, the specified number of descriptors distributed into each category being, respectively: 5, 8, 12, 16, 18, 16, 12, 8, and 5. Thus, at one end of the nine-step continuum are placed the appraiser's five descriptors deemed most characteristic or most salient of the person being described. At the other end of the continuum are placed the appraiser's five descriptors deemed most uncharacteristic or most "salient" in a negative sense for describing the designated person.

After the sorting, the category placement of each of the CQ descriptors is recorded. The categories into which the statements have been placed are themselves numbered, from 9 through 1, with 9 by convention referring to the most characteristic end of the continuum and the number 1 to the least characteristic end. For each CQ descriptor, the number of the category in which the descriptor was placed is recorded as that descriptor's value in the particular person description. With all the data entered in this fashion, ready for subsequent computer entry and analysis, the procedure is completed. The CQ cards are then reshuffled, preparatory to another sorting.

TWO ILLUSTRATIONS OF THE CQ PROCEDURE APPLIED

Research and teaching possibilities of the CQ procedure have been mentioned but only in highly general, allusive terms. Here are offered in more detail two illustrations of how the proposed standard language brings about a useful otherwise unachievable comparability of appraiser evaluations and how it can provide important substantive understandings not otherwise attainable.

The Case of "The Optimally Adjusted Person"

The first illustration contrasts subjective evaluations of a person that are offered when no restrictions are set on the way the descriptions are expressed as compared with subjective formulations of that person offered through the CQ method. So that the reader can bring personal knowledge and perspective into play in evaluating the relative merits and deficiencies of the two descriptive approaches, it is convenient to portray a vivified concept—*the optimally adjusted person*—as a "subject" rather than an actual person.

Two clinicians were asked to describe, in their own words, the nature of the optimally adjusted personality. Following this exercise, each clinician again described the optimally adjusted individual but this time by means of the CAQ-descriptor set. About 15 or 20 minutes were required for the second description, appreciably less time than was required for the first, freeform, personally constructed characterization. It is informative to contrast these two kinds of descriptions.

Clinician G, in writing his description, had the following to say:

First of all, the optimally adjusted person may be characterized by having a heightened tolerance for dissonance. Stated simply, this means that he can be comfortable in situations that others would attempt to avoid. Within himself he may sense certain unresolved conflicts and seeming inconsistencies, but he is at ease with this kind of dissonance. In fact, he is more often fascinated than perplexed by these inconsistencies both in himself and others.

A great deal of this tolerance stems from a perception and appreciation of the relativity concept, especially the relativity of social behavior. He is a master of "role playing." Often he performs the conventional and socially expected in a "tongue-in-cheek" manner. However, he would never deliberately disturb others by flouting convention. This does not imply that the optimally adjusted person lacks a sense of commitment. On the contrary, his commitments are strongly reinforced by rational considerations.

In his social relations with others, the optimally adjusted person selects his friends with care. He is more concerned with quality than quantity. He is generally friendly and outgoing with people but he does not strive to please everyone. He is no "back-slapper" or "glad-hander." To many, his seeming casualness is often misinterpreted as aloofness.

Intellectually, the optimally adjusted person is above average. In his field of concentration he is more the generalist rather than the specialist. His interests are broad and he has contact with many aspects of experience. In fact, many of these interests may appear "off-beat" to some but to him they have value and meaning. This does not imply that he glorifies the esoteric; he merely pursues those lines of interest that are most congruent to him.

Rather than being religious in the conventional sense of the word, the optimally adjusted person tends to be humanitarian in his outlook. Religion (either of the institutional variety or not) means doing something for others. He is not preoccupied by metaphysical dilemmas or verbal quibbles. He has a broad concern for others and continually searches for ways of realizing an inner need for compassion.

In conclusion, it appears that the concept of the optimally adjusted person expounded here is not at variance with the related concepts of the self-actualized individual, the creative personality, or the fully functioning personality. In the last analysis, all of these concepts may be synonymous for a common personality structure.

Clinician N, in her conception of psychological optimality, wrote the following:

An optimally adjusted person is one who has an understanding and acceptance of self and society, both with their limitations and strengths. This acceptance is not a passive submission to limitations that could be overcome but an insight that distinguishes evitable and inevitable ones. He is relatively free of defenses and compulsions and as such is also free to enjoy the utilization of his energies, which gives him a feeling of self fulfillment, enriches his environment and helps overcome avoidable limitations. He does not resort to work as a means of escape nor are his energies paralyzed leading him to inactive means of escape. He is free from inner compulsions and excessive need for outer controls. He is not embarrassed to conform nor afraid to differ. He can accept criticism and appreciation and is also objective in his evaluation of others.

He is not free from problems because he is actively engaged in life. He recognizes problems and tries to understand them. He has developed independent skills but does not find it difficult to seek help when needed. He enjoys working alone and does not find it difficult to work with others. He can play the role of receiver and giver comfortably. He accepts his role as an individual in an interdependent society.

When differences exist between his conception of his role (age and sex role) and that defined by society, he has an understanding of the differences and their reasons and he is not afraid to differ within reasonable limits and still maintains an acceptance from society because he can communicate with them. When differences are greater he moves toward the direction of bringing changes in society. When there is lack of clear definition or a variety of ways of finding a role, he does not feel lost and shows sufficient self-insight and flexibility to work out the role best suited to his abilities. There is not a big gap between his level of aspiration and his abilities. His controls are internalized, providing a relatively consistent value system that is neither too restrictive for spontaneity nor too loose for organization and control.

Each clinician offered a considered, personal effort to characterize the concept of optimal adjustment. These formulations read well and possess intrinsic merit. But do they suffice and how do they compare? The first exposition emphasizes such attributes as "tolerance for dissonance," "role-playing (ability)," "a sense of commitment," "breadth of interest," and "humanitarianism." The second effort describes optimal adjustment in terms of freedom "from inner compulsions and excessive need for outer controls," the ability "to accept criticism and appreciation," and "also objective in evaluation of others." Is there an equivalence or similarity in these two evaluations? If so, then how is such similarity to be recognized?

The uncertainty in evaluating these respective formulations comes from two sources. The first source is the inevitable circumstance that clinicians have personal linguistic styles of expression that consequently present an appreciable interpretive problem to a would-be comparer. The second (and not less important) problem arises because the two clinicians have not focused their perceptions on the same set of attributes in describing the hypothetical subject. The first clinician says nothing in regard to, for example, the ability to accept criticism, a quality stressed by the second clinician. Conversely, one can only guess as to the second clinician's views on the place of "tolerance for dissonance" in her conception of optimal adjustment. The two concept describers each focus on different aspects of the construct, neglecting others that might have been considered. Yet, intuitively, there does appear to be appreciable congruence between the two characterizations. Consider now how the description problem is treated through the CQ procedure.

The 26 most salient descriptors—positive and negative—in Clinician G's formulation of the optimally adjusted person are listed in Table 2.1. Also to be read from Table 2.1 are Clinician N's 26 most salient—positive and negative—descriptors. For reasons of brevity, the order of the remaining 74 descriptors in each description is not given.

As can be seen, both clinicians have now expressed themselves by using the same comprehensive set of CQ attributes. The comparison task at this point is straightforward. The two separately offered characterizations of optimal adjustment can simply be correlated. In this instance, the two independent CQ characterizations of the optimal personality correlate .77, indicating quantitatively an impressive convergence between the two respective conceptualizations of the construct. Indeed, by the Spearman–Brown prophecy formula, the composite of the two construct conceptualizations has a latent reproducibility (reliability) of .87, testifying to their deep equivalence.

Contentwise, both judges agree that the optimally adjusted person is *warm, productive, insightful, ethically consistent, perceptive,* and *candid.* Their definitions, at the negative end, exclude such attributes as *hostility, anxiety, fearfulness, pervasive guilt feelings, distrust, self-pity,* and *the use of repressive mechanisms.* These descriptors constitute the core of their substantial agreement.

There are also some instructive differences discernible between the two conceptions. Clinician G places more value on such attributes as *intelligence, esthetic reactivity,* and *autonomy* than does Clinician N. Clinician N, however, emphasizes *appropriateness* and a *lack of projectivity* more than does Clinician G. Other differences exist, but these few perhaps indicate the commonality and also the different flavors of the alternative conceptualizations.

With the initial freely rendered essays, one could only attempt to sense the nature and extent of the equivalence and difference between the characterological formulations. However, the CQ procedure, by its enforced commensurateness, permitted easy and instructive comparison to be realized. By requiring

TABLE 2.1
CQ Descriptors That Fall in the Highest Two and Lowest Two Categories
for Clinician G and Clinician N

Q category	Clinician G	Clinician N
Most characteristic (5 descriptors)	(3) has a wide range of interests (35) has warmth; has the capacity for close relationships; compassionate (51) genuinely values intellectual and cognitive matters (64) is socially perceptive of a wide range of interpersonal cues	(26) is productive; gets things done (28) tends to arouse liking and acceptance in people (60) has insight into own motives and behavior (70) behaves in an ethically consistent manner; is consistent with own personal standards (75) has a clear-cut, internally consistent personality
Quite characteristic (8 descriptors)	(96) values own independence and autonomy (17) behaves in a sympathetic or considerate manner (26) is productive; gets things done (60) has insight into own motives and behavior (66) enjoys esthetic impressions; is esthetically reactive (70) behaves in an ethically consistent manner; is consistent with own personal standards (71) has high aspiration level for self (77) appears straightforward, forthright, candid in dealings with others (83) able to see to the heart of important problems	(2) is a genuinely dependable and responsible person (32) seems to be aware of the impression s/he makes on others (33) is calm, relaxed in manner (35) has warmth; has the capacity for close relationships; compassionate (64) is socially perceptive of a wide range of interpersonal cues (77) appears straightforward, forthright, candid in dealing with others (80) interested in members of the opposite sex (93) behaves in a masculine (or feminine) style and manner

(10) anxiety and tension find outlet in bodily symptoms
(12) tends to be self-defensive
(25) tends toward overcontrol of needs and impulses; binds tensions excessively; delays gratification unnecessarily
(34) overreactive in minor frustrations; irritable
(42) reluctant to commit self to any definite course of action; tends to delay or avoid action
(45) has a brittle ego-defense system; has a small reserve of integration; would be disorganized or maladaptive under stress or trauma
(68) is basically anxious
(78) feels cheated and victimized by life; self-pitying

(38) has hostility toward others
(40) is vulnerable to real or fancied threat, generally fearful
(47) has a readiness to feel guilty
(49) is basically distrustful of people in general; questions their motives
(86) handles anxiety and conflicts by, in effect, refusing to recognize their presence; repressive or dissociative tendencies

Quite uncharacteristic (8 descriptors)

(23) extrapunitive; tends to transfer or project blame
(30) gives up and withdraws where possible in face of frustration and adversity
(40) is vulnerable to real or fancied threat, generally fearful
(45) has a brittle ego-defense system; has a small reserve of integration; would be disorganized or maladaptive under stress or trauma
(49) is basically distrustful of people; questions their motivations
(61) creates and exploits dependency in people
(78) feels cheated and victimized by life; self-pitying
(86) handles anxiety and conflicts by, in effect, refusing to recognize their presence; repressive tendencies

Most uncharacteristic (5 descriptors)

(10) anxiety and tension find outlet in bodily symptoms
(38) has hostility toward others
(47) has a readiness to feel guilty
(59) is concerned with own body and the adequacy of its physiological functioning
(73) tends to perceive many different contexts in sexual terms; eroticizes situations

each judge to attend to the complete range of person attributes included in the CQ language, the dangers of differential focusing were avoided. Where previously, comparison of evaluations was not readily feasible, the CQ procedure explicitly and simply provides it—a most useful achievement.

There remains the question of whether this accomplishment has not been achieved at excessive cost. Perhaps the objectification of comparisons is no more than that. If by this effort at objectivity, the achievement has been at the cost of relevance, of course the procedure is defeated by its victory. The reader should form a personal impression as to how, in the example presented previously, the written essays and the CQ descriptions compare in their usefulness in conveying the similarities and differences in the conceptions held by the assessors. In later chapters of this volume, this essential question—of the balance between the costs and the gains accruing from the CQ procedure—is referred to often. In the evolvement of the CAQ- or CCQ-set, there has been sensitivity to this issue and the procedure has been shaped accordingly. The ultimate judgment on this matter, of course, must come from the crucible of empiricism.

Creativity in Women Mathematicians

As a second demonstration of the CQ method and its capabilities, research that focuses on creativity in women mathematicians is of appreciable substantive interest (Helson, 1971).

Each member of a most unusual, highly selected, homogeneous group of 40 women doctorate mathematicians had been carefully evaluated on a 7-point scale as to her mathematical creativity by a panel of eminent university mathematicians. A female doctorate mathematician was considered creative if her average rating was 5 or higher; all others from this already highly select group were deemed relatively uncreative.

Separately, each woman had been intensively assessed in weekend groups of 10 by a staff of assessment psychologists, none of whom were practicing clinicians. It was known to the observers that all of these women held a doctorate in mathematics. The assessment the women experienced was comprehensive in scope and included a variety of perceptual–cognitive and experimental procedures, a battery of standard psychological tests, and some specially designed interpersonal situations (e.g., charades, group discussions, interviews). Each member of the psychological staff, after the weekend assessment, described each woman mathematician by means of an early version of the CQ procedure. Of course, none of the assessing psychologists had information as to the judged mathematical creativity of the women subjects nor did any of the psychologists possess the personal mathematical competence to project a subject's likely creativity rating. The several CQ descriptions for each woman mathematician were then arithmetically averaged to provide a composite-based description for everyone.

For each CQ descriptor, the 40 scores of these women mathematicians were then correlated with their independently derived categorical numerical ratings of mathematical creativity. Obviously, subsequent connections observed between judged mathematical creativity and the independently evaluated CQ descriptors are of substantive empirical import as well as demonstrational interest.

Table 2.2 reports the CQ descriptors significantly and statistically correlated with judged mathematical creativity level in this unusual group of women mathematicians.

These empirical CQ results have appreciable intrinsic interest. Considering the great homogeneity of the sample and that the sample consists of women rather than men, as had been the case in earlier studies, the findings

TABLE 2.2
CQ Descriptors Significantly Correlated With Creativity
in Women Mathematicians

Positively correlated

Descriptor 39.	Thinks and associates to ideas in unusual ways; has unconventional thought processes. (.64)
Descriptor 57.	Is an interesting, arresting person. (.55)
Descriptor 62.	Tends to be rebellious and nonconforming. (.51)
Descriptor 51.	Genuinely values intellectual and cognitive matters. (.49)
Descriptor 8.	Appears to have a high degree of intellectual capacity. (.46)
Descriptor 99.	Is self-dramatizing; histrionic. (.42)
Descriptor 82.	Has fluctuating moods. (.40)
Descriptor 1.	Is critical, skeptical, not easily impressed. (.38)
Descriptor 94.	Expresses hostile feelings directly. (.36)
Descriptor 53.	Various needs tend toward relatively direct and uncontrolled expression; unable to delay gratification. (.35)
Descriptor 46.	Engages in personal fantasy and daydreams, fictional speculations. (.34)
Descriptor 50.	Is unpredictable and changeable in behavior and attitudes. (.31)
Descriptor 65.	Characteristically pushes and tries to stretch limits; sees what she can get away with. (.30)

Negatively correlated

Descriptor 63.	Judges self and others in conventional terms like popularity, the correct thing to do, social pressures, etc. (−.62)
Descriptor 2.	Is a genuinely dependable and responsible person. (−.45)
Descriptor 17.	Behaves in a sympathetic or considerate manner. (−.43)
Descriptor 7.	Favors conservative values in a variety of areas. (−.40)
Descriptor 41.	Is moralistic. (−.40)
Descriptor 24.	Prides self on being objective, rational. (−.37)
Descriptor 9.	Is uncomfortable with uncertainty and complexities. (−.35)
Descriptor 11.	Is protective of those close to him/her. (−.35)
Descriptor 70.	Behaves in an ethically consistent manner; is consistent with own personal standards. (−.33)

are theoretically most implicative in regard to the general nature of mathematical creativity. Of the 100 CQ-descriptor correlations with the creativity criterion, 22 pass the statistically set cutting point. The descriptors positively correlated with mathematical creativity in women doctorate mathematicians appear to describe a relatively *unusual, amoral, flamboyant* person who, although *impulsive* and *direct in her expressiveness*, is also *moody* and *introverted*. The descriptors negatively correlated with mathematical creativity portray a very different kind of woman—one relatively (but not necessarily absolutely) *tied to conventionality, internalized moral standards* and *the safeguards these provide against impulse expression and uncertainties* in the world. These intriguing empirical findings serve to further instance the convenience and fruitfulness of the CQ method.

On the basis of these two empirical demonstrations, the reader may be encouraged to go on to later chapters.

II

THE CALIFORNIA Q-SORT PROCEDURE: EVOLVING A LEXICON AND A SYNTAX

3

DEVELOPING THE CALIFORNIA ADULT Q-SET DESCRIPTORS[1]

If a restricting basic vocabulary is to be used, then the restrictions should be chosen most carefully. The initially agreed-on fixed language cannot rise above its insufficiencies. It was because of this recognition that effort was concentrated on establishing a "good" set of person descriptive variables. With full awareness that generalizations would be limited by the California Adult Q-set (CAQ) descriptors finally selected, the expectation was that care and corrections coming from extensive preliminary experience and sequential revision would be importantly corrective.

Having recognized the primacy of establishing a comprehensive set of person Q descriptors, how does one begin? What are the rules to follow in ensuring achievement of this desideratum? The literature did not provide guidance

---

[1]The orientation here toward Q-set construction differs markedly from that advocated by Stephenson and his subsequent adherents. Early on, Q-sets were created ad hoc, improvised quickly as a function of convenience and personal, unsupported preference. In a later approach, all of the statements in an arbitrarily demarcated universe were said to be collected. Then, from this restricted universe, strictly at random, samples of statements were selected to serve as Q-sets. Of course, random sampling from a questionably complete, unilaterally specified universe offers no guarantee of sufficient coverage. A third, ambitious Stephenson approach aspired to theory testing through an analysis of variance design said to be embodied by a "structured" set of Q statements. This aspiration proved to be doomed by its failure of credible implementation (Block, 1961, pp. 49–51; Cronbach & Gleser, 1954).

along the way. The sole remarks on the fundamental problem of Q-descriptor content are those by Stephenson (1953), the innovator of the Q-sort method. However, his recommendations do not provide a sufficient basis for the present purpose of developing a set of person Q descriptors. Aside from a few "practical considerations" to be respected in establishing Q-sets—considerations such as understandability, conciseness, and so on—Stephenson said little on this crucial feature of his technique. He expressed satisfaction with a "rough-and-ready universe of statements" from which, with "a certain art" and with "certain precautions," a sample "suitable to the needs of a particular study" can be compiled. Especially, Stephenson considered it "a mistake to regard a sample (of Q descriptors) as a standardized set or test of statements. . . ." (1953, pp. 76–78)—a view contrary to the present orientation.

With anticipation of the contribution a competent set of Q descriptors could make, the enterprise began. Some 90 Q variables were expressed in descriptor form, aiming at comprehensive coverage of the person domain. This initial assembly of variables was of course an unspecifiable function of the writer's personal theoretical preferences and scope.

Several a priori principles were used in writing California Q-sort (CQ) descriptors:

1. Each Q descriptor was written in a theoretically neutral form. Although a broadly psychodynamic orientation frankly underlay the intended Q-set, the descriptors themselves were committed to no special theoretical viewpoint. No Q descriptor embodied a concept linked exclusively to one theoretical orientation and therefore the person formulations built up by a Q-descriptor configuration were compatible with any of several theoretical viewpoints.

2. Each Q descriptor was written to imply a continuum, rather than suggest an either–or, yes–no categorization. It was intended that the salience or cruciality of a descriptor would be expressed by its sorting placement rather than directly by wording; for example, "is distrustful of people in general" would imply paranoia when placed as extremely, conspicuously salient.

3. Each Q descriptor was written to express a single psychological "element" to avoid equivocal interpretation engendered by double-barreled, indeterminate phrasings. For example, the statement "is talkative and self-assured" was considered a poor descriptor in that the person being evaluated could be talkative but not self-assured or self-assured but not talkative. Partitioning such descriptors into their constituent elements eliminated what otherwise would be an insoluble problem for the sorter while still permitting the expression of complex conjunctions of separate univocal elements.

4. An effort was made to include only Q descriptors conceptually independent of each other, even if these descriptors were functionally related in the usual instance. By conceptual independence is meant that the psychological sense of each descriptor could not be coordinated with or derived from the psychological sense of any other descriptor or conjunction of descriptors. Thus, the CQ descriptor, "Is skilled in social techniques of imaginative play, pretending, and humor" is appreciably correlated with the CQ descriptor, "Appears to have a high degree of intellectual ability." However intellectual ability need not imply imaginative play and humor: The descriptors are empirically related asymmetrically. Of course, given awareness of the complications within the descriptor domain, realization of this principle could be only an aspiration, not an assured achievement. Deliberation, experience, and psychometric analyses of the provisional Q descriptors were counted on for important refinements. The finally fixed-on CAQ-set profited a great deal from earlier semantic and statistical analyses.

5. Related to this concern with the conceptual independence of Q descriptors was the stance taken with respect to a certain redundancy of Q statements. The presence of empirical correlation among descriptors was not judged as totally undesirable. Although a redundancy may exist when two Q descriptors usually correlate appreciably, it was considered worthwhile to often carry along this redundancy to preserve the possibility of registering within the Q arrangement for a person those crucial instances in which the usually expected correspondence between descriptors does not hold. Thus, the CQ descriptor, "Favors conservative values in a variety of areas," and the CQ descriptor, "Is uncomfortable with uncertainty and complexities," may be expected to correspond fairly well within most persons but certainly not perfectly. It is important to be able to describe the individual with the one characteristic but not the other. When a usual intraperson relation fails to exist, it is often important for this unusualness to be recorded. To express the many exceptions to usual correspondence—exceptions that could influence the cast of an entire person formulation—it was considered desirable to include related (but not fully equivalent) Q descriptors. Obviously, careful and consensual value judgments were required in implementing this respect for inconsistencies in syndromes. The advisability of this particular emphasis in developing the CAQ-set may best be evaluated after actual use of the procedure. For the present, it is important to note that this

orientation also guided development of the CAQ-set from its inception.

6. A further facet of the redundancy issue arises from recognition that certain attributes may not have clear behavioral opposites. For example, "submission" did not remove its verbal opposite, "dominance," because there exists a kind of person for whom both of these variables are positively salient, the so-called pecking order person who is deferent to individuals of higher status and imperious with individuals of lower rank. As another illustration, the characteristic of "impulsivity" did not displace the necessity of including an opposite characteristic on "constriction." Descriptors expressing both characteristics are needed to be able to describe the individual whose pattern of impulse control is *bimodal*, that is, both undercontrolled and overcontrolled. It was also noted that a person descriptor could have divergent reversals: A person who is not "self-abasing" may be "self-accepting" or, alternatively, "critical of others." If the nuances and complexities of character could not be mapped sufficiently by words in a sometime relation to other words, then a component of redundancy was incorporated into the CAQ-set to cope with equivocal possibilities.

7. A final concern in Q-descriptor writing was to minimize degree of value judgment in observer Q descriptions of individuals. Ideally, observers should be dispassionate in their perceptions. In reality, however, their frailties of opinion are ever present. One way to prevent value judgments from infiltrating the descriptions offered by appraisers is to provide a language that diminishes values from prime consideration. Toward this end, effort was made to compose descriptors in a neutral, non-evaluative form. Necessarily, however, a number of descriptors selected for inclusion in the eventual CAQ-set carry positive social implications whereas a number refers to socially negative or undesirable personal properties. Some evaluative descriptors are unavoidable; they are conceptually required if a comprehensive description is to be offered (Block, 1965). As judged by raters, neutral, positive, and negative descriptors exist in the eventual CQ-set in the ratio, approximately, of 2:1:1. In usage, the positive and negative CAQ descriptors do not appear to be especially susceptible to or dominated by stereotype effects. There is appreciable psychological heterogeneity within the set of positive CAQ descriptors and also within the set of negative CAQ descriptors. A global, undifferentiated, adulatory, or condemnatory evaluation of an individual there-

fore is readily identified by its caricature of psychological health or disorder.

It cannot be claimed that in all regards the principles of Q-set construction were followed with complete success. Undoubtedly, certain CAQ descriptors can still be interpreted ambiguously or as double-barreled. For some users, the CAQ descriptors may be viewed as jargon laden. Deliberately, interpersonal and intrapersonal CAQ descriptors have been merged and levels of inference mixed; for some purposes or for some inclinations, such decisions may be unacceptable. The balance struck on redundancy is also open to question: Does too much redundancy remain? Have Q descriptors excised as excessively redundant removed the possibility of reporting fine discriminations?

The labors involved in forming, evaluating, and progressively refining Q descriptors were appreciable. But it must be recognized that, in the nature of an imperfect world, there is no way of evaluating the extent to which these reasoned albeit arbitrary principles of Q-descriptor writing have been satisfied. The Q descriptors were developed frankly by using a broad base of psychiatric and psychological opinion, and earlier uses provided an opportunity to study and refine the Q descriptors. Certainly, many difficulties and insufficiencies observed in earlier Q-sets have been reduced. Consequently, a broad spectrum of potential users may well find the present version useful and versatile. Now, to historical details.

EVOLVING THE CAQ-SET, FORM I

Ninety descriptors, earlier assembled with the foregoing orientation in mind, constituted a starting point. This provisional set was then the focus of intensive and prolonged discussions with two other clinical psychologists and a psychiatrist. In some 60 hours of meetings, each descriptor was taken up in turn and discussed with respect to its clarity, its psychological importance, and its implications for the sufficiency of the total Q-set.

The task of achieving clarity was simply an editing job. The guiding editorial principles were several: conciseness when possible, amplifications when judged necessary, elimination of unrequired or multiply understood jargon, descriptor phrasings that stayed within the conceived universe of discourse.

The psychological importance of a CAQ descriptor was the judgment, by consensus after discussion, of the information value and general relevance of the particular descriptor in describing persons. By virtue of this consensual basis, the initial collection of CAQ descriptors took its first step away from idiosyncratic emphasis and toward the goal of a wider acceptability.

As descriptors were reworked and reconsidered, they became familiar in meaning and in capability. The final criterion was then invoked: namely, were the CAQ descriptors—now clear and agreed to be important—sufficient in themselves or in combination to encompass the full range of person constellations?

No analytical method for testing the adequacy of the CAQ-descriptor set, of course, existed. Therefore, an empirical effort was made by the constantly changing CAQ-discussion group to find weaknesses in the immediately current CAQ-set. Illustrations out of experience and hypothetical, albeit conceivable, instances were invoked to embarrass the descriptive capabilities of the CAQ-set as it existed at that moment. Whenever it was judged that a gap or inadequacy had been demonstrated, whenever some facet of people judged important proved inexpressible by an existing descriptor or some conjunction of existing descriptors, suitable descriptor revisions were made or an appropriate descriptor was added to the CAQ-set.

Attention to the descriptive possibilities residing in conjunctions of CAQ descriptors was an important evaluative strategy. Thus, the descriptor "is fatherly" was not directly included in the CAQ-set because a conception of "fatherliness" could be expressed by conjoining such CAQ descriptors as "Is turned to for advice and reassurance," "Is protective of those close to him," "Behaves in a masculine style and manner," "Is calm, relaxed in manner," "Has warmth; has the capacity for close relationships; compassionate," and others. Many proposed Q descriptors were excluded when referenced against a constellation of existing CAQ descriptors.

After the initial group had deliberated extensively and offered its descriptor changes, the resultant CAQ-set was submitted to a second group of clinical psychologists. Clinical psychologists were invoked because of the presumption they would have catholic views of humankind. In a series of seminars, the CAQ descriptors were discussed again and again with this new group. Discussion was oriented toward issues of clarity, importance, and sufficiency. Appreciable further change to the CAQ descriptors came from these meetings, as the challenge was taken up by the group to find person-relevant descriptors not already included.

With the completion of this second set of discussions, it was decided to "freeze" the CAQ-set as it stood at that point. The beginning collection of descriptors had been broadened considerably in perspective and acceptability. It seemed opportune to test the CAQ-set's research utility and its psychometric properties. Accordingly, for a 14-month period, the revised array of now 108 descriptors, labeled as the *CAQ-set, Form I,* was used without further change in several studies.

EVOLVING THE CAQ-SET, FORM II

In the course of using Form I, various psychologists and psychiatrists offered additional critique and suggestions for improvement, suggestions growing out of actual practice, research, or teaching experience with the procedure. The suggestions were a fundamental resource in guiding the revision made at this time.

A primary basis for shaping the revision came from a psychometric analysis of 240 CAQ-sorts, using Form I. Each CAQ descriptor was evaluated to find descriptors showing little variability over a wide range of persons. Such CAQ descriptors conveyed little differential information. If the small dispersion for a CAQ descriptor was judged to reflect a universal human property rather than the special homogeneities of the particular person sample providing the data, then that descriptor was considered not differentially important and was eliminated in the revision.

The CAQ-set, Form II, benefiting from additional intelligences and returns from experience, was another step in the direction of achieving consensual utility—a descriptive capability sufficiently versatile to permit person descriptions by a wide range of psychodynamically oriented observers. It consisted of 115 descriptors and was used for several years until replaced by Form III of the CQ-set.

EVOLVING THE CQ-SET, FORM III

A tentative revision of Form II of the CQ-set was prepared by incorporating the suggestions accumulated from users in the preceding years. This tentative revision was then the basis of yet another series of discussions by person assessors. At these meetings, the group discussed each CAQ descriptor, evaluating them—singly and in conjunction—against the criteria described earlier.

Concomitant with this further evaluation, an extensive psychometric analysis of CAQ descriptors from Form I and II was again conducted. For each CAQ descriptor, means, dispersions, and correlations with all other descriptors were generated in four quite different samples.

These data were examined to further identify uninformative descriptors, that is, descriptors manifesting little dispersion or correlating too highly with other descriptors in the set. In this scanning, it was required that a descriptor's uninformativeness had to exist in more than one of the several data matrices. This condition was set as a safeguard against prematurely concluding that a CAQ descriptor was unnecessary. If a CAQ descriptor did not consistently demonstrate uninformativeness, then this could only mean that different patterns of descriptor covariation existed in the several person groups. In these instances, the inclination was that such a finding needed to be respected, even at the cost of including a descriptor usually (but not always) uninformative.

Another criterion used in evaluating the then CAQ-set was that the average interperson correlation within each sample be quite low, of the order of .10 or .12, with a reasonably uniform distribution of interperson correlations. As the average interperson correlation within a sample increases, there is obviously less discrimination among individuals. A relatively high average interperson correlation legitimately may exist when the sample is of a rather homogeneous nature. However, in a sample judged heterogeneous, a relatively high average interperson correlation arises only when CAQ descriptors are placed relatively equivalently for all individuals. Such CAQ descriptors can be called *universals* because they are salient (or not salient) for all people. Universal descriptors introduce no special bias, but they are wasteful because they are less useful as discriminators or may misleadingly suggest the existence of important homogeneities in the sample studied. When descriptors of little variance in multiple samples were found, they were either eliminated or restated to enhance their potential for reflecting genuine variance.

With the completion of psychometric analyses and another evaluative gauntlet for the CAQ descriptors, Form III was formalized. Form III contains 100 CAQ descriptors and has been frequently and productively used in a wide variety of studies over the years. A number of these studies are described or reported later. Computer literature searches will identify many more.

No fundamental change of the CAQ-set, Form III seems warranted now, but derived experience has suggested some further tweaking of CAQ-descriptor phrasing. The current version—CAQ-set, Form III–R—remains aligned and fully comparative with the earlier Form III version. At some future time, when this version has been found seriously wanting, a more fundamental revision may be in order.

Strategically, another Q-set has been carefully derived from the adult-oriented CAQ, that is, the California Child Q-set (CCQ). It is more applicable to children, many of the CCQ descriptors deriving from the CAQ. Some CCQ descriptors are applicable only to children, but many are connectable to the CAQ descriptors for adults. The CCQ descriptors are listed in Appendix B.

4

THE CALIFORNIA ADULT Q-SET
DESCRIPTORS: CRITICISMS
AND REJOINDERS

As noted earlier, if a common language is to be substituted for individual freedom of expression, then assurances are required that the vocabulary and the grammar of the imposed language are sufficient for its intended purpose. Failing a general sense that this requirement has been achieved, the effort is properly rejected. Given confidence in the California Adult Q-set (CAQ) as descriptively versatile, the appeal of uniquely phrased expression may perhaps wistfully be abandoned for many purposes.

Questions of what may be called *syntactic rules* are left until chapter 5; in chapter 4, vocabulary alone is considered. Are the CAQ descriptors rich enough in their conjunction and aggregate to accomplish sufficiently well their descriptive purpose? What are the constraints imposed on the perceptive observer limited to subjective expression only by means of the descriptive phrases that happen to be within the CAQ-descriptor set?

Such constraints, restrictions, oversimplifications, arbitrary exclusions, and so on as may be said to characterize the CAQ-set must be countered. Therefore, now, I describe the particulars of criticism and rejoinder.

1. Implied in criticisms of the CAQ-set is that the results it issues are a function of the particular Q-descriptor set involved. With

a different Q-set, it is suggested that observed relations conceivably could be importantly different. If the instrument for character description by its happenstance properties restrictively shapes reporting, then there can be little faith in its findings. To change the Q-set would mean the findings it issues would change as well.

This criticism could, in principle, be true and, if true, would be devastating. A Q-set assembled quickly without care or sophistication certainly may have special, unspecifiable peculiarities. Massive redundancies or unacceptable lacunae could tilt the relations perceived.

However, this almost automatic, a priori criticism is substantially confronted by the repeated use of a broad consensual and successive basis for descriptor suggestion and descriptor modification. The evolutionary course of the CAQ-set and the scope of its phrasings went through a long, developmental process. Such bias as may be said to remain survived scrutiny from a sizable Bay Area sample of contemporary character describers, that is, clinicians. Potential users now of the CAQ-set should therefore find it reasonably suitable for expressing configurationally their own evaluations of persons.

Would another sizable sample of clinicians evolve a Q-set with appreciably different functional properties? Of course, such a separately constructed Q-set is unlikely to duplicate exactly any existing locution in the CAQ-set. Nevertheless, the functional relations educed by a second, well-based clinician-evolved Q-set can be expected to be similar to the functional relations that appear through the present clinician-evolved Q-set because both would be targeting the same domain of character description.

Because the multiplication of equivalent Q-sets ad libitum would simply add anarchic confusion, it is reasonable to settle on one widely ranging and judged sufficient set of Q descriptors that fit the needs of many. By fixing on one good, consensually developed Q-set as sufficient for widespread use, the subsequent interchange and comparison of information is made easy.

2. Another criticism voiced against the CAQ-set is that the observer is constrained in the number of discriminations that can be made. There are, it is argued, many more facets to persons than the CAQ-set (or any Q-set) can express. Three different rejoinders respond to this contention. The first countering argument is a numerical one, the second justification introduces considerations of relativism, and the last suggests a compromise course when this criticism is most passionately held.

(a) It is possible to compute the number of different ways in which the 100 descriptors in the CAQ-set can be arranged into the designated nine categories (Ferguson, 1949). This number proves to be 6.45×10^{85}, an astronomically large figure. In computing the number of possible descriptor constellations, independent placement of each descriptor has been assumed and this assumption is known to be incorrect. By how much, it is impossible to say, because empirical estimates of descriptor covariation vary greatly from sample to sample. However, reduce the previously mentioned figure by a factor of 10 or 100 or a million or a hundred million and there still is available an immensely large array of different descriptor configurations. As reflected by the number of permutations and combinations available to the user of the CAQ-set, it seems that a sufficient number of configurational possibilities exist if the judge can use them reliably.

(b) The response of relativism makes a simple if disputatious claim, namely, the discrimination constraints entailed by the use of the CAQ-set are slight relative to the constraints imposed on person study by other methods. When one considers the uncertain or rough reliability of other measures in psychology, when one recollects the fallibility of criterion measures or the uncertainties of checklist diagnosis through the American Psychiatric Association's *Diagnostic and Statistical Manual of Mental Disorders* (e.g., Kirk, 2004), it would seem the numerical constraints on discrimination imposed by the CAQ-set are not the weakest link in the inferential chain. This is not to say that limitations of the CAQ-set are unimportant. It is only to suggest that comparatively the number of discriminations afforded by the CAQ-set is not especially limiting.

(c) There inevitably will arise circumstances in which a description solely through CAQ phrasings will be viewed by an observer as inadequate; important information and perceptions unconveyable by the CAQ procedure will be seen as being abandoned. At such times, a freely written characterization by the appraiser of the actual individual may be desirable or politic. In studies in which the authors choose to use the CAQ procedure, it is important that this option be exercised in addition to rather than instead of a CAQ description. By using both procedures as needed, observers need feel no sense of communication constraint. There is extra effort required, but this is the cost of conviction, the conviction that the free description attains a goal not achievable otherwise. An interesting side benefit of this option is the opportunity it provides to examine the judged discrepancy between the standard language California Q-sort (CQ) description and freely expressed views, as exemplified in chapter 2 when I described the optimally adjusted person both freely and through the CAQ procedure.

3. Another criticism of the CAQ-set questions whether the CAQ phrasings are indeed comparably understood by appraisers. Because the intention of the CAQ procedure is to provide a standard language so that comparison of person descriptions becomes possible, it is pernicious if the standard language is not used in equivalent ways.

   In response, consider the prolonged and careful evolution of descriptor phrasing, described earlier. The exacting scrutiny and rephrasing as necessary of each descriptor helped achieve greater clarification and commonness of understanding than would have been the case with rapid or casual Q-descriptor construction. When a descriptor was elaborated, care was taken that these extensions be consonant extensions. The advent of CAQ-set, Form III–R further testifies to this concern. Therefore, it seems fair to say that such problems of interpretability as could be anticipated were confronted.

   Nevertheless, in actual use the interpretability problem may still arise. Different observers may come with radically different language backgrounds, conventions, emphases, and so on. A fruitful practice in these instances is to have the several appraisers calibrate themselves by describing the same person. Discrepant observers then can come to identify the basis of their disagreements; they can separate disagreement due to genuine differences in evaluation from unwanted discrepancies due to differing interpretations of descriptors. A series of calibration sessions can do much to converge the verbal understandings of observers initially not attuned to the CAQ descriptors. In preliminaries to research in which the CAQ-set is to be used, such calibration sessions can be helpful to the appraisers involved.

4. A final concern voiced in regard to the CAQ-set has to do with the problem of behavioral levels and inferences from observation. Although most of the CAQ descriptors require of the observer only direct, culturally grounded inferences in description of the person's behavior, other CAQ descriptors demand the appraiser's far-ranging, psychodynamically deep inferences as to the person's latent motivational structure. Sometimes,

observers express uneasiness about the extrapolations asked of them.

The problem posed by highly inferential judgments is, of course, not limited to the CAQ-set. It is a problem generated by accepting the conceptual necessity of using *genotypical* or *metapsychological* notions for a deeper understanding of a person. Contemporary psychological orientations have chosen—and the CAQ procedure adopts this conceptual choice—to use abstract, directly unspecifiable constructs as an explanatory means of making sense of behavior that is otherwise unexplainable. Accordingly, the problem of hazarding inferential judgment must be lived with if this conceptual orientation is used.

The process of *psychological inference*—of how an understanding develops or is projected from an accretion and integration of separately insufficient observations—involves profound theoretical considerations that cannot be considered here. The immediate practical dilemma confronting the CQ observer, however, is what to do when it is felt there is an inadequate observational basis for inferring an individual's characteristics.

Obviously, when a judge has had no reasonable opportunity to form understanding of a person, it would be ridiculous to compel a person evaluation. The resulting CQ description is likely to describe Everyman. In appropriate observational situations, however, observers should have had reasonably sufficient opportunities to appraise the individual under scrutiny.

If the observer still has opportunity to extend observations of the insufficiently known person, it should be done. When time must have a stop, however, the course of action for the observer is to do as well as possible. Using implicit person theory as guide, the observer should let extrapolations proceed as they will. That is, the complete set of CQ descriptors should continue to be used; descriptors should not be deleted to make life easier for the observer if only because different observers would be hesitant in regard to different CQ descriptors. Such deletions would defeat the very intentions of the CQ procedure—comparability with corresponding CQ data.

The observer who is uncertain about the salience of certain CQ descriptors may extrapolate unwisely or well. At worst, some random discrimination noise may be introduced; at best, some insistent, intuitive hunches about the person may be forced into CQ visibility and prove to have a veridical basis. If conjectures do not issue with disproportionate frequency from certain observers, and if these conjectures are not focused on certain classes of persons, then the wildest of speculations will introduce little systematic bias. Relations with other independent information (including entirely separate CQ data) will be statistically more difficult to obtain, but no systematic errors will have been introduced.

It has long been recognized that an observer's personal feeling of sufficient or insufficient information about a person is based more on a characteristic intrinsic to the observer than of a characteristic of the person being appraised. Some observers are comfortable with grand extrapolations that are based on flimsy data; other assessors are never satisfied they know enough to evaluate a person. Studies have shown the degree of certainty *habitually* held by an observer in appraising individuals—the professional appraiser's "response style"—carries little implication for the subsequent accuracy of that observer's evaluation. However, the observer—whether characteristically certain or characteristically tentative—varies in evaluative *confidence* in regard to particular persons. Some persons are believed by an observer to be relatively well understood and other persons are not believed by that observer to be relatively well understood. Although the observer's habitual certainty has no larger implication, the observer's degree of relative confidence in regard to a range of particular persons has proven to have substantial consequence (Little, 1961; McNiel, Sandberg, & Binder, 1998). It appears that an uncertain observer, although perhaps bewailing informational insufficiencies, may still be able to offer a most valuable evaluation of the subject.

Overall, the criticisms and concerns expressed about the CQ descriptors, then, do not seem formidable.

5

Q-SORT METHODOLOGY

Over the years, questions in regard to the methodology of Q-sorting person descriptors have provoked much discussion and presumption but little analysis and rationale. The problems to be discussed are not unique to the Q-sort method; they are problems of judgment generally. Only by understanding these issues can the California Q-sort (CQ) procedure as it has responsively evolved be appreciated.

JUSTIFICATION OF THE CQ DISTRIBUTION

The Reason for a Fixed Distribution

A central question is whether the CQ-set is to be freely, spontaneously arrayed by the observer along a continuum of person salience or whether the observer should be required to fit evaluations to a prescribed distribution (Block, 1956). The imposition of a standard, fixed, prescribed, or forced distribution of CQ descriptors on all CQ-sorters has been a controversial feature to some[1]

---

[1]In the early primer on *Q methodology* (McKeown & Thomas, 1988, p. 34), it is asserted that idiosyncratic Q-distribution shapes are inconsequential in their effect. As the earlier reference to Carroll (1961) makes algebraically clear, this assertion and belief is indisputably incorrect.

(see chap. 2, this volume). Why should the appraiser of a person be compelled to sort CQ descriptors into an arbitrary and perhaps personally uncomfortable distribution and use a prescribed suit of categories perhaps felt to be unnatural?

The logic underlying the requirement of a fixed-descriptor distribution needs to be recognized, because it serves a fundamental and absolute requirement—achieving the goal of creating fully commensurate person descriptions. A compelling illustration of this necessity is by demonstrating the consequences when a prescribed distribution is *not* imposed.

Suppose in evaluating an individual, one observer evaluates many more attributes as extremely characteristic or extremely uncharacteristic of the person than does a second observer, who is evaluatively more moderate. Some might naively and incorrectly presume the more emphatic assessor knows more about the person being evaluated than does the more cautious assessor. Moreover, if a CQ composite that portrays the person is subsequently to be developed, the observer who manifests response extremeness (and a therefore larger variance of CQ-attribute placement) will have more influence on the subsequent CQ consensus than the more diffident observer. However, as noted earlier in this volume, there is much evidence that indicating assuredness of judgment does not also augur accuracy but is more often expressive simply of an appraiser's response style (Little, 1961; McNiel, Sandberg, & Binder, 1998). Accordingly, it is better to avoid this unwarranted basis for disproportionate weighting of assessors.

Consider now a second kind of problem, this time arising from differences in the way judges spontaneously segment a continuum. Suppose we know a priori that two observers in characterizing a given person identically rank the descriptors of a 100-descriptor CQ-set; that is, the descriptors chosen by the one assessor as characterizing the person exactly correspond in their ordering to the descriptor sequence chosen by the second assessor. In this unlikely but exemplifying situation, the correlation of agreement between the two observers is obviously unity (1.00), expressing perfect assessor congruence.

However, suppose the two identical descriptor continua are each to be recorded not as full rankings but are segmented into dichotomies. The observers separately are asked to divide the descriptors into two categories: those qualities the observer deemed characteristic of the person and those qualities deemed not characteristic. One judge, with stringent personal standards as to what shall be called "characteristic," identifies only 10 descriptors as characteristic and 90 as uncharacteristic. The second assessor, more generous or lax, partitions the 100 descriptors into 90 as being characteristic and 10 as being uncharacteristic. The correlation table that illustrates these two conjoined dichotomous evaluations is shown in Table 5.1.

In the resulting fourfold table, by definition both assessors agree perfectly on the 10 descriptors considered as characteristic, and they agree perfectly on the 10 descriptors considered as uncharacteristic. However, the

TABLE 5.1
Illustration of the Effects on Latent Full Agreement
of Radically Different Dichotomization

		Judge B		
		Characteristic of subject	Uncharacteristic of subject	Sum
Judge A	Characteristic of subject	10	0	10
	Uncharacteristic of subject	80	10	90
	Sum	90	10	

assessors disagree on the remaining 80 descriptors that the one observer labels as characteristic whereas the other observer labels them as uncharacteristic.

Now, in this particular circumstance of widely discrepant segmenting of a continuum, the two judges correlate only .11. Although the two judges indeed are latently identical in their evaluations, because of the different ways each has opted to overtly partition the underlying continuum, the subsequently computed manifest correlation between them is markedly reduced and importantly misleading.

This lowering of an index of appraiser agreement as a function of different—often fortuitously different—segmentation of the underlying judgment continuum will always be the case. Only if both judges segment the underlying continuum identically will the degree of their underlying correspondence become fully apparent. To the extent that clinicians differ in regard to their categorizing proclivities, their manifest correlation will be lowered—never raised.

This point is entirely general, not limited to the particular vivid example mentioned earlier. Whenever the number of Q descriptors exceeds the number of sorting categories, the calculated correspondence between different Q-sorts is adversely influenced to the extent the *shapes* of the two contrasted Q distributions are different. The greater their divergence with regard to distribution shape—with descriptor ordering held constant—the lower their index of agreement. Never, *algebraically*, can the correlation between two observers be falsely elevated (Carroll, 1961, Appendix A). This logical recognition is of fundamental importance, although it often goes unrecognized by Q-oriented (and correlational) investigators. It necessarily entails use of a common, universally applied distribution for a Q-set if the resulting Q-sorts by appraisers are to be commensurate and thus fairly compared.[2]

---

[2]For analyses resting solely on correlations, such as factor analysis, small differences between Q distributions may not prove especially important in the analytical context. However, large distribution differences can importantly affect correlation analyses, and they defeat efforts at analyses involving Q-sort comparisons.

A hasty response suggested for this troublesome lowering problem is to have every Q-sorter completely rank the focused-on set of Q descriptors. By so doing, appraisers would have identical distributions, and the intercorrelations among them would fairly represent their degree of correspondence; Q-sort intercorrelations would not be lowered by differences in distribution shapes. However, complete ranking of Q descriptors is an impractical, even foolish demand to impose on observers. The time required of the evaluator increases markedly the more pair-discriminations are demanded. Moreover, the finer the discriminations called for, the less the assuredness of the appraiser in regard to the position in which a Q descriptor is placed, especially with regard to Q descriptors falling into the midrange—to the point that Q-descriptor placements may show little stability in midportions of the ordering spectrum.

For these several reasons—the greatly increased time required, the extreme personal difficulty judges have in reliably making fine discriminations especially in midrange of the distribution—complete rank ordering does not present itself as a solution to the problem posed by different shapes of Q-descriptor distributions.

A less-than-complete ordering would lessen Q-sorting labors, that is, categories would remain ordered relative to each other, but within each category further descriptor discriminations are not made. This tactic nevertheless would introduce a lowered correlation between Q-sorts if Q-sorters are permitted to freely—and variably—choose the number of Q descriptors to be placed within each score category; different distribution shapes would then arise and therefore correlations between Q-sorts would be adversely influenced.

The only remaining solution is thus to mandate that all judges place identical numbers of descriptors into each of the ordered categories—hence the prescribed, fixed, or forced-sorting method. By using a universally prescribed distribution for Q descriptors, comparisons and correlations among Q-sorts become straightforward and commensurate. Confounding, inevitably muddling response styles of assessors are prevented from arising.

The Potential of Differential Informational "Pull"

Despite the rationale for a universal fixed Q distribution, a remaining argument invoked against prescribing the Q-descriptor arrangement has been that this approach loses certain "information" that would be retained if an unprescribed distribution of judgments was tolerated. The presumption here has been that something important is being expressed about a person being appraised when the assessor's description results in an unusual shape for the free arrangement of Q descriptors. This supposition would be relevant indeed if one person reliably tended to elicit one kind of distribution from judges whereas another person pulled a reliably different distribution form.

This hunch has merit and plausibility, but it is a conjecture that properly requires empirical evaluation. It is not sufficient to simply assert that a methodological constraint loses information. With the assertion devolves a responsibility to specify of what this information consists and just how important in the overall analytical scheme this information may be. There is information and there is *information*. Not all of the reliable facets of behavior are worthy of consideration or are uniquely expressed; some information is trivial or irrelevant to the descriptive purpose at hand. Other information, although important, may be reflected more completely or more directly by alternative means. A priori, the suggestion that the prescribed distribution Q-sorting procedure excludes certain channels of communication should be interpreted not so much as a criticism but rather as a call for investigation of the weight and uniqueness of the eliminated information.

A study was designed that bears on this question (Block, 1956). Assessors were asked to Q describe a set of public personages in a free and unrestrained way before the procrustean fixed distribution was further imposed on them. The design of the research permitted evaluation of the relative contributions of the judges and of the personages involved to the shape of the unforced distribution.

The primary and clear finding was that assessor idiosyncrasies explained, almost completely, the various shapes of the unconstrained descriptor distributions. Judges differed among themselves radically and, except in one instance mentioned next, not as a function of the person being described. An important ancillary finding was that, in the unrestricted sorting situation, judges did not volunteer certain discriminations they subsequently were able to reliably make when pressed to the task.

In one instance, however, a described person did appear to influence systematically the extempore Q-descriptor arrangements of the judges. The several Q-sorters, when in the unconstrained-sorting situation, tended to use extreme scale categories significantly more often for this one person than for the other persons being described.

This finding requires attention because when a mandatory distribution is used such findings are precluded from existence. What then is the importance and psychological meaning of the finding that a particular person pulls an especially extreme reaction from appraisers?

This characteristic of a person has unknown significance until it is related to other and separate information that lends meaning to what otherwise remains only an observational fact. To discern the implications of this person-based influence within the unregulated Q distribution, it was convenient and relevant to analyze the quite independent data from the *prescribed* distribution situation. By comparing the prescribed descriptor ordering for the extremely viewed person with the prescribed descriptor orderings for the other persons, the unique impressiveness of the one person stood revealed as a result of his being perceived to be Machiavellian, assertive, affectless, flamboyant, and so on.

Although there may be other implications of this individual's unique pull, the number and nature of the differentiating Q descriptors indicate the implications of this person's tendency to elicit extreme reactions were well expressed within the mandatory Q arrangement. If the person's pull, revealed when unconstrained sorting was permitted, had been precluded by use of the fixed-distribution procedure, it appears that little psychological information would have been lost. Much of the meaning of this person's pull, discerned through an unregulated Q distribution, was alternatively available from the prescribed Q ordering.

This instance is not an isolated finding. In almost all anticipatable Q-sort circumstances, the psychological meaning of reliable person-based pull differences that issue from an unconstrained Q-descriptor distribution would be available as well from Q descriptions based on constrained Q distributions. The reason why this assertion is likely to be true is that each of the recognized or conceivable person characteristics that create distribution differences in the unconstrained Q-sorting situation is alternatively conveyable through an appropriate CQ descriptor within the distribution-specified CQ-set. Already noticed or conjectured as creating distribution differences in "free" circumstances are such attributes as *favorableness–unfavorableness* of evaluations, amount of information the sorter feels is available, and the *colorfulness–drabness* of the person being described. Each attribute can be expressed by suitable descriptors within the prescribed CQ distribution. If wide dispersion in the unforced CQ sort reflects a person's colorfulness, then a Q descriptor, "Is colorful," by its placement within the prescribed Q-sort of that person will convey similar meaning. If the average scale value for descriptors in the unconstrained Q distribution is related to the favorableness of the assessor's evaluation, then descriptors bearing upon favorable and unfavorable characteristics will by their positioning within the forced sort provide equivalent information.

The only limitation on this stratagem for eliminating consideration of psychologically relevant distribution differences in the unconstrained situation is that the Q-set being used with a prescribed distribution must be comprehensive enough to include the various psychological implications of potential shape differences. But this is only another way of saying the CQ-set must permit comprehensive personality description—a requirement already taken to heart.

Reasons, condensed, for use of prescribed as compared with freely evolved Q distributions are as follows:

1. The free Q-sorting procedure lowers the correspondence among Q-sorts, whereas the prescribed, forced Q-sorting procedure permits fully commensurate, unambiguous assessments of the agreement among Q-sorts.
2. The unconstrained Q-sorting procedure allows assessors to not make discriminations they indeed are able to make under the prescribed distribution condition.

3. The free Q-sorting procedure does not provide information inaccessible through the prescribed Q-sorting procedure.
4. The free Q-sorting procedure provides methodologically unwieldy data, whereas the prescribed Q-sorting procedure provides data in a convenient and readily processed form.
5. The prescribed Q-sorting procedure empirically provides somewhat more discriminations than the free CQ-sorting procedure.
6. The free Q-sorting procedure, by its susceptibility to bunching Q descriptors at both ends of the salience continuum, is more susceptible to the Barnum effect, the tendency to attribute global, unindividuated characteristics to an individual (Meehl, 1956).

For these several reasons, Stephenson's initial but previously unrationalized stipulation that the Q-sorts adhere to a fixed, specified distribution is reaffirmed. The gains accruing from this methodological recommendation seem unquestionable.

The Shape of the Prescribed Distribution

With the decision to prescribe a Q distribution, concern shifts to the question of just what shape distribution to fix on. This question is not an especially pivotal one. There are enough pertinent observations in the literature and arising out of Q-sort experience to suggest a tenable distribution form that enjoys broad acceptability and is therefore unlikely to warrant appreciable change.

Thus, Q descriptors have relevant negative as well as relevant positive salience. It follows, then, that the sorting dimension must have psychological meaning at both of its ends and discrimination throughout the full salience continuum.

A second decision is concerned with the number of categories to be used for the salience continuum. Obviously, the more categories used, the more discriminations are made. However, use of too many categories creates difficulties for the assessor who may have difficulties making salience decisions in the category midrange. A Q distribution therefore should have a fixed but humanly sensible number of discrimination categories.

For implementation of this desideratum, there is abundant and pertinent information. Guilford (1954, chap. 11) provides an old but still excellent discussion of studies on rating methods. For the CQ procedure, after trial and error, nine categories have been judged sufficient and yet not excessive. A nine-interval continuum, although demanding of the appraiser, still elicits reliable discriminations. Other Q investigators have used alternate numbers of categories, and Stephenson himself has used as many as 13. Admittedly, the choice might have gone otherwise; nothing fundamental would have changed. However, the need for standardization is paramount and, for that reason alone, the decision to fix on nine categories for the CQ distribution continues to control present practice.

A third decision is concerned with the essential shape of the decided-on nine-category, double-ended distribution. By a misinterpretation of Stephenson (1953), there has developed a view that a distribution of Q descriptors must be normal or Gaussian. This is not so, as Stephenson (1953, p. 60) pointed out. The distribution may be of any nonbizarre, symmetrical shape. Pragmatically, the selected shape depends on just how congenial or affronting the evaluators who are using the prescribed distribution will find it to be.

The two serious alternatives for a Q distribution are a unimodal, normal distribution or a rectangular, uniform distribution. In a unimodal distribution, there is a piling up of descriptors in the middle categories of the continuum; in a rectangular distribution, there are an equal number of Q descriptors in each of the designated categories.

With the number of scale intervals or categories fixed, the number of discriminations in a Q description is solely a function of the shape of the distribution used, with the maximal number of discriminations stemming from a rectangular distribution. To the extent that descriptors pile up in any category, the total number of discriminations decreases.

Empirically, the natural distribution offered by judges in an unforced situation averaged across a number of judges, turns out to be a symmetric, somewhat unimodal one. It is definitely not normal in form, verging instead toward platykurtosis but short of rectangularity.

Consequently, for the CQ-set in particular, the number of descriptors in each of the nine categories—5, 8, 12, 16, 18, 16, 12, 8, and 5—has been set in-between rectangularity and normality. As computed by Ferguson's (1949) method, the number of discriminations offered by this distribution does not especially differ from the maximal number of 4,400 discriminations offered by a nine-interval rectangular distribution. The prescribed CQ distribution contributes 4,349 discriminations. Given the psychological reasons for deviating toward a centered unimodality, this slight numerical difference is unimportant.

Thus, some introspective considerations and some statistical ones converge on an equivalent recommendation. Because midrange discriminations contribute less salience information and, as already noted, are more difficult to make, it is easing on Q-sorters if these midrange discriminations are made fewer in number. This end is accomplished simply by deviating somewhat from rectangularity toward a centered unimodality.

From the statistical quarter, unimodality makes sense as well. Analysis of Q data often requires the use of a similarity index between Q-sorts. Usually, this similarity index is a correlation coefficient, an index especially sensitive to extreme Q-descriptor placement and giving relatively little weight to descriptors placed close to the distribution's central tendency. Because such similarity indices are compellingly useful, it is unreasonable to generate finely grained, midrange discriminations not weighted subsequently by the similarity indices used.

In sum, the reasons for the chosen shape of the CQ distribution are as follows:

1. Empirically, studies have suggested appraisers prefer a distribution with a shape between rectangularity and unimodal symmetry.
2. Q descriptors placed in middle categories are psychologically less salient than extremely placed Q descriptors in evidencing the psychological portrayal of a person.
3. Moreover, descriptors placed in the middle categories are the most difficult and also the most time-consuming judgments for the appraiser to make.
4. Conventional indices used to express the similarity between Q-sorts give relatively little weight to discriminations made in the distribution midrange.

For all of these reasons, the descriptor distribution chosen for Q-sets tends to be unimodal but flatter by far than a bell-shaped distribution.

6

CALIFORNIA Q-SORT
PSYCHOMETRICS

INDIVIDUAL CALIFORNIA Q-SORTS (CQS)
AND THEIR REPLICABILITY

Having provided the reasoning that leads to the decision for a prescribed, symmetrical, unimodal distribution, a next question is "How dependably can an appraiser describe a person through the established CQ procedure?" If the mental operations involved in formulating a CQ-sort are importantly aleatoric, the entire enterprise fizzles. First, then, some assurance of the substantiality or replicability of an evaluator's CQ-sort is required.

Herewith is some accidental, unreproducible (even amusing) evidence on the reproducibility of a CQ-sort by an appraiser. Some years ago, at an assessment center, a research staff evaluated sets of persons over a series of weekends, grueling for both the assessees and the staff assessors. Immediately after a weekend, each staff member CQ described each of the 10 persons just observed. Seriously characterizing 10 different persons all in the course of a single day is a fatiguing, necessarily absorbing chore.

By a slip of the mind, on one occasion a staff member completely forgot that he had already CQ-sorted a particular subject. Toward the end of a long day, he CQ-sorted that person a second time, for what he thought was his 10th

CQ-sort of the day. On discovering his unnecessary duplication, he cursed tiredly because it meant he still had a last person to describe, who he then conscientiously CQ-sorted.

The incident is anomalous and not planfully repeated. It is of unique interest because in a pure sense it meets the theoretical but unattainable requirement of *test–retest reliability*: reliability calculated without the passage of time and unaffected by residual memory. Certainly, the forgetful staff member would not have done the second (unnecessary) CQ-sort had he at all remembered his prior, hours-before appraisal. Additionally, this assessor had experienced much retroactive inhibition from his various intervening CQ-sorts of other assessees. It may safely be presumed, given the happenstance, that the forgetful assessor represents a "pure" test case for evaluating test–retest reliability: He had absolutely no memory of how, in the hours just before, he had placed the CQ descriptors in evaluating the person involved.

How well did the two CQ-sorts of the same individual by the same but memoryless assessor correlate? The answer is an impressively high .94. Of course, a single and so special an instance should not be incautiously generalized; one cannot know how other similarly forgetful assessors would have fared.

This single finding, however, receives further support by implication from the frequent finding of extremely high correlations (circa .75) among CQ-sorters in describing a well-understood "target" conceptual person (e.g., "the optimally adjusted person, exemplified" or "the paranoid person, exemplified"). Such agreement among CQ-sorters could not arise unless the target concept as understood by each CQ-sorter was both reliably and similarly held. Together, these findings testify to the essential dependability of seriously expressed CQ-sortings.

The consistency with which an individual CQ-sorter can order descriptors along an abstract and complex "salience" dimension indicates the sorter has a definite cognitive basis for offering a character evaluation. This is a striking, implicative, necessary finding. It suggests that, in the course of a developing life, individuals develop multitudinous episodic memories of persons and events. Subsequently, they find it heuristically simplifying to cognitively condense or generalize these remembrances into character understandings or portrayals; impinging memories are abstracted into reliable attribute ascriptions (Peevers & Secord, 1973).

THE "WISDOM" OF COMPOSITES, CONSENSUS CQ-SORTS, AND THEIR REPLICABILITY

It should be remembered, however, that the reproducibility or reliability of a recorded subjective impression does not necessarily mean the subjective impression has veracity; the *reliability* of an individual appraisal does not necessarily mean an accuracy of that appraisal. The *plausibility* of an individual appraisal depends on the larger, surrounding nomological framework of subjective impressions held by a broader base of individual appraisers. The plausibility of an individual appraisal is enhanced when multiple, operationally independent, diversely based subjective impressions of the same person prove to all manifest some sufficient degree of positive intercorrelation. Although by no means a foolproof credibility principle, the congruence among multiple, separate appraisals from diverse observers of the same person offers a persuasive inductive basis for considering their center of gravity—a composite—as having verisimilitude, a kind of truth.

Long recognized has been the heightened cogency or wisdom afforded by judgments issuing from group composites. Agreement among a mixed bag of independent observers has proven empirically to be largely—if not always— creditable. If many appraisers attribute "warmth" or "intelligence" to a person, then this generalized view is justly given more credence than a single appraiser's attribution of warmth or intelligence to that person. By virtue of its broader judgmental basis, a consensus of assorted observer impressions of a person will be more believable—and empirically likely more accurate—than the impression afforded by a single observer of that person. Surowiecki (2004) recounted numerous instances in the wider world wherein the consensus opinion or judgment of large groups of people on sundry matters proves to be more prescient than estimates based on an elite few. Closer to the immediate circumstance is the clever, instructive study by Dawes (1977, p. 267) who asked, "Suppose we measured height with rating scales instead of rulers?" He had faculty members guesstimate the heights of departmental colleagues and averaged their guesses. Correlating these averages with actually measured faculty heights, the coefficient proved to be .98, virtually perfect; the consensus height estimate was more accurate than the height guesses of any individual faculty member. Why is this so?

A first reason devolves from psychometrics. Multiple measures or indicators (e.g., different intelligence test items or, in the present instance, independent appraisals by different observers of the same target person), when aggregated, always *cumulate* the common variance (from the various intelligence items or from the different appraisals of a person) and reduce the presence within the aggregate of irrelevant *noise* (intrinsic to the diverse individual intelligence items or to the several individually subjective appraisals of the same person). The logic underlying this psychometric process has long been known and is formally embodied in the Spearman–Brown prophecy formula. Compositing multiple, commonly intended indicators always heightens the stability or reproducibility of the composite, thus enhancing the implicativeness of the derived consensus for an ultimate, often latent criterion (i.e., validity or accuracy). Whereas each of the commonly intended indicators (intelligence items or person appraisers) might not correlate well with each other or with the implicit accuracy criterion, the democratic summation of them all markedly improves the chance of achieving the desired connections.

However, although the Spearman–Brown effect is well-known, multiplicity of indicators per se may not alone be sufficient. The multiple indicators should also represent—in variety or diversity—the *domain* of possible intelligence test items or, in the present instance, the domain of possible person appraisers. Otherwise, the psychometrically reliable composite may be too narrow in compass to have large or interesting signification. If all of the intelligence test items are limited in scope to the same facet of intelligence (e.g., vocabulary knowledge, alone) or all the appraisals of the same person stem from rigidly conforming disciples of the same doctrinaire clinician, the high reliability of the composite is unlikely to represent a broad view of intelligence or a broadly based portrayal of a person. Representative sampling of the domain of intelligence test items or the domain of CQ appraisers of the target person therefore is also required. Anticipation or prejudgment can help ensure that the multiple indicators used, whether of intelligence items or CQ portrayals of the same target person, include diversity and result in a broader, more representative, more believable—and by inference—more accurate view.

In sum, a happy consequence of a consensus or composite that is based on multiple, entirely separate appraisers divergently experiencing a target person is that, psychometrically, it is a more generalized impression than the subjective impressions offered by any solitary appraiser. If based on diverse appraisals, the composite more closely approximates "truth" or at least its verisimilitude. Conjoining multiplicity and domain sampling of appraisers, the composite therefore has a statistically improved likelihood of achieving connection and correspondence with other quite different dependable data.

REQUIREMENTS FOR A CONSENSUS

In forming a consensus from separate appraiser CQ evaluations, two related requirements must be met. The first requirement is an obvious one—the subjective impression CQ-sorts by each of the observers must be stable and well-based rather than chancy. The opening section of this chapter indicates this requirement can be expected to be met.

The second requirement is that the CQ consensus formed must not be overly influenced by the singular CQ contribution of any participating observer. It should be remembered that the observer or appraiser is being used only as a "measuring instrument," providing unique subjective impressions of the attributes of a designated person in commensurate form. It must be reasonable to believe that, in combining multiple CQ-sorts of the same person, the resulting CQ consensus fairly represents the general views of relevant observers about the person's authentic disposition.

FORMING A CONSENSUS

How—specifically—may the several, entirely separate CQ appraisals of a person be pooled to best or fairly describe the person's character? In one form or another, a whole host of methods have addressed this question because it is the long familiar psychometric problem of how to form a composite judgment or group decision in the absence of a criterion. Conveniently, the simplest pooling procedure has been shown to closely approximate optimality (Dana & Dawes, 2004; Wainer, 1976).

The composite of a number of separately formulated, commensurate CQ evaluations of the same individual can be well expressed simply by arithmetically averaging the separate CQ-sorts for that individual. The averaging method issues an objective and more representative expression of observer evaluations; it is psychometrically sound and democratic as well because none of the observers can justify being awarded special interpretive weighting.[1]

If based on several appraisers, a composite-based Q-sort tends to quickly achieve substantial reliability. The kind of reliability meant here is *reproducibility*, the correspondence to be expected when the composite Q-sort is correlated with a composite Q-sort based on an equivalent set of observers.

Table 6.1 specifies the reproducibility of a composite Q-sort for varying numbers of assessors and for varying degrees of average intercorrelation among assessors, as estimated by the familiar and powerful Spearman–Brown prophesy formula. From the table, it is clear that respectable reliabilities are readily obtained in typical contexts as observers tend to agree and/or the number of observers increases. It should be noted that as the number of appraisers increases, even with tiny appraiser intercorrelations, reliability asymptotically approaches 1.00.

As a group composite, an averaged CQ-sort shares the properties of all averages in having considerable sampling stability. Simultaneously, because the CQ composite has a limited correlation with each of the individual CQ-sorts

---

[1] In psychiatry, there has been preference for the case conference or "diagnostic council" (Murray, 1938) method of formulating and then diagnosing a person. A group of clinicians will meet to discuss a patient and formulate an evaluation of the person (usually, a diagnosis). Certainly, it may be informative and reinforcing for the group to come together to compare and extend individual formulations. In training or educational contexts, the conference method of formulating evaluations has a special value because the give and take of information can be instructive. But for research purposes, judgments issuing from group interaction are inadvisable. Conclusions coming from group debate are influenced by a variety of unspecifiable (or at least unreportable) group dynamic factors such as the relative status or prestige of the various judges, their relative persuasiveness, the fortuitous interpersonal contagions that may develop and linger, and so on. "Consensus" conclusions in this context are confounded in unknown ways and their true consensuality is not ascertainable. This criticism of staff diagnostic conferences could be neglected if the conferencing method regularly demonstrated its larger validity. In fact, however, the very little empirical evidence on the matter strongly suggests that no predictive gains are contributed by the conference method (Kelley & Fiske, 1951; Westen & Weinberger, 2004). In the dynamics of group discussion, the participants in the conferencing situation do not appear to contribute additional acuity in the consensus judgment finally reached.

TABLE 6.1
Reliability of Composite CQ Evaluations as a Function
of Number and Intercorrelation of Judges

Average judge intercorrelation	Number of judges					
	2	3	5	8	100	1000
.10	.18	.25	.36	.47	.92	.99
.30	.46	.56	.68	.77	.98	1.00
.50	.67	.75	.83	.89	.99	1.00
.70	.82	.88	.92	.95	1.00	1.00

from which it derived, it is relatively unaffected by any single clinician contributing to the average. In principle, the CQ-sorts of individual assessors may be interchanged at random with those of other nominally equivalent observers, without expecting appreciable influence on the CQ composite. It would appear, then, the requirements for a composite CQ evaluation are achievable—reproducibility and relative autonomy of the averaged CQ array from any single contributing observer.

THE LIKELIHOOD THAT INDIVIDUAL PERCEPTIONS
WILL BE LOST IN THE CONSENSUS

Although the doubtful metascientific admissibility of solitary, nonconsensual observations has already been remarked on, what is the empirical likelihood of the CQ composite losing special insights dependably afforded by the separate impressions of individual evaluators? The chance is quite small. It is not widely recognized that the composite evaluation does surprising justice as well to separate, unique observer evaluations.

A correlation coefficient can be computed between an observer's CQ evaluation and the composite Q-sort, including that appraiser's Q evaluation, resulting in a part–whole correlation. Obviously, as this part–whole correlation approaches unity, there is less and less opportunity for a meaningful difference to exist between the discriminations provided by the individual observer and the discriminations provided when the composite includes that observer.

The part–whole correlation is a function of two factors, the intercorrelation of the observers and the number of observers. Table 6.2 cites the part–whole correlations when the average intercorrelation of observers is zero, .50, and .71; and the number of observers is 2, 3, 5 and 8. These combinations probably bracket the various situations empirically encountered.

The conclusion to be drawn from this table is that, although the possibility may conjecturally exist of an individual observer who is offering dis-

TABLE 6.2
Part–Whole Correlations Under Various Conditions

Average observer intercorrelation	Number of observers			
	2	3	5	8
.00	.71	.58	.45	.35
.50	.79	.71	.64	.59
.71	.87	.82	.78	.75

criminations that are importantly different from those contained in the consensus, the part–whole correlations in likely situations tend to be high enough that there is small likelihood that separate analyses would be dependably worthwhile. With few or even a moderate number of observers, and even with relatively low interobserver agreement, analysis of the composite CQ array will discern almost all of the relations conceivably discernable through individual evaluations.

Moreover, in unpublished work, I have found that a single assessor occasionally bettering the CQ composite in regard to one person is not dependably superior to the CQ composite in regard to other persons and indeed often is worse. By and large, then, the composite CQ array appears to be a fair and sensitive way of representing individual CQ evaluations. It has the happy faculty of empirically being more consistently discriminating than any of the individual CQ evaluations of which it is composed. In chapter 7 of this volume some intriguing, coherent substantive findings afforded by such CQ composites will be evidenced.

IN REGARD TO THE STILL UNREQUITED PREFERENCE
FOR UNIQUE JUDGMENTS

Despite the attractiveness of combining commensurate information to establish a well-based reliable composite, the idea of forming a composite—of empirically combining judgments—may be anathema to the sensitivities of some person observers; there often still remains a tendency among clinicians to reflexively reject the notion.

The anticombining plaint that separate analyses of individual CQ evaluations would reveal valid perceptions lost or otherwise diluted in the combining process has been advanced rhetorically but never tested; it claims that respecting each observer evaluation separately will provide important information forever lost when all of the observers are combined into a *mean* mean.

This argument raises both pragmatic and philosophical issues not really considered. Pragmatically, what is the likelihood that individualized Q-sorts will indeed issue more cogent understandings than a brute force composite that is based on arithmetically combining observations by appraising peers? This question has perhaps already received sufficient, relevant response: empirically, the CQ-sorts of single assessors are not dependably more discriminating than the combined CQ composite. As Table 6.2 makes clear, because individual Q-sorts tend to correlate highly with the composite of which they are a part, there remains a small possibility that an individual Q-sort will dependably differ from the broader-based composite.

The philosophical question is, given that more positive results might dependably emerge from separate analyses of individual observers than from the analysis of a group consensus, what does this mean scientifically, and where do such individual findings leave us or rather take us? This is a point that relates to the nature of science.

If, in fact rather than in speculation, one particular assessor discriminates more than the composite derived from combining all of the observers, this finding would have to be respected. But, in and of itself, the phenomenon would have no consequential meaning until investigated and its why and wherefore understood. The distinction important here is that between prediction and understanding. The first is helpful in providing leads to, and checks on, the second. However, they are not the same. There can be prediction without understanding, and there can be understanding without the ability to predict.

If it is agreed that science must have a deep consensual basis, then although an individual observer's perceptions may be uniquely acute, they are mysterious until it is known how their greater keenness is *dependably* achieved. An exclusive acuity has scientific importance only if its basis can be discerned. Otherwise, it remains simply a, perhaps useful, curiosity piece; it is not a datum of science. It is by this reasoning that solitary, ineffable observer evaluations are seldom usable as antecedents of understanding. As a basis for hypothesis and "discovery," such perceptions of course are irreplaceable. Their status is questioned, however, when they are used as proof or "justification" (Reichenbach, 1951).

7

ON THE PROCESS OF
CHARACTERIZING A PERSON BY
THE CALIFORNIA Q-SORT METHOD

The immediately preceding several chapters of this volume describe the development of an encompassing set of person descriptors and a rigorous methodology to assure their commensurate descriptive usage. Moreover, in several ways, the dependability and coherence of resulting California Q-sorts (CQs) have evidenced their firm cognitive and empirical basis. Chapter 7 discusses the subjective judgmental basis that underlies the interpretation of CQ descriptors, obviously at different conceptual levels, as coordinate and scalable.

Can phenotypical CQ descriptors such as "Initiates humor, makes spontaneous funny remarks" be intermixed meaningfully with more inferential descriptors such as "Has a readiness to feel guilty"? What is the nature of the complex dimension along which CQ descriptors are ordered? What is the deep meaning of *psychological salience*, the personally unique, intuitive, formally unspecifiable criterion held in mind by the CQ-sorter?

Salience is an unspecifiable term idiosyncratically conceived but also commonly understood. The thesaurus offers multiple gleanings or connotations for the word: for example, *arresting, notable, striking, prominent, significant, jutting, centroidal, dominant, crucial,* and *paramount*.

For the present purposes, perhaps the effective notion of psychological salience, positive or negative, can best be conveyed when considered within an informational context. By "informational," reference is to the sense in which the concept of information is used in information theory (e.g., Attneave, 1959) and in measurement logic (Cronbach, 1953a). The information (i.e., understandings) projected by the appraiser may be viewed as efforts to reduce uncertainty about the character and behavior of the person of focal interest.

Thus, of two Q descriptors, the descriptor that excludes the most behaviors or alternative characteristics (or believed by the observer to do so) is, by definition, the more informative or salient, whether placed positively or negatively. A descriptor is not salient to the extent it is understood as failing to narrow the range of behaviors or characteristics of the person being described. The limiting cases, according to this definition, are where a descriptor is viewed as permitting or entailing or predicting only one behavioral possibility or characteristic (and is therefore uniquely salient) and where a descriptor does not delimit at all the set of behaviors or characteristics (and is therefore irrelevant in the person formulation).

For many, the notion of specifying as informational what it is an individual will not do or will not be may seem unnatural and therefore a few remarks here on the rationale are in order.

To predict that an individual, as a function of personal anxiety level, will manifest a highly specific behavior is a pinpoint prediction. Highly specific predictions are either right or (usually) wrong. Pinpoint predictions have proven empirically to be a premature psychological effort.

To predict that an individual, because of anxiety, will go through a radical reorganization of personality is a delimiting but not a pinpoint prediction. In general, it is impossible to seriously offer specific behavioral predictions about people. One can only narrow the range of possibilities. This is not to deny pinpoint prediction as an ultimate aspiration; it is simply to recognize the many complexities—usually unresolvable—of anticipating the specifics of future behavior in unanticipated contexts. Moreover, in the isolated instances in which perhaps pinpoint prediction may be feasible, it is but a special case of the alternative definition favored here.

Appraiser acumen in regard to person functioning usually operates within a delimiting perspective. In practice, however, predictions that are delimiting tend to be neglected even though they may substantially narrow behavioral alternatives. Although an infinite amount of acquaintance and knowledge is required to say what someone is or will be, much less understanding and knowledge is required to begin to meaningfully say what someone is not or will never be. The approach of excluding alternatives is more humble but allows approximations of understanding to be registered. The appraiser might anticipate the likelihood of a patient's suicide per se without predicting whether sleeping pills, a leap from a bridge, or a .38 caliber revolver will be used.

To illustrate this informational approach, consider a hypothetical game wherein a person is to be described by one and only one statement. Perhaps a graduate student is briefly messaging home for the first time intimations about imminent marriage. The parents wish to know what sort of person their offspring is marrying. What one descriptive statement would provide the most information to the parents?

The adult child could write, "Getting married to member of human race." Such a statement would provide no information because it is not delimiting. The child might say, "Getting married to a member of the opposite sex." This message would be better but likely would not much reduce the uncertainties of the parents. Neither of these messages would give the parents a useful clue as to the kind of person their child is marrying.

A better message—better in the sense that closer specification of the nature of the imminent mate is provided—might be, "Getting married to sociology graduate student" or "Getting married to graduate student majoring in computer science." Certainly, sociology or computer science graduate students are each more homogeneous groupings than graduate students in general and, accordingly, this message would leave the parents more informed and somewhat less uncertain. The message has a degree of salience and has eliminated some potential behavioral alternatives. An even more informative message might be, "Getting married to acutely disturbed hebephrenic schizophrenic." The message—distressing as it might be—is extremely specifying of the mate's characteristics. Individuals in a group of acutely disturbed schizophrenics are importantly similar. Such a descriptive statement, if it applied, would be an extremely salient one. By further refining the description of a person, character is delineated ever more closely. The observer who describes a person in multifarious, salience-ordered terms is conveying personal understandings and information.

Returning now to the CQ procedure, 100 conjunctively related messages are provided for the appraiser to "send." Judgments of salience are strictly constrained by the particular descriptors made available. Descriptors not included in the specified ensemble—because they are judged inherently universal in nature ("is a member of the human race") or too molecular ("has a reaction time of .12 second to a supra-threshold electric shock") or merely unfortunate omissions—are irrelevant to the immediate problem confronting the observer, namely, sorting the salience of the particular set of CQ descriptors available. Because judgments and comparisons can be made only with the descriptors included in the CQ deck, to avoid post hoc regrets here again is a reason for exhaustive coverage by a Q-descriptor set.

A final complicating remark on salience is in regard to what may be called *metasalience*. Many CQ descriptors are critically informative for the very reason that they are judged not salient for the particular person—these descriptors may be called metasalient. For example, if a descriptor such as

"Has high aspiration level for self" is sorted into a middle category, the meta-information has been conveyed that this person is viewed as not dominated or driven by ambition, nor yet as a passive, defeated individual. By the descriptor's placement, the assessor is expressing an evaluation that, for this particular person, concerns in regard to aspirations do not provide a central theme. Certainly, such an impression is important to convey. Its importance, however, derives from a different level of understanding than the direct salience context in which judgments are initially offered.

This, then, is the dimension of salience along which the CQ descriptors take on meaning. A person is portrayed by the descriptors the observer evaluates as important, characteristic, defining, delimiting, or implicative for the person being described. In practice, the foregoing rationale operates only implicitly, and judgments proceed apace. For this reason, it is important every so often to call attention to the meaning of the sorting continuum, if only to resensitize the observers to the purpose of their task.

III

THE CALIFORNIA Q-SORT PROCEDURE: RESEARCH APPLICATIONS AND CLINICAL RELEVANCE

8

CALIFORNIA Q-SORT
RESEARCH APPLICATIONS

A diligent reader of this volume should now be in a position to carry out and record a California Q-sort (CQ), even if not on a routine basis. The procedure, however, is not designed simply to provide data in a special format. CQ data have unusual and versatile uses. What are some ways these commensurate evaluations can be used? In what kinds of research are CQ data likely to prove useful? Four kinds of research use are described: (a) comparing two CQ sortings, (b) relating CQ data to independent categories and variables, (c) using CQ prototypes, and (d) discerning personality types through the CQ-set.

COMPARING TWO CQ-SORTINGS

A frequent use of evaluations is simply to contrast a pair of CQ descriptions to identify the descriptors placed differently in the two orderings. Two CQ-sorting psychiatrists or psychologists may wish to describe their conceptions of, say, the borderline personality to gain from their descriptor similarities and differences a recognition and articulation of their respective conceptual understandings. Or it may be of interest to compare the CQ-sortings by two separate clinicians of the same person (client) to see where they agree and disagree in their appraisals. Multiple such examples could be listed.

To know whether a descriptor in one CQ ordering is placed differently in a second CQ arrangement, it is necessary to have some idea as to what discrepancy in descriptor placement is to be considered interpretively important. If one sorter places a descriptor at CQ Position 3 and a second sorter places the same descriptor at CQ Position 4, is this a difference worth attending to, or does the difference between the placements of a descriptor have to be two intervals, three intervals, or how many?

An informal criterion is sufficient to evaluate what differences between the placements of the same descriptor in two Q-sortings are to be considered interpretively substantial. The more formal statistical way involves greater assumptions and labors than the integer differences warrant. The informal method involves simply lining up the two CQ-sortings that are being compared and then noting the CQ-descriptor pairs that differ by two or more intervals. After arranging these differentiating descriptors by their direction of difference and by magnitude of placement difference, a reading of these descriptors portrays directly the nature of the differences between the two CQ evaluations. In circumstances in which two CQ-sorts are to be compared descriptor by descriptor, this decision method for selecting the differentiating descriptors is precise enough. For the very occasional interest in a more formal statistical criterion, Block (1961, pp. 90–94) can be consulted.

This informal analytical approach is sufficient because the placements of CQ descriptors can take on only integer values, and therefore differences in descriptor placement also will be expressed only in integer terms. When a computationally complicated statistical derivation indicates that a non-integer difference is important, it cannot be invoked. Instead, the next higher integer must be used as the criterion. By moving to the next higher integer, a more stringent criterion of importance is necessarily used.

For the range of reliabilities usually encountered and for the statistical levels of importance conventionally used, experience indicates that difference between CQ values of three intervals or more will almost invariably be statistically important. Indeed, a difference of two intervals will quite frequently prove to be statistically discriminating as well. Thus, the quick and approximate method works well, erring, when it does, on the side of conservatism; the highlights of the differences between two CQ-sorts are quickly and readily discerned.

In achieving an understanding of the CQ descriptors that distinguish the two CQ arrays, it is useful to keep in mind also the absolute as compared with the relative placement of these descriptors. A descriptor dependably distinguishing two CQ arrays may, in absolute scaling terms, still not be extreme. For example, a CQ descriptor may discriminate between two CQ arrays, but in one array the placement for that descriptor may be in an intermediate category, whereas in the other CQ array the placement of that descriptor may be three categories away but still be in an intermediate category (e.g., a value of 3 for the one and a value of 6 for the other). Thus, although the descriptor reliably distinguishes the two CQ arrays, it may not be especially salient in an absolute sense (or the descriptor may have absolute implication in only one of the CQ-sorts). It makes interpretive sense in reporting to distinguish between descriptors that have absolute salience and those that are only relatively salient.

RELATING CQ DATA TO INDEPENDENT CATEGORIES AND VARIABLES

Two somewhat different but essentially similar analytical approaches have been used: (a) two groups of CQ-sorted individuals that are categorically different on some independent basis (e.g., men vs. women, Republicans vs. Democrats, English majors vs. computer majors) are statistically compared on each of the 100 CQ descriptors and (b) CQ-sorted individuals each with scores on an independently defined continuous variable (e.g., susceptibility to the Stroop inhibition effect, frequency of drug use, systolic blood pressure) are evaluated by correlating each of the 100 CQ descriptors with the independent dimension.

CQ-descriptor analysis is extraordinarily simple in this computer age. When two categorically different groups are to be compared, for each of the 100 descriptors the distribution of California Adult Q-sort (CAQ) values for individuals in the first group is compared with the distribution of CAQ values for individuals in the second group. If the one distribution is statistically different from the other, then that descriptor distinguishes the two groups. For example, for descriptor j the scale values established for individuals in the first group may be 3, 4, 3, 5, 2, 3, 2, 4, 7, and 4. For individuals in the second group, the scale values established for this descriptor may be 6, 5, 7, 6, 6, 5, 9, 8, 6, and 7. It is clear that the second distribution has a higher average value than the first. Accordingly, that descriptor j may emerge as statistically more characteristic of individuals in the second group. The essential requirement for comparison is that the groupings be established independently of the CQ-sorts.

When the CQ-sorted individuals differ on a continuous variable, each CQ descriptor is correlated with the independent variable. The resulting statistically important correlations convey the personological implications of the independent variable.

In psychological assessment contexts, CQ analyses relating to independent groups or variables have been frequently used although seldom within psychiatric settings in which such analyses also would have appreciable interest. It is therefore instructive here to illustrate the methodological versatility of this kind of analysis in psychology. A half-dozen diverse examples are presented now, centering on—for reasons of immediate citation convenience—my past studies.

Some Illustrative Psychological Studies

One study compared, revealingly, the CQ-sort character formulations of "ineffective liars" with "effective liars" (Block, 1957b). An experimental procedure identified, from a larger sample of medical school applicants, 20 individuals who were autonomically reactive when asked to lie and 20 individuals who were autonomically unreactive when asked to lie. Decision in regard to reactivity or nonreactivity was based solely on extent of electrodermal response when deliberately lying. For each of the 40 persons, and on the basis of prolonged and divergent observations, there had existed five independent CQ-sorts by person appraisers who had absolutely no knowledge of the separately determined autonomic reactivity categorization. For each person, the CQ-sorts were arithmetically aggregated into a composite CQ-sort. Contrasting the CQ composites of the two groups identified many CQ-descriptor characteristics associated with autonomic Reactors (Ineffective Liars) as compared to Nonreactors (Effective Liars). Reactive individuals had been independently described as more likely to be: *anxious and tense, readily dominated by others, giving up and withdrawing in adverse situations, ethically consistent,* among other attributes. Unreactive individuals had been described as more likely to be: *valuing their own independence, nonconforming and rebellious, directly hostile, not easily impressed.* The findings have reciprocal implication in regard to the strengths and uncertainties of a traditional polygraph lie-detection procedure and independently achieved subjective impressions.

Another categorical study investigated, through comparison of CQ-person descriptions, the personological implications of hyperconfident, hypercautious, and reality-warranted decision making in a psychophysical experiment (Block & Petersen, 1955). The task involved estimating over a number of repetitions whether a varied line was longer or shorter than a standard, invariant line. Sometimes the length of the varied line was perceptually indistinguishable from the length of the standard line, and sometimes the varied line was grossly different in length from the standard. Each time, however, the participant made a decision and expressed his degree of confidence in that decision. On the basis of decision performance, a sample of Air Force officers was classified into three groups: (a) the first group contained individuals who certainly expressed confidence in decisions made when line-length comparisons were easy but who also expressed confidence even when making inordinately difficult line-length comparisons, (b) the second group contained individuals who expressed uncertainty when line-length comparisons were most difficult to make but who also expressed uncertainty even when decisions were extremely obvious, and (c) the third group contained individuals who expressed confidence when decisions were obvious but who expressed uncertainty when decisions were very difficult to make. Separately, 8 assessment staff members had independently, from subjective impressions gained in variegated social interactions, CQ sorted each of the officers, and for each officer a composite CQ-sort had been arithmetically aggregated. Statistical evaluation of the descriptors indicated the overly confident individuals in the line-decision task separately had tended to be evaluated as *constricted, blustery, dogmatic, less self-reliant, less intelligent,* and *with little tolerance for the complexities of life.* The individuals experimentally classified as overly cautious had separately been evaluated as: relatively *introspective, lacking in ambition and self-reliance,* and *socially nonparticipative.* The third group of individuals—expressing confidence when decisions were easy and lacking in confidence when decisions indeed were difficult—tended to be viewed by assessors as *self-reliant, socially perceptive, intellectually active, as having good sense,* and as *adapted and adaptable.* These findings were coherent, socially cogent, and connect experimental behaviors to independent subjective impressions.

Another study evaluated the differences between young women and young men all with high self-esteem (Block & Robins, 1993). Psychologists have long studied the self because one's self-perceptions are both a reflection of the life that has been led and an influence on the life that will be lived. Self-esteem was indexed by the congruence between a person's self-description and the person's description of a personally ideal self. Conceptually, the extent to which one sees one's self as being similar to one's personal ego ideal may be viewed as operationally reflecting one's self-esteem.

CQ-composite aggregations of each participant were available, on the basis of CQ-sorts made by six independent observers each observing the participant on one of six separate occasions. Although for both sexes, individuals with high self-esteem were evaluated in somewhat similar descriptor terms, self-esteem was manifested in different terms as a function of gender. Young women high in self-esteem, compared with young men high in self-esteem, tended to be CQ evaluated as relatively "warm," "giving," "protective," "sympathetic," "gregarious," "talkative," "conventional," "moral," "straightforward," "cheerful," "poised," and "interested in the opposite sex." Young men high in self-esteem, compared with young women high in self-esteem, tended to be CQ-viewed as relatively "critical," "self-defensive," "hostile," "keeping of people at a distance," "sensitive to demands," "concerned regarding their personal adequacy," "likely to have unconventional thought processes," and "likely to be esthetically sensitive." There certainly is a personality core of self-attributed self-esteem common to both sexes, but the genders appear to aspire to quite different values. These findings are profoundly implicative in regard to the different foundations of self-esteem in America for the two sexes.

The Stroop Color–Word Interference Test (Stroop, 1935) has been used in more than 2,400 studies of perception and cognition. It has been called "the gold standard of research in attention" (MacLeod, 1991, p. 160), fundamental to understanding cognitive interference effects. The Stroop paradigm can be quickly described. First, a set of printed *color names* (e.g., the words *red*, *green*, *blue*, *yellow*) is presented and read aloud by the participant. Second, a set of varying *color hues* (e.g., *red*, *blue*, *green*, *yellow*) is presented and each hue is verbally named. Third, a set of color words is presented wherein each color word is printed incongruently, in a contrary color hue (e.g., the word *red* is printed in blue; the word *green* is printed in yellow) and the task involves the naming of the color hues of the printed words. All three procedures are timed. The primary measure of interest, known as the Stroop effect, is the degree of response interference (RI) or response slowness in the last, incongruent task wherein what is expectably salient (attending to the printed color words) cognitively interferes with the present specific task demands (attending to the color hues in which the words are contrarily printed).

Four assessment psychologists who used the CQ procedure to encode their individual subjective impressions had earlier described each participant, and CQ aggregates had been arithmetically created for each person. The many CQ descriptors evidencing sizable correlates with RI convey the personological context that surrounds resistance to interference, reliably different according to gender. Adolescent girls who are relatively resistant to RI independently tended to be characterized as "having a wide range of interests and competencies"; "possessing self-esteem and personal confidence"; "having insight into both self and others"; "having positive, rewarding, and satisfying interpersonal relationships"; and as being "candid, ethical, persistent, and energetic." The distinguishing descriptors of RI for boys presented a quite different picture. Adolescent boys who are relatively resistant to RI independently tended to be characterized as "in firm control of their impulses" and "relatively unsusceptible to environmental distracters" (the key interfering element in the Stroop task). They were also evaluated as "relatively submissive," "conservative," "troubled by their introspectiveness," "guilt-ridden," and "with an anxious sense of vulnerability" (Block, 2004).

One of the great concerns of our cultural time has been the problem of understanding the provenance of substance abuse. Within the course of a longitudinal study, a number of participants had become involved with some of the drugs widely available in the current culture.

It was readily possible to go backward in time and relate adolescent drug use to nursery school California Child Q-sort (CCQ)-aggregated evaluations garnered from 6 entirely independent nursery school teachers. Through CCQ-descriptor analyses, preschool children subsequently using drugs at age 14 tended earlier to be characterized as "undercontrolled," "restless and fidgety," "emotionally labile," "disobedient," "lacking in calmness," "domineering," "behaving immaturely when under stress," "reluctant to yield and give in," "aggressive," "overreactive to frustration," "teasing," "unable to recoup after stress". These very early antecedents of drug use have large import for contemporary views in regard to adolescent drug use and, consequently, social policy. It would appear that the roots of adolescent substance abuse are discernible, and perhaps modifiable, in early or later childhood (Block, Block, & Keyes, 1988).

Psychologists and political scientists have long been interested in the relations between personality and politics. Longitudinal study permitted an unusual analysis, first ascertaining political orientation of the persons as young adults and then looking backward in time to the CCQ composites developed for each participant during the nursery school years when they were not yet political beings.

At age 23, participants had been administered a variety of indicators of political values to identify conservative or liberal attitudes. When aggregated, their composite provided a reliable and coherent political attitude measure.

This measure was related to CCQ-aggregated composites of the individual participants formed 20 years earlier from the subjective evaluations contributed by six separate nursery school teachers. Many child descriptors of subsequent conservatism or liberalism in young adulthood were found. Preschool children (both boys and girls) subsequently relatively conservative at age 23 were described as more likely to be "inhibited," "uncomfortable with uncertainty," "susceptible to a sense of guilt," and "rigidifying when experiencing duress." Preschool children who 20 years later were relatively liberal impressed their nursery school teachers as more likely to be "self-reliant," "energetic," "prone to develop close relationships," and to be "somewhat dominating." Some interesting gender differences seemed to exist. Although more needs to be done to refine and extend these analyses, the connections between person descriptions formed in very early childhood and the adult political orientation subsequently solidified obviously have significance for political thought (Block & Block, 2006a, pp. 740–743).

The Research Versatility of the CQ Procedure

The CQ procedure can provide comprehensive and commensurable descriptions in a wide variety of circumstances. Comparison can be between good versus mediocre officers, chess players versus dice throwers, cheerleaders versus accountants, psychotherapists versus neurologists, the children of elderly parents versus the children of young parents—the possibilities are endless. They require only theory or imagination, an independent basis for identifying or classifying individuals, and of course proper CQ-sort data.

In the field of psychiatry, applications of the CQ procedure are potential rather than fait accompli. For a conjectured example, suppose a psychiatric hospital or clinic asks such questions as (a) What are the differences between patients who subsequently are successful in a suicide attempt and patients who make only abortive efforts toward suicide? (b) What are the differences between patients who improve with an antidepressant and patients who do not? or (c) What are the differences between patients whose illness changes for the worse with time as compared with those who return to a kind of adequacy? Further instances of useful or interesting contrasts can of course be multiplied.

In response to such questions, CQ-sorts previously collected on a routine basis could provide abundant, relevant, easily analyzed information. Crucially, the CQ information would be temporally prior to the subsequent basis for constituting the groups to be compared. Consequently, the analysis of previously collected CQ data would have substantial, unequivocal, forward implication.

This research possibility is in principle not organizationally difficult to implement. The simple requirement is that, after a designated expert clinician has evaluated a patient, the patient routinely is described by means of the CQ procedure, an appraisal task requiring 15 or 20 minutes from the clinician per patient—once clinicians who formulate such descriptions have gained familiarity with technical details of the method. The CQ evaluation could be based on psychological tests, intake interviews, psychotherapy reports, life history accounts, or other sources of person information. If CQ descriptions of a patient are available from multiple clinicians, then a composite CQ description could be developed; however, even a single CQ description of a patient would be worthwhile in circumstances when the accumulated sample becomes large. Over time, accruing a substantial number of clinical judgments in CQ form would serve as a multifaceted informational resource for statistical analysis, whenever some interesting independent basis for establishing comparison groups is noted.

Statistical Considerations Important in Evaluating CQ Data

For each CQ descriptor, a correlation with the independent dimension is required or a test of the difference in descriptor placement between the groups being compared. For the 100-descriptor CQ-set, therefore, 100 statistical tests are required. As noted earlier, what formerly involved onerous calculation has become almost trivial in these computer times.

In evaluating whether a CQ descriptor differentiates two groups, a variety of parametric or nonparametric statistical tests can be called on. When descriptors are to be related to an independent dimension, conventional correlation is often informative and informally instructive. However, several additional matters require explanation to clarify and more rigorously analyze the Q data.

In the comparison of groups with respect to their respective descriptor placements, it should be noted that Q data are being treated as normative although originally collected ipsatively (cf. chap. 1). Initially, for each individual, descriptor j for individual i was evaluated vis-à-vis the remaining

99 descriptors, and in this context it was assigned to a category, that is, given a scale value. In the present comparative or correlation research application, individual i's value for descriptor j is being merged with the ipsatively earned values for descriptor j of all other individuals. This now involves normative measurement, and some concern as to the appropriateness of this use was early expressed (Cattell, 1944, p. 296; Guilford, 1954, p. 528).

This methodological concern proved accessible to empirical study. The propriety of using ipsatively collected scores as normative scores proved to be well justified (Block, 1957a). The kinds of discriminations afforded by normative data and by ipsative data treated normatively appear to be fully equivalent and functionally interchangeable, at least in the one direction when ipsative scores are used as normative scores. Apparently, the ipsative understanding of a person has strong, controlling implications for normative judgments.

A larger concern stems from the recognition that CQ descriptors correlate with each other, to a greater or lesser degree. This circumstance complicates interpretations drawn when each of the 100 CQ descriptors is separately statistically analyzed. The lack of independence between descriptors in a Q-sort is created in two ways. The first of these is a purely logical one, with unimportant effect in the present context. The second way is a substantive one that can have uncertain implications and is crucial to evaluate.

The logical basis for an interdependence among Q descriptors stems from the otherwise warranted use of a prescribed Q distribution. By the placing of a descriptor into a category, the likelihood logically is lessened that other descriptors also will be placed into that category. This point is most readily seen by an extreme example. Thus, with a two-descriptor Q-set, having placed one descriptor, the placement of the second descriptor is fully determined; it correlates -1.00 with the placement of the first descriptor. The reciprocal effect in this context is total. However, as the number of descriptors increases, and consequently the degrees of freedom available to the sorter, the negative correlation among descriptors moves toward zero, almost to the vanishing point. For the prescribed 100-descriptor CQ-set, the entailed average correlation between Q items can be computed to be no greater than $-.01$ (Haggard, 1958, pp. 17–18). Consequently, this minute built-in negative correlation can be ignored in subsequent analyses.

The second kind of interdependence among Q descriptors is more important and ubiquitous, coming from psychological realities that exist well beyond the CQ-sort method. Psychological variables may validly correlate with each other, to a greater or lesser extent. Thus, in general (but not without important exception), the person quality of *dominance* goes along with *assurance*, *empathy* with *warmth*, *impulsivity* negatively with *constriction*, and so on. And because CQ descriptors are intended to reflect underlying attributes, they too will often correlate with each other. Consequently, if a statistical test indicates that a descriptor is an important differentiator, then statistical tests that involve Q descriptors related with this first descriptor may be expected to have some tendency also to be important. The converse applies as well; if a Q descriptor is not a differentiator, then all Q descriptors associated with this first descriptor also will tend not to be differentiating.

Now, in analysis of the relations of CQ descriptors with an independent criterion, 100 statistical tests are calculated. If all of these tests were fully independent of each other, then classical statistics expects, for example, an average of 5% of them to be at or beyond the .05 level of significance just by chance. In evaluating a set of 100 truly independent significance tests, an investigator would insist that at least 5% of the tests be statistically suggestive. Otherwise, there would be no basis for believing the set of results qua set is based on anything other than chance.

However, when statistically evaluating a set of Q descriptors to discern which descriptors relate in an important way to an independent criterion, the multiple statistical tests of Q descriptors are not independent of each other. The results from one Q-descriptor analysis do have implications for the results stemming from other Q-descriptor analyses. How then can the investigator form, from these numerous separate but nonindependent evaluations, a proper evaluation of the full set of results? How does one know that the overall findings are not most parsimoniously ascribed to the workings of chance? As suggested before, this kind of problem—analyzing multiple nonindependent variables—occurs often in psychological and other research; it is not a problem peculiar to the CQ method.

Mathematically, the problem a priori is intractable; conventional statistical models do not and cannot provide an appropriate basis for inference. The correlational structure underlying a set of nonindependent Q descriptors is inordinately complicated, varies from one study to the next, and is unspecifiable in advance. How can such a correlational structure be evaluated for its substantive implication?

Extrapolating from Pitman's (1937) permutation test, an unbiased, empirical, Monte Carlo method for deciding whether a set of findings qua set is worth or not worth considering has been evolved for this kind of context (Block, 1960).

In brief, a computer is iteratively used to randomly generate empirically a sampling distribution of the number of correlations expected to reach a set level of importance simply on the basis of chance. The originally obtained variance–covariance matrix of variables (i.e., the 100 CQ descriptors) is used as the appropriate seed to delimit the range of sets of chance findings. Instead of comparing two meaningfully different groups with respect to the set of Q descriptors or relating a potentially meaningful criterion variable to the set of Q descriptors, the two groups or the criterion variable are iteratively randomized and then related to the set of Q descriptors. With sufficient iterations of this procedure, and recording of the observed findings, a stabilized, randomly based empirical sampling distribution is established. This empirically established sampling distribution provides a relevant frame in which to evaluate chance findings and against which the actually obtained set of Q-descriptor correlations can be referenced and appraised. This resampling method is completely general and indicates whether the obtained findings are internally valid for the particular instance being evaluated.

Increasingly, the empirical sampling or Monte Carlo approach to data analysis has come into use. A more general treatment of its applicability is discussed as *resampling* (Simon, 1974, 1999) or as *bootstrapping* (Efron, 1979; Efron & Tibshirani, 1986).[1]

In practice, the investigator will require computer access (and perhaps—even likely—a sophisticated data analyst to arrange the relevant analyses). The necessary computer arrangement is simple to set up and subsequently can be easily and often invoked to establish a clear contextual basis for identifying the chance or nonchance nature of the full set of targeted results. It simply involves running a personal computer overnight.

THE USE OF CQ PROTOTYPES

A popular, convenient, and nomologically supported application of the CQ procedure involves referencing the CQ-sort of an individual against what is called a CQ *prototype* (for early references, see Block, 1957a, 1961). A *prototype* (also called a *criterion CQ-sort*) is a definition of a theoretical or experience-based concept expressed in CQ terms; it is an idealized view of what behaviorally and intrapsychically a construct entails; it expresses a psychological reference frame comprehensively articulated by a criterion array of CQ descriptors. In brief, a prototype represents a theoretical construct, a diagnostic label, or an apperceived recognition—old or new—expressed in terms of CQ descriptors.

To establish a CQ prototype, it is necessary to enlist a number of individuals (at least 5 or 6 but a dozen is better) unquestionably knowledgeable about the chosen concept or reasonably assumed to seriously know about the concept. Each expert separately describes the paradigmatic person who exemplifies the designated concept through a CQ-sort. If the designated concept is well understood, then the several idealized CQ descriptions can be expected to correlate highly with each other because of commonly held, deep recognitions. If this empirically is the case, these several CQ descriptions are then arithmetically

[1]Relevant software is readily Internet available from http://www.resample.com. The reader is referred to these sources for extended discussion of the problem and the procedural logic of the proposed solution.

pooled to create a composite (i.e., averaged) Q description better grounded than any of the individual prototypic CQ descriptions from which it was derived.[2] This CQ composite becomes the criterion prototype—the psychological standard or ideal type—representing that concept. A composite-formed CQ prototype cancels away the idiosyncrasies within each individual conceptual characterization and, as an average, has psychometric reproducibility far superior to any of the individual CQ prototypes from which it derives.

Having available or having created desired prototypes, it is then readily possible to correlate the CQ-sort of an actual person with the CQ prototype of a concept. The value of the correlation can be taken as a *similarity score*, expressing the degree of correspondence of the particular person with the conceptual criterion or standard. The higher the correlation, the more that person can be presumed to be similar to or behaves similar to that prototype. Such similarity scores have proven for a half century to be highly useful and versatile in various research contexts (e.g., Block, 1971; Funder & Block, 1989; Haviland & Reise, 1996; Klohnen, 1996; Kobak, Cole, Ferenz-Gillies, & Fleming, 1993; Kremen & Block, 1998; Mischel, Shoda, & Peake, 1988; Westen & Shedler, 1999a, 1999b).

Many CQ prototypes have been constructed; many others can be created. CQ prototypes have long existed for such psychiatric entities as, for example, the depressed individual, the paranoid, the narcissist, the psychopath, the borderline individual. Q prototypes also were early derived for the resilient individual, the undercontrolled individual, the introvert, the construct of self-efficacy, individuals reflecting Loevinger's autonomous stages, alexithymia, generativity, wisdom, and about 40 more person-constructs, indicating the broad convenience and applicability of the prototype approach. Contrasting associated prototypes can be quite instructive in conveying their conceptual differences and similarities as, for example, between *antisocial personality* versus *undercontrol* (Block & Gjerde, 1986b), *intelligence* (IQ) versus *ego-resiliency* (Block & Kremen, 1996), and between *wisdom* versus *creativity* (Helson & Srivastava, 2002). A few depictive prototypes are listed within several of the appendices.

---

[2]The basis of a composite is the combining of multiple individual CQ-sorts of a person. Often, simple aggregation of the individual Q-sorts is sufficient. When the number of multiple CQ-sorts of a person varies from one person or context to another, it is helpful to convert the aggregations into averages. Doing so places all the composites within the same numerical frame of reference. This is accomplished easily by dividing the aggregated sums by the number of CQ-sorters contributing to the aggregate. Indeed, sometimes, it is even useful to "re-Q" the composite distribution of descriptor means to achieve absolute commensurateness. For each CQ composite, the descriptors with the 5 highest means are given category scores of 9, descriptors with the 8 next highest means are awarded category scores of 8, descriptors with the 12 next highest means are given category scores of 7, and so on through the prescribed CQ distribution. In reassigning descriptor means, any ties should be arbitrarily placed into the adjacent category. By converting descriptor means to fit a CQ-sort distribution, the composite then resulting will change slightly but becomes absolutely commensurate.

Some Illustrative Uses of Prototype Similarity Scores

Prototype similarity scores, developed from each of a set of persons, may be correlated with different measures quite far removed. For example, the similarity scores of a sample of persons with respect to a particular prototype can be correlated with the Stroop RI scores of the persons or their scores on a conservatism or liberalism measure. A sizable correlation betokens the importance of the prototypic construct for understanding the nature of Stroop RI or conservatism or liberalism or whatever non-CQ variable is at hand.

A sample of CQ-sorted individuals can itself form an empirical CQ composite, characterizing the nature of that particular group of persons. This group-based empirical composite can in turn be correlated with a construct prototype. The higher the similarity, the more the group is characterizable by that prototype.

Another application of CQ prototypes is in connection with studies wherein the conceptualizations or interests of the investigators change after the basic CQ descriptions have been collected, for example, in longitudinal or assessment research. Often, in such studies, persons are not evaluated at the time of their availability with respect to certain concepts that later appear to be important. It may not be possible to redeem this deficiency because the persons may be unavailable for restudy or may be 20 years older. Yet the investigator wishes to evaluate them retrospectively with reference to prototype constructs not anticipated at the time of original data collection (Block, 1957a).

In such circumstances, if the persons already have been described by means of CQ descriptions, their prototype scores on the omitted concept can be obtained easily. A number of qualified experts would be asked to formulate the personality implications of the new concept in CQ-descriptor terms. Their composite CQ-sort could then serve as a belated criterion definition of the added concept. By correlating the actual Q-sorts of the now-departed persons against the just-evolved criterion, scores ordering the persons on this new concept become available. The resourceful researcher may wish to keep this procedure in mind. The method has been used in a number of research instances and appears to provide useful scores well after the fact.

For certain theoretical purposes, it may be implicative to know whether persons in one group exemplify or correlate more with a criterion than do persons in a second group. For example, a question may be, "Do persons responding on self-report measures as culturally and politically highly reactionary prove separately to have been CQ-described as having the personality structure delineated in *The Authoritarian Personality?*" (Adorno, Frenkel-Brunswik, Levinson, & Sanford, 1950). The answer in one study appears to be affirmative (Block & Block, 2006a).

In teaching psychiatric or personality assessment students, some expert judgment of the appropriateness of the interpretations offered by each student is often involved. This can involve a time-consuming, uncertain, often repeated undertaking. How shall these multifarious psychological interpretations by students be evaluated and compared? If the instructor is willing to serve as a criterion or can enlist a number of acknowledged experts to serve as criteria, the problem is readily confronted. The instructor's criterion CQ description or the aggregated criterion CQ descriptions of presumed experts may serve as a standard of veridicality. Each student's interpretation, conveyed by means of the CQ language, would be evaluated against the available criterion of truth, the evolved CQ prototype. The correlation between these two sorts—the student's CQ-sort and the criterion-defining CQ-prototypic sort—provides a convenient index of the congruence of the student's interpretation with the criterion afforded by expertness, thus easily providing the necessary evaluation of each student.

An especially implicative—and ambitious—potential application of the CQ procedure involves the professional evaluation of mental health. The American Psychiatric Association has created a set of categories (the *Diagnostic and Statistical Manual of Mental Disorders* [DSM]) into which a patient can be placed by an individual who is serving as diagnostician. Diagnosis is made if the assessor estimates that the person manifests a threshold number of the checklist symptoms that define the category.

In its various versions, the *DSM* has had a controlling influence on American psychiatry and mental health providers. It has become the way of diagnostic life—for psychiatrists, clinical psychologists, social service agencies, pharmacologists, reimbursing insurance companies, lawyers and relevant courts, and the like. It provides authoritative if questionable "recipes" for mental health diagnoses and in its most current version, the *Diagnostic and Statistical Manual of Mental Disorders, Fourth Edition, Text Revision* (American Psychiatric Association, 2000), contains well over 400 categorical diagnoses and numerical codes.

However, the *DSM* in everyday clinical practice still reveals appreciable, often alarming disparities and uncertainty in diagnostic evaluations. Indeed, because of frequent diagnostic doubtfulness in a professional world wherein definite diagnosis is now absolutely required, the category, "personality disorder not otherwise specified," has become a wastebasket. It is the most frequent *DSM* diagnosis invoked by mental health practitioners, a "copout" invoked to avoid uncertain or difficult decisions. Moreover, the *DSM* issues challengeable estimates of the frequency and comorbidity of mental disorders. Accordingly, the *DSM* "bible," deferred to religiously by many, has brought forward many agnostics (e.g., Kirk, 2004; Kutchins & Kirk, 1997; Widiger & Clark, 2000). It has been revolutionary for the mental health community, but not all revolutions advance the world.

Diagnoses based on partially meeting the full set of checklist criteria are methodologically troublesome because two patients receiving identical diagnoses can have very different sets of symptom manifestations. Even more important is the use of categorical, present–absent diagnoses when manifestly the mental disorder is better viewed conceptually as lying along a psychiatric dimension. Compare, for example, the distinct *DSM* diagnoses of *schizoid personality disorder* and *schizotypal personality disorder*. How reliably, really, can clinicians truly make a distinction between these two similar diagnoses?

Presuming that psychiatrists can construct diagnostically descriptive CQ prototypes—and prior efforts indicate the feasibility—composite prototypes of the basic psychiatric diagnoses could readily and reliably be formulated. Given a comprehensive set of consensually based prototypes of mental disorders (and more could later be added as required or desired), subsequent diagnosis would objectively follow simply by correlating a patient's actual CQ description with each of the amassed diagnostic CQ prototypes. The set of correlation values would provide a quickly obtained, quantitative profile of the patient's predilections and mental status. In this way, diagnostic Q prototypes can provide a convenient, objective, and conceptually attractive alternative to the currently dominant but disjointed, confusing *DSM* approach favored by American psychiatry.

Admittedly, the pragmatic inertial problems involved in moving away from the ensconced *DSM* are enormous, but an objective, reproducible, dimensional approach to the problem of mental disorder is logically needed. The CQ-prototype approach if applied within the psychiatric context may warrant consideration as an improvement over perpetuation of the long muddle with the *DSM*. Also, as is seen in the next section of this chapter, it may set the stage for a fundamental restructuring and improvement of the current mental health classification system.

A Caution in Regard to the Similarity Coefficients Between CQ-Sorts

It is crucially important to recognize that the similarity coefficient between two Q-sorts is not entitled to reference the theoretical sampling distribution conventionally used in evaluating correlation coefficients. The similarity coefficient between two Q-sorts is not strictly a correlation coefficient in the usual statistical sense.

The Reason Why Is Not Widely Recognized

The theoretical sampling distribution for true correlations expects that any two arrays of Q descriptors taken at random will correlate zero, on the average. With random interperson Q correlations, however, correlation coefficients are likely not to average zero. Certain universally applicable descriptors may have been included within a Q-set, thus building in positive correlations among Q-sorts. Or the persons in the group being studied may have certain substantive similarities that tend to create positive interperson correlations.

For many purposes, informal evaluations of similarity coefficients may be descriptively sufficient. However, because the average correlation among actual

Q-sorts cannot be expected to truly be zero, if it is wished to go beyond simple description—to know whether two Q-sorts are indeed unusually related— a reference frame must be developed by the resampling, Monte Carlo approach previously described. By empirical resampling, the distribution of similarity coefficients among all the actual Q-sorts can easily be developed and subsequently referenced to see if an obtained similarity coefficient is indeed statistically unusual. As already noted, general resampling software is readily available through the Internet although a statistical consultant may also be needed.

DISCERNING PERSONALITY TYPES THROUGH THE CQ-SET

The availability of many CQ-sorts, variously developed, opens the possibility of unusual, engaging further analyses. This section presents a rationale, its consequent methodology and associated cautions, some illustrative research applications, and details some convenient analytical procedures.

The Rationale for a Personality Typology

Psychiatrists, psychologists, and indeed people in general often think and talk in categorical terms, if only because of the abstractional convenience such language provides. Thus, psychiatrists may diagnose categorically between *major depressive personality disorder* and *dysthymic personality disorder*, between *schizoid personality disorder* and *schizotypal personality disorder*, between *histrionic personality disorder* and *narcissistic personality disorder*. Psychologists may distinguish *repressors* and *intellectualizers*, *introverts* and *extroverts*, *achievers* and *affiliators*, *undercontrollers* and *overcontrollers*. Lay people may classify persons with such bland words as *nice* or *annoying*, *interesting* or *dull*.

These and similar characterological distinctions are often uncertain in implication. Some of these contrasts may reflect no more than linguistic categorizations imposed on, and better understood in terms of, continuous characterological dimensions. However, others may, at least in principle, reflect a genuine typological, discrete difference in the way certain kinds of individuals are psychologically organized. By a "type" is meant here "a subset of individuals characterized by a reliably unique or discontinuously different pattern of covariation with respect to a specifiable and nontrivial set of variables" (Block, 1971, pp. 109–110).

This definition is not new—it derives from earlier formulations of the idea of type (Block, 1955; Cattell, 1952; Cronbach, 1953b; Stephenson, 1953). It approximates Meehl's (1962, 1992; Waller & Meehl, 1998) complex and complicated notion, long pursued, of *psychological taxons*. Tucker (1966) also, in a different way, has resonated to the importance of testing whether relationship uniformity exists over all individuals. If indeed there are types, this recognition implies that the psychological laws or relations that characterize one type of personality may be quite different from the psychological laws or relationships that characterize a different personality type.

The study of personality types is a beckoning venture, but the implications of a typological approach are not immediately obvious, as Cattell (1952) early pointed out. The typological approach has been alluring because it asserts an argument many are inclined to accept or at least test—that a nomothetic, monolithic view of psychological functioning as applying to all individuals is presumptive and likely wrong in fundamental ways.

To illustrate the argument, consider gender. Psychological research often presumes there are no disjunctive sex differences or that such differences as exist are only quantitative. However, the relations among psychological variables for men and for women are frequently crucially different. For example, IQ correlates positively with depression in young American women but correlates negatively with depression in young American men (Block, Gjerde, & Block, 1991). Generalizations that reliably apply to the one sex often do not apply to the other. Therefore, with respect to various matters, the two sexes may not be combined; they indeed are different types in important ways.

Within each sex as well, there can be bases for partitioning samples into subgroups, each relatively homogeneous but typologically different from other homogeneous subgroups, for example, overcontrollers and undercontrollers, depression caused by failures in intimate relations and depression caused by failures of aspirations, dissonance enhancers and dissonance reducers, field-dependent and field-independent individuals. Highly lawful relationships that characterize one subsample may not characterize another subsample equally but differently determinate.

In suggesting the same functional behavioral principle may not apply to all persons, the converse idiographic position is not being implied. Although there may not be a single view of person functioning that can be used across the board, persons cannot be organized in an infinite number of ways. All person organizations are directed toward achieving a temporally tenable system for perception of and response to a complex and fluxional world. However, some arrangements within a person may be seen as submitting the individual to such extremes of anguish as to not be tenable; they exist, if at all, only transiently before being replaced by other system designs with more stable properties. These are durable modes of person organization and are likely reasonably few in overall number—there are not endlessly unique ways of achieving the psychoeconomic requirements of the person. Although we are all unique at the level of historical incident and in the content of experience, although the idea of uniqueness may be a satisfying phenomenological belief, when persons are looked at in terms of modes of adaptation, we are none of us so exquisitely different as to defy a rather useful categorization.

The categorization may often use blurred boundaries so that some persons cannot be cleanly located in any one category. The defining properties for category membership may be gross and imprecise so that it seems inappropriate to consider all members of a category as interchangeable or equivalent. However, these concerns are simply (sic!) matters of practice and implementation. They do not deny the principle and usefulness of the pigeonhole.

Given this preamble, it becomes of interest and consequence to use the CQ procedure for research on issues in this domain, to analysis of matrices of interperson CQ correlations. On the basis of the intercorrelations among CQ-sorts, individuals may be algorithmically and conceptually grouped. For exploratory studies especially, when there is not already a schema with which to view the personological world, the algorithmic approach is attractively compelling. Cluster analysis, with its "tree" representations, has sometimes been used but as Goldberg (2006, p. 347) noted, when person description is the goal, cluster analysis cannot fairly represent the complex relationships existing among descriptors. Therefore, the emphasis here is on the method of factor analysis as the primary way of typologically grouping interperson CQ correlations.

The Use of Factor Analysis With CQ-Sorts

Seventy-five years ago, William Stephenson (1935) introduced the idea of correlating persons across variables as an alternative and productive preface to the method of factor analysis. Correlations among the orientations of persons reflect a person-centered emphasis (cf. chap. 1).

Factor analysis had been—and usually still is—based on a matrix that expresses the correlation of variables across persons. Burt (1937) dismissed Stephenson's idea and a controversy developed, was extended into a full-scale but confusing debate (Burt & Stephenson, 1939), and subsequently was joined in by others (Block, 1955; Cattell, 1952; Cronbach, 1953b; Eysenck, 1954). Stephenson's approach was early arbitrarily labeled by Burt as *Q-factor analysis*, and traditional factor analysis he designated as the *R approach*, names that have existed over the years and also account for the name of the Q-sort.

For Burt, the issue existed solely in the restricted algebraic realm: given a two-dimensional numerical matrix wherein each entry reflected person *j*'s score on variable *i*, the matrix transpose required for correlating persons across variables was only a mathematical reciprocal of the results provided by the traditional approach of correlating variables across people. Stephenson argued that there was indeed a fundamental difference in the results provided by the two approaches. Both were correct, given their very individual construals of the issue.

Burt had presupposed "objective" data based on the external behavioral manifestations of individuals, subsequently encoded as numerical scores (e.g., IQ, number of repetitive pushups, credit card indebtedness, drug use, political leanings, and so on). Regarding a correlation matrix based on such data, there indeed was mathematical reciprocity between Q- and R-factor analyses.

Stephenson, however, was focused on quite a different data matrix, resulting from a different kind of information—the opinions and attitudes of persons on various matters (e.g., a set of portraits of objects of art, a set of statements expressive of Jung's theory, a set of statements on global warming, a set of political candidates). This scaling was accomplished by a procedure—later known as *Q-sorting*—Stephenson devised to permit relativistic expression of the subjective perspectives of persons in a form suitable for his Q-factor analyses. This subjectivity-based matrix issued different substantive structures than was provided by Burt's objective kind of matrix. It was this different kind of data and its resultant structures that Stephenson, not always clearly, focused on.

The original Stephenson–Burt controversy was a function of their different orientations and interests. For Burt, the matrix entries were objective scores, whereas for Stephenson the matrix entries represented subjective opinions relevant to the domain defined as of interest; the two adversaries were concerned with qualitatively different data matrices.

Separately, as interest moved toward a person-centered approach for understanding character, variable-centered R-factor analyses for many seemed empirically unsatisfying. Factor analysts had always been aware that R-factor analysis results were a function of the particular sample of individuals on which the data were based. It was also recognized that person samples, from one R-study to another, were often differently composed and that the R-factor results based on one sample could be markedly different, even absent, from the R-factor results issuing from another sample; the correlations between identical variables in different R-factor analyses often fluctuated appreciably, sometimes even wildly, from one R-factor study to another. For this disquieting reason, Cattell (1952) suggested "Q technique has its chief use as a classificatory device for finding the subpopulations in a nonhomogeneous population" (p. 502). Cronbach (1953b) wrote an important chapter on "the place of correlation between persons in science" wherein he noted that "nonchance relations cannot be perceived when fundamentally different organisms are shuffled together in a sample" (p. 388).

Given the climate of the times, Q-factor analysis was recognized as an apt way of identifying the *subpopulations* (i.e., types) within nonhomogeneous populations. Also, as attractive, person-centered data suitable for Q-factor analysis, the Q-sorts of a person by competent appraisers gained recognition. Focusing on patterns of person organization arising within each of various samples, consistent patterns of findings of interest could be better revealed and perhaps conjoined.

Exploratory factor analysis (EFA)—the analysis of communal variance— is a widely used method, variously understood and applied. It is heuristically useful when large masses of correlation data exist—data too extensive and intertwined to permit immediate understanding—and a coherent interpretation of the order underlying the myriad empirical connections is attempted. It generates potential explanatory interpretations of the underlying structure of a correlation matrix. Haig (2005) provided philosophical perspective on the abductive or conceptual implications of the method.

The variety of methods and procedures of factor analysis may be found in a number of texts and articles (Comrey & Lee, 1992; Finch & West, 1997; Gorsuch, 1983; Harman, 1976; Mulaik, 1972; Thurstone, 1947). For knowledgeable recent overviews of the technical decision problems or choice points besetting exploratory factor analysis, the articles by Goldberg (2006) and Fabrigar, Wegener, MacCallum, and Strahan (1999) are strongly recommended to the beginning factor analyst.

As a cautionary note, it should be remembered that factor-analysis writings usually presume or are presented in terms of the *correlation among variables*—over the person sample involved. They are R-oriented, and therefore the factor analysis results in various groups of highly related variables. For the less usual procedure of *correlations among persons*—over the descriptors involved—the factor analysis results in various groups or types of similar persons. In reading the R-factor analytic literature but, with Q analyses in mind, the factor-analytic novice is cautioned to constantly remember this transposed difference. Mentally and empirically, data transposition is usually required when reading on conventional factor analysis: R variables should be viewed as Q persons, the R-person sample should be viewed as the set of Q descriptors. Transposition is easily accomplished once and for all on a computer but is often verbally confusing in speech, whether inner or interpersonal. Attention is required here.

Computer software permits EFA to be readily available through widely available statistical packages, such as SAS, SPSS, and SYSTAT wherein data transposition is easily accomplished. Also relevant are the computer packages, PQ Method and PCQ for Windows, expressly designed to record Q data directly in proper transposed format and for Q-factor analyses. Although computationally, factor analysis is now easily accomplished, knowledge and perspective continue to be necessary in understanding the procedure and its implications. In embarking on this approach, statistical knowledge or a statistical resource person may well be required.

The highly technical choice points in proceeding through a factor analysis include (a) the specific factoring method to be used, (b) the communality estimate chosen, (c) the number of factors extracted, (d) the particular rotational procedure used, and (e) consideration of the computation or necessity of factor scores. Especially, it should be noted that the default arrangements automatically invoked in many computer factor-analysis packaged programs are often statistically and conceptually questionable in the way they unilaterally shape the ultimate results. However, escaping the defaults is usually an easy option for the forewarned analyst.

The less technical, unwary, but would-be factor analyst may find helpful some quick, savvy, sometimes philistine views on the process:

1. Usually, and considering the quality and underlying precision of the data being analyzed, the various factoring procedures produce surprisingly equivalent results regardless of the specific methodological choices invoked. However, it may be helpful to try alternative methodological procedures, the aspiration being to attain pretty much the same results regardless of method used. The finding that one's results are essentially invariant over methodological changes is reassuring and persuasive.

2. More important than confirmation over a variety of procedures is a sufficient replication or an attractive abduction conceptually in support of the obtained factoring. Thoughtfully applied and interpreted, factor-analytic methods are powerful computational procedures for cogently structuring relationships otherwise impossible to encompass.

3. In addition to worrying about the nature of the person sample, it is well to be concerned about the nature of the variables being factor analyzed. Thus, consider the apocryphal R-factor analysis of 99 different but essentially equivalent finger dexterity measures combined with one good measure of intelligence. A naïve factor analyst might be impressed by the emergent, coherent, general, and therefore seemingly paramount dexterity factor that explains almost all of the variance in this 100×100 correlation matrix. The solitary, unredundant, and therefore not communal intelligence measure, although in real life of great importance, might be discarded by an unthinking factor analyst as simply a residual of no consequence. As another illustration of the interpretive problems that may intrude on a factor analysis, consider Thurstone's (1944) factoring of all of the then extant perceptual measures. A champion of representative design complained that Thurstone had not sampled the perceptual tests not yet created and therefore complained that Thurstone's correlation matrix was not sufficiently heterogeneous. The interpretation of a factor analysis is not automatic and straightforward; it always depends on psychological sagacity.

4. The number of factors extracted is critical and sometimes, without justification, is chosen arbitrarily. However, overextraction of factors especially but underextraction also can be misguiding. The default rule still often residing in statistical factor-analysis packages, of automatically accepting all factors with eigenvalues greater than one, should be rejected. Insofar as the actual data should be determining, the method advocated by Horn (1965)

to establish the proper number of underlying factors impresses many as logically attractive and empirically accurate.

5. The emergent factors must be rotated, seeking meaning through what is called "simple structure," a positioning of the factors wherein each person (in a Q-factor analysis) has a relatively high or relatively low factor loading on a putative type. These rotations may be orthogonal (wherein all factor-based types are simultaneously uncorrelated with each other) or oblique rotations may be sought (permitting different types to be more or less related). There are a variety of rotational procedures in the literature, some algorithmically objective and some based on subjective perceptions conjoined with abductive conjectures. The most frequently used rotation procedure (varimax) has often not been the one to use. Any subjective rotation requires consensual corroboration.

6. Factors require names or labels. This naming should be by separate independent factor interpreters, subsequently compared and integrated to ensure the general tenability of the factor interpretations.

Some Illustrative Applications of CQ-Factor Analyses

In *Lives Through Time* (Block, 1971), the 170 participants (84 men, 86 women) in the Institute of Human Development Longitudinal Study initiated around 1930 in Berkeley had each independently been CQ-sorted in regard to their junior high school (JHS) years by at least 3 experienced clinicians, regarding their senior high school (SHS) years by another set of 3 independently functioning clinicians, and again in their mid-30s, well along their life paths, by yet another set of 3 independent clinicians. For each of the three age periods, the CQ-sorts for each person were aggregated into a composite. Then, for each sex separately, the large matrix of interperson correlations was calculated.

It was reasoned that factoring the JHS CQ interperson correlations alone would have only sculpted a typology of early adolescent character structure. Factoring the mid-30s interperson correlations alone would have only delineated a typology of adult character structure. However, given the longitudinal context, and interest in courses of personality development, it was decided to factor analyze the adjoining of the JHS CQ composites with corresponding mid-30s CQ composites to reflect development trends over 20 years.

Five personality types algorithmically emerged from Q-factor analyses of the male sample and were loosely labeled, *ego resilients, belated adjusters, vulnerable overcontrollers, anomic extraverts,* and *unsettled undercontrollers.* Six types issued from factor analysis of the female sample and were christened, *female prototypes, cognitive copers, hyperfeminine repressives, dominating narcissists, vulnerable undercontrollers*, and *lonely independents*. Their CQ descriptors richly described each type. Moreover, and in particular, the several types linked impressively and provocatively with various data completely independent of the CQ data on which the typologies were based. Those especially interested in this complicated study should refer to the original source.

A number of investigators have reported CQ- or CCQ-related typologically oriented factor and cluster analyses. The samples studied are of both genders, use somewhat different methodologies, and have come from diverse countries far removed from each other. Remarkably, the investigators have come up with surprisingly replicable findings. Three personality types have been repetitively discerned: *resilient*, *overcontrolled*, and *undercontrolled* (e.g., Asendorpf & van Aken, 1999; Hart, Hofman, Edelstein, & Keller, 1997; Robins, John, Caspi, Moffitt, & Stouthamer-Loeber, 1996; van Aken, van Lieshout, Scholte, & Haselager, 2002). Further subtypes latterly have been differentiated, with consequential psychosocial adjustment implications. These empirical findings are noteworthy because, in psychology, there have been few replications. In addition, moreover, the types seem to relate to data quite outside the methodological basis of the typologies. Thus, the three types appear to display different cortosol levels and reactions (Hart, Burock, London, Atkins, & Bonilla-Santiago, 2005) and the types prove to relate to perceived parental rejection, depression, and aggression (Akse, Hale, Engels, Raaijmakers, & Meeus, 2004). For an edifying introduction to this research movement, the reader may wish to consult Scholte, van Lieshout, de Wit, and van Aken (2005).

Over the years, the *DSM* has evolved in a topsy-turvy, untidy fashion. The development of an extensive set of reliably formed psychiatric prototypes may provide a long-needed regularization, clarification, and simplification of current psychiatric nosology. The ready method of factor analysis is required, and three sequential procedural steps are involved:

1. Working from the *DSM* diagnostic categories, CQ prototypes need to be formulated, as described earlier, to characterize the various conjectured or defined psychiatric entities. For each of many psychiatric entities, 10 clinicians each knowledgeable enough of the psychiatric concept to portray it with CQ descriptors would be required for definitiveness. For any accepted psychiatric disorder, it should be feasible to locate professionally trained and accepted clinicians to say what it is. This venture would be an arduous, slow, costly endeavor but well within practical feasibility.

2. Intercorrelating the 10 independent CQ descriptions of a single psychiatric entity would indicate empirically the actual agreement among credentialed professionals in their understanding of the specified mental disorder. If their agreements are appre-

ciable, then the 10 separate CQ-sorts could be aggregated into a composite CQ prototype of that particular psychiatric concern. The reliability of this composite could readily be estimated by a Spearman–Brown calculation. Such composite prototypes would be created for all psychiatric disorders judged or suggested as relevant, thus, would accrue a host of psychiatric CQ-prototypic composites, each with reliable definition.

3. These conceptual prototypes could then be intercorrelated and factor analyzed. Factor analysis of these conceptual prototypes, expressed at different levels of factor extraction (Goldberg, 2006; Waller, 2007), would provide a new, hierarchical conceptual organization (and perhaps reorganization) of psychiatric nosology. This approach has the promise of at least simplifying psychiatric nosology and perhaps revealing different levels of psychiatric understanding.

Provisional exploration along these lines in preceding decades has been most encouraging, but this enterprise properly awaits future energy, wider funding resources, and enlarged cooperation with mental health practitioners.

9

SUBJECTIVE IMPRESSIONS
IN CLINICAL PSYCHOLOGY

Since Meehl's (1954) transforming review of the clinical versus statistical prophecy issue, many subsequent studies have entered the lists, seeking to further test and perhaps improve the dismaying empirical record of individual clinician judgment expressed as prediction (e.g., Dawes, Faust, & Meehl, 1989; Grove & Meehl, 1996; Sawyer, 1966; Sines, 1970). Some meta-analyses (Ægisdottir et al., 2006; Grove, Zald, Lebow, Snitz, & Nelson, 2000) have, perhaps definitively, corroborated earlier conclusions—over a wide variety of comparisons, individual clinical prediction fares no better than and is often inferior to statistical prediction. This chapter takes absolutely no issue with this long and wide literature. It does, however, seek to introduce reconsideration of the way this research interest has been studied and the larger issue framed. Also, it perhaps offers a way by which subjective impressions by appraisers can contribute empirical understandings not available by other means.

SOME CLINICAL PSYCHOLOGY HISTORY

What has been meant by "clinical prediction"? Clinical prediction has been characterized as involving an appraiser's impressionistic, subjective, intuitions—informally expressed—in regard to a person, used to make a prediction about that person's behavior in the real world (Dawes et al., 1989; Meehl, 1954).

What has been meant by "statistical prediction"? Statistical prediction has been characterized as involving mechanically applied rules—actuarial or algorithmic—issuing routinized, impersonally offered prediction about a person's behavior in the real world.

By an imperfect but commonly held analogy, clinical judgment may be said to involve the "right brain" (the hemisphere presumably of subconscious, spontaneous apperceptions, intuitions, and imaginative thought) and statistical prediction may be said to involve the "left brain" (the hemisphere of coolly logical, analytical, quantitative calculation).

Although there have been many studies in various medical and other substantive fields on the clinical judgment versus mechanical prediction issue, here focus is on studies in psychology and psychiatry whereby the question of the accuracy of individual clinical judgment has been a special preoccupation.

In the development of psychiatry and clinical psychology subsequent to World War II, psychodiagnosis was a primary focus. The confident temper of the times led to high expectations for clinical acumen. However, ineluctably, clinical judgments were empirically compared with actuarial/statistical information.

The subsequent findings proved remarkably one sided. Subjectively based impressions formulated by a psychologist offered no advantage over a labor saving, algorithmic judgmental procedure and frequently fared worse (although the statistical approach cannot be said to perform very well). Consequently, the informal subjective impressions of a clinician have come to be viewed by many as scientifically offering little or nothing of serious informational value. Curiously, most mental health practitioners seem to have remained largely unaffected by or ignorant of these empirical findings.

Retrospecting on that historical time, clinical versus statistical prediction studies can be recognized as having been overly pragmatic, generally resorting to existent or readily invoked person classifications for criteria and existent or readily drawn-upon person classifications as predictors. Criteria and predictors were both often only administratively convenient and conceptually were usually far from ideal.

On the criterion side, criteria were usually rough-and-ready, imperfect, appreciably unreliable diagnoses of various kinds. By themselves, undependable criteria by introducing "noise" lowered the accuracy achieved in *all* subsequent evaluative analyses.

But it was on the prediction side that these comparative analyses showed their fundamental operative difference. Informally reached individual clinical judgments—based in unknown, idiosyncratic, fluctuating, summary ways on a clinician's subjective impressions—were conspicuously adventitious and introduced an appreciable unreliability component into their predictions. On the other hand, algorithmic predictions about an individual—by their very nature—were uniformly reproducible or reliable in their predictions. Accordingly, *ceteris paribus*, the unreliability present in individual clinical judgments inevitably attenuated their anticipations of the available criterion. Such attenuation effects were early recognized as a cardinal reason for the poor showing of clinicians (e.g., Goldberg, 1970, 1991). In retrospect, it is not surprising that, although neither predictive approach worked well, ambitious clinical predictions were matched by and often even bettered by the more pedestrian actuarial approach.

In the flurry of competitive studies on clinical versus statistical prediction, there were many, often unrecognized, compromises. Ideally, in a well-planned research study, the criterion would have sufficient reliability and be conceptually interesting; the predictive information would also have sufficient reliability and be conceptually relevant. However, in taking up conveniently accessible data, these research requirements often were not met or evaluated. Indeed, the effort at clinical prediction may have been doomed in major ways from the outset.

SOME REFLECTIONS ON THE CLINICAL VERSUS STATISTICAL PREDICTION ISSUE

Given the sustained bootlessness of empirical appraiser efforts at person predictions auguring the future, the very notion of "prediction," per se warrants closer consideration. Philosophically, the problem besetting observer-based person prediction needs to be recognized as an existential one. Although prediction is often viewed as "the gold standard test of understanding," person predictions from individual subjective impressions into an unspecifiable future can only be dicey. There are simply too many situational and circumstantial variables—many of them unforeseeable to consider and integrate into a predictive formulation. There is the further sticky, practical problem of explicitly cogitating reliable, relevant signs in regard to what often are situations beyond calculation. Despite the extravagant faith certain clinicians sometimes have claimed in their own forecasting powers, no one can truly envisage the protean outcomes that arise in an uncertain world. Therefore, individual clinical predictions into the unknown future are fundamentally risky; they will tend to be divergently based and ineffable. A more humble but perhaps more useful approach is needed.

Within empirical science, the beginning thrust of much research is simply to establish dependable empirical connections among intriguing phenomena. The scientific goal is to establish interesting and *nonspurious* links among different events, circumstances, developments, data, milestones, whatever attracts attention. For example, within psychology, different phenomena have varying degrees of intrinsic interest and theoretical possibility. Thus, interest in buttoning rate arouses little attention; depressive moods are of great human concern.

Furthermore, the temporal distance between two phenomena is of no special logical importance as long as their relation is nonspurious and is of interest. Terminologically, if a datum is empirically connected to a later datum, the finding is termed *predictive*; if a datum is empirically connected to an earlier datum, the finding may be termed *postdictive*. Empirical connections among essentially concurrent data can be just termed *concomitant findings*.

The theoretical understanding and conceptualization of dependable and interesting connections is, of course, a primary scientific endeavor. However, no less important is the parallel objective of empirically establishing such interest-arousing, reliable findings. The advance of science involves the reciprocal interplay of both theorizing and empiricism.

CONJOINING THE CLINICAL AND THE STATISTICAL— CONCENTERING SUBJECTIVE IMPRESSIONS

Within the indefinitely broad study of person dispositions, the scientific problem may not be so much that of conceiving psychological theory as of achieving firm, communicable findings of intrinsic psychological interest and consequence. In that search for findings worth psychologically thinking about, the empirical benefits accruing from individual clinical observers—varying as they do in sagacity, astuteness, and foresight—has been obscure. Although in the last half century, individual impressionistic person evaluations have remained ubiquitous, they have not earned widespread confidence.

Yet the tradition of incommensurate, impressionistic, unevaluated, usually solitary, clinical appraisals has continued with no or little evidence-based support. However, numerous empirical studies using the California Q-sort (CQ) *compositing* procedure have appeared over the years demonstrating that commensurate clinical observers, suitably concentered or focalized, provide an unusual resource of perceptivity not previously recognized or well-plumbed. The mosaic of subjective impressions held by person–appraisers, when enlisted differently, often leads to composite-generated, nonspurious, and intriguingly nomological findings. In effect, the indubitably subjective impressions of clinical appraisers can become a new form of clinical research data.

The historical evolution of the CQ procedure merits mention here. Reacting early to the disappointment of conventional clinical predictions, a different research tactic was used. It stemmed from the recognition that individual subjective impressions of persons by appraisers, as used in psychological research and clinical judgment studies, were idiosyncratic, arcane, unspecifiably predicated, and noncomparably expressed. For the subjective impressions of person observers to have consequence, however, it was reasoned they are better registered by a formal, specifiable, articulated method, providing an essential commensurability between appraisers—for example, the CQ procedure (Block, 1961).

The practice of registering in a wide-ranging, commensurate way the subjective impressions of a person as held by a number of independent appraisers proved most attractive. Immediately, it provided intrinsically interesting comparisons among the several CQ descriptions. Such comparisons were informative and thought provoking in the evaluative similarities and differences they displayed. But, of even more consequence, the appreciable commonalities appraisers usually manifested regarding a particular person suggested invoking the psychometric logic of aggregation to achieve a more central descriptive representation of the particular person.

Historically, aggregation had already long demonstrated, by empirical applications of the Spearman–Brown prophecy formula, that it enhanced the dependability of a composite. This increased reliability of the composite increased its potential probability of connecting with other quite separate and independent happenings or events. Applied to multiple, commensurate, equally weighted CQ descriptions of the same person, the very idea of aggregation suggested it could provide a higher consensual "truth"—a concentering of the varying subjective impressions from the several, functionally independent appraisers.

The algebraic basis for the force of aggregation is well presented in psychometric texts. A layperson's understanding of the basis for this aggregational research strategy is to be found in the sagely evolved life principle that the characterization of a person should not depend exclusively on the particular subjective impression held by any one appraiser. Personological truths about a person are more likely to be conveyed through the common thread that underlies the subjective impressions of several presumably perceptive appraisers quite independently characterizing the person. This is the cardinal underlying aggregation principle: It justifies creating a composite from the multiple, commensurate, subjective impressions available for each person. These apperceptions indicated the way subjective impressions of person appraisers could be seriously brought into the research process as a unique kind of relevant data. The collective contribution of appraisers could be represented through a particular data-generating procedure.

Research emphasis was routinely placed on having a number of clinicians or lay observers each independently have appreciable opportunity to experience a particular person and then to psychologically portray, through the CQ procedure, contemporary descriptions of the person studied; behavioral prediction per se was nowhere attempted. This procedure was followed with regard to each sample participant. These arduously developed multiple CQ descriptions were aggregated for each person studied to create, for each, an individual composite. Subsequently, the set of person composites was related multidirectionally to available and interesting criteria.

In several early studies, this procedural approach proved remarkably generative empirically (Block, 1957b; Block & Bennett, 1955; Block & Petersen, 1955; Helson, 1971); therefore and thereafter, the procedure became prescriptive. It is of interest to note that perhaps influenced by earlier mutual correspondence in the late 1950s (Block, 1961, p. 75), Meehl (1959) once opined, "It is . . . possible that interview based judgments at a minimally inferential level, if recorded in standard form (for example, Q-sort) and treated statistically, can be made more powerful than such data treated impressionistically as is currently the practice" (p. 124). The concentering approach from the mid-1950s and as just described has, over the years, provided ample support for Meehl's conjecture.

A further revelation of this approach incidentally arose in the course of a later longitudinal study (Block, 1971). Psychological clinicians, informally formulating predictions into the future on the basis of their individually sensed understanding of an adolescent, displayed little accuracy in their anticipations of the adult adjustment status of these adolescents evaluated 20 years later. However, the quantitatively commensurate, contemporary CQ descriptions of each adolescent, made by three independent clinicians and then aggregated, proved consistently to be appreciably better related to adult criteria in four samples. The difference intimated that contemporary person Q descriptions, aggregated and used as predictors into a then undefinable future, could be more connecting than intuitively based augurings.

Further emboldened, the decreed approach was extensively used in a 3-decade longitudinal study (Block & Block, 2006b) that depended heavily on this research strategy. The results are all predicated on contemporary subjective impressions of each person, separately CQ expressed in quantitative and commensurable terms by multiple independent appraisers, then arithmetically pooled to form a composite-based, concentering CQ description of each person.

These composite CQ-sorts repeatedly generated appreciable, arresting, nomologically related connections with a variety of independent, far-removed reference or criterion variables. In a diversity of contexts—predictive, concurrent, and postdictive—the approach was productive whether, for example, predicting subsequent drug use from childhood California Child Q-set (CCQ) descriptions (Block et al., 1988) or finding CQ descriptors synchronous with autonomic activity while lying (Block, 1957b) or looking backward from political orientation as young adults to CCQ-sorts collected 20 years earlier when participants were in nursery school and not yet political beings (Block & Block, 2006a). Beyond these studies, many more in the literature testify to the fecundity of this research way (e.g., Block, 1957b; Block, 1965, 1971; Block & Baker, 1957; Block, Block, & Harrington, 1974; Block & Gjerde, 1986a; Block et al., 1991; Block & Kremen, 1996; Block & Petersen,

1955; Block & Robins, 1993; Donahue, Robins, Roberts, & John, 1993; Helson & Srivastava, 2002; Helson, 1971; John, Cheek, & Klohnen, 1996; Kremen & Block, 2002; Siegelman, Block, Block, & von der Lippe, 1970). The number and variety of the findings consequent on this research analysis process attests to its value. It provides much of the support for Hofstee's (1994) appraisal that "The averaged judgment of knowledgeable others provides the best available point of reference for . . . assessing someone's personality . . ." (p. 149).

THE MODUS OPERANDI FOR CONCENTERING APPRAISALS

The methodological recipe that underlies the emergence of a psychological percipience from a host of different but commensurate subjective appraisals of a person is similar to but also crucially different from previous ways that purport to represent clinical psychological judgment. The specific recipe entails the following points:

1. A person-centered, ipsative judgment of the individual. Person evaluation should not be narrowly conditional or relativistic.
2. Use of a comprehensive, atheoretical array of person descriptors. The CQ-set, long developed and well-tested, has proven to be an apt choice. Normative ratings usually are not exhaustive in their coverage and are not conjunctively stated.
3. Person judgments are expressed dimensionally (on a 9:1 scale). It is recognized as conceptually inappropriate to think of person attributes as being of an all-or-none, present or absent, categorical nature.
4. Multiple observers are necessary. Each appraiser, inevitably possessing a different personal evaluative perspective and experiencing the person in singular circumstances, weighs the person through a unique pair of eyes.
5. Person appraisal by an observer is based on subjective impressions gained in variegated contexts. The assessor has generous time to observe the person, usually but not necessarily, in a planned and prepared observation situation.
6. Each appraiser functions entirely independently, without reference to or knowledge of the evaluations held by other observers. There can be no influence whatsoever of any observer's views on those of any other participating observer.
7. The required use of the prescribed CQ distribution compels the person impressions of each observer to be commensurate. Person judgments by different observers are in an identical reference frame and thus prevent response sets and unequal influences on the final composite for that individual.

8. The several appraisals by the different assessors of a particular individual are arithmetically aggregated or pooled to form a composite CQ description for that person.

Aggregation provides both concentering—the coming together of subjective impressions to a common center of understanding—and as foretold by Spearman–Brown logic—an improved reliability of description. Although individual CQ-sorts, because of observer idiosyncrasies coupled with inevitable random error, may demonstrate relatively scant, unimpressive, uncertain relations with various reference phenomena, the derived CQ-composite description of a person emerges as representing collective perceptivity and, by virtue of its better dependability, has a far better likelihood of relating statistically to other phenomena.

9. The set of composite person descriptions—a unique, concentered CQ composite for each individual—provides reliability-improved, appraiser-based, wide-ranging, contemporary personality descriptions of each member of the sample.

The assembled set of CQ composites provide data that exist at a new analytical level. As evidenced through the numerous coherent earlier citations and their fit within an overall nomological network, appraiser recognitions suitably developed and processed may frequently contribute valuable and statistically firm findings not achievable by other means.

Composite Q-sorts can be expected to further serve in a variety of analyses with other quite independent, reliable, and far-removed indexes of individual differences. As in data analyses generally, obtained CQ findings must demonstrate their nonspuriousness by statistical evaluation. Such evaluation is conveniently established; as necessary, suitable empirical CQ-sampling distributions are readily computer derived to serve as the reference context for particular analyses. This statistical tactic, described earlier, is now readily implemented.

THE ANTICIPATED PRACTICAL CONSEQUENCES OF THIS CONCENTERING APPROACH

The various ingredients of this long-used approach are each required; no ingredient alone is sufficient. Properly sequenced, the descriptive uniqueness of each person is usually reliably portrayed from what initially began as the individual subjective impressions of various observers.

This methodological sequence, in its necessary entirety, does not appear to have been generally used earlier. There do not appear to have been prior instances of the systematic aggregation of subjective impressions comprehensively expressed in commensurate form.[1]

The sequence provides a singular way of adding the strengths of the statistical approach to a clinical appraisal approach. The newly introduced features are that previously informal subjective impressions are first explicitly and comprehensively expressed through the CQ-set and in a commensurate form. Then, the logic of aggregation creates the reliable emergence of collectively surmised discriminations. Although the discriminations of individual observers separately may be insecure, the aggregation effect is formidable. The procedural sequence has worked dependably well in many applications and can be expected to be useful in further circumstances. It speaks out for the latent, recondite presence of potentially relevant discriminations expressed through compositing carefully elicited and commensurate appraiser evaluations.

Admittedly, this research course is burdensome and perhaps can only be used in specially favored research circumstances. The very arduousness involved in implementing the formula can be dispiriting, and it is a research avenue that is often unfeasible because of its special logistical, methodological, and funding demands. Only the rare research program is likely to have both the motivation and resources for its implementation.

Thus, for many clinical contexts, this approach may be of only demonstrational interest rather than practical, everyday implication. Whether its empirical attainments will develop appreciation of the inexpressibles in clinical understandings remains to be seen. The concentering procedure may be seen only as an existence proof that there is indeed something inherent that is not artless in clinical judgment. It is certainly difficult alternatively to conjecture how the unthinking, impersonal statistical, mechanical, algorithmic approach might establish the remarkable diversity of reliable but coherent behavioral connections clearly established through quantitative, articulated, commensurate, aggregated subjective impressions.

EVALUATING CLINICAL EXPERTISE

An expert may be thought of as someone with extensive knowledge and experience in a particular field, one able to call on this cognitive store rapidly and relevantly. The expert's knowledge includes not only close information

---

[1]Horowitz, Inouye, and Siegelman (1979) noted how averaging ratings increased the reliability of a composite and therefore the likelihood of establishing its external validity. However, the further requirement of commensurateness was not recognized. The report on "the value of pooling" (Schulz & Waldinger, 2005), instanced by a study on intuitively apprehended emotion (Waldinger, Schulz, Hauser, Allen, & Crowell, 2004), also adds support to the aggregation research strategy but again was not cognizant of the distorting effect of noncommensurateness. The work on the principles of forecasting (Armstrong, 2001) also warrants mention in regard to the value of aggregation.

about the problems usually encountered but also savvy as to how to dynamically deal with unusual situations. The expert is presumed to be better than a novice at the same task. In psychology or psychiatry, clinical expertise is considered to develop as a function of clinical training, clinical experience, acumen, and the character tempering provided by life.

The perspicacity of the clinical expert's judgment and intuition has long been assumed and even vaunted by clinicians (and often their clients). Experienced clinicians in their self-perceptions, and as usually viewed by the public, are expected to have superior acuteness of perception and understanding of the psychology of persons. Westen and Weinberger (2004) gave voice to this point of view when they described how clinical experience and sophistication can bring important insights into person evaluations that are otherwise undetectable.

However, the inescapable empirical question remains: Are clinical experts indeed superior to socially intelligent lay observers in their skill at psychological inference? As noted by Westen and Weinberger (2004), "We know very little about how expert versus lay observations of personality or psychopathology fare in predicting . . ." (p. 599). They suggest that contrasting what Meehl (1960) has called the "cognitive activity of the clinician" with its counterpoint, the "cognitive activity of the socially intelligent lay observer," would be most edifying.

Relevant here is the remark, suggested by their research, of Schulz and Waldinger (2005):

> There are some domains . . . in which those with the greatest expertise are neither specially trained observers nor self-reporters but, rather, lay observers who have a native or learned ability to detect complicated social and psychological phenomena and make subtle discriminations. This type of expertise is thought of as intuitive because it uses implicit knowledge that is not always accessible to conscious awareness or capable of being fully articulated. (p. 556; see also chap. 1, this volume)

To more definitively investigate the professional assumption of the presumed superiority of credentialed clinical experts, is it necessary to specify what is meant or should be meant by reference to a "socially intelligent lay observer?" If one insists on reasonable standards of cognitive and perceptive competence, we are reduced to, perhaps, 10% or 15% of all available adults. Professional mental health providers are almost universally drawn from this thin slice of the population, and it seems fair to consider the remainder of this slice as representing the self-reflective socially intelligent lay observer (e.g., nonclinical graduate students, graduates of 4-year universities, etc.).

In specific regard to evaluating the distinctive contribution of clinical expertise, the CQ method may provide an attractive evidence-based medium. The CQ procedure contains many descriptors that involve character surmises but is not abstruse, convoluted, or impenetrable. Contrasting a group of clinical experts with a group of socially intelligent lay observers—both assessing the same diverse sets of patients and nonpatients through the CQ procedure—would provide intriguing and implicative analytical opportunities. The comparison would confront the far-reaching, long-lingering question as to the veridicality and special contribution of clinical expertise, per se.

From the positive demonstrations afforded by the methodological recipe earlier described, two conclusions follow:

With the first conclusion, given the empirical relations of CQ composites with a wide array of separate individual differences, there appears to be definite person information latent in the subjective impressions of observers when these are expressed commensurately and subsequently pooled.

With the second conclusion, it apparently is not necessary to depend on credentialed clinical psychologists. The subjective impressions, expressed in CQ form by clinically inexperienced but socially intelligent lay observers (e.g., graduate students and nursery school teachers) have provided many empirical instances that demonstrate that CQ observers need only be bright, motivated, and with culturally cognizant experience.

In regard to the conjectured clinical expert versus nonexpert distinction, two straightforward hypotheses would seem to follow:

- *Hypothesis 1*: Clinical experts—individuals credentialed within the mental health community—should be expected to manifest greater uniformity among themselves in their descriptions of a person—and over a set of persons—than socially intelligent lay observers without clinical training and experience. This hypothesis is readily testable.
- *Hypothesis 2*: Person-CQ descriptions offered by clinical experts, when aggregated into composites, should be expected to manifest stronger connection with various external criteria than the person-CQ descriptions offered by socially intelligent lay assessors, when aggregated into composites. This expectation also can be empirically tested.

In addition, the contentual similarities and differences between CQ composites derived from credentialed clinical experts and those derived from bright, motivated, culturally aware, value-neutral nonprofessionals would be especially instructive to behold. Perspective on the particular efficacy of clinical expertise in perceiving mental health problems would be gained by this study.

In talking about clinical expertise, the vague term "intuition" is often alluded to as at the very heart of clinical judgment. The variously used notion of intuition warrants closer, more insistent attention and articulation than it yet has received. A most thoughtful, cogent analysis of intuition—bringing together what it means and what it does not mean—has been offered by

Epstein (2007). Epstein fundamentally ascribed intuition to automatic, inexpressible, learnings from experience and elaborated the concept in useful logical and psychological ways. Grounded in his *conceptual–experiential self-theory* (Epstein, 1993, 1994), he distinguishes between two interacting modes of mental functioning—an experiential or intuitive mode and a conceptual or analytic mode. The beginning clinician must have native talents of psychological perceptivity. In addition, over time and experience, the learning clinician develops rationally based expertise that increasingly becomes experiential, responsively adjusting to the meaning of subtle cues. The serious and experienced clinician is certainly conceptual in many ways but also intensely sensitive in the face-to-face apprehending of a client. In the person CQ formulations registered by a clinician, it seems fair to presume that evaluations of descriptor salience may be thought of as importantly experientially influenced. Accordingly, in evaluating the same set of persons, the CQ-sorts by credentialed clinicians should differ from those provided by intelligent nonclinicians along such lines.

More thinking and empirical testing is needed to establish and test the parameters of what is called intuition. At present, the confronting question remains: Is clinical "expertness" actually demonstrable? The question is logistically and temporally beyond serious empirical address here. However, future investigators can and should take up the issue, and the CQ procedure may be able to provide the medium. The challenge represented by studying clinical expertise, if proven out, will demonstrate its justification. If the belief in clinical expertise—studied relevantly—proves empirically unwarranted, the implications will be most sobering. Dare the challenge be empirically pursued?

10

A SALMAGUNDI OF Q AND A SALUTATION TO STEPHENSON

This last chapter first brings forward for further or new consideration the various California-evolved Q-sets. It then briefly discusses some alternative approaches in the literature to the usage of Q-sorting. Finally, it explicitly acknowledges the creative spirit of Stephenson, to whom much is due.

VARIOUS CALIFORNIA-EVOLVED Q-SETS

Over the past decades, the California Q-sort (CQ) procedure with its person-centered orientation and content has shown discriminative efficacy in many settings. It has demonstrated it can quantitatively accommodate to many informational resources, for example, clinicians of various schools, judgments from videotapes, reasonably extensive file records, self-views, peer-views, views from parents or close relatives, diverse but integratable information and data, and biographies. Because of the procedure's absolute insistence on commensurateness, it excludes troubling appraiser judgmental idiosyncrasies and its methodological logistics—admittedly more demanding than simple, convenient, but questionable self-report—generates credible, dependable data. The approach therefore has encouraged extension into relevant, largely unplumbed domains.

This section sets the stage for the subsequently offered completing appendixes. Here, the various California Q-sets are most briefly characterized. In the appendixes themselves, the several Q-sets are more detailed and extensively described. Readers may find these additional home-grown Q-sets of interest, if only as points of departure. All have seen prior effective use in earlier studies.

The California Adult Q-Set (CAQ)

Extensively exemplified earlier, the full list of CAQ descriptors is provided together in Appendix A with convenient instructions for CAQ administration. Also, Appendix A includes some illustrative and useful examples of CAQ prototypes.

The California Child Q-Set (CCQ)

The full list of CCQ descriptors is provided together in Appendix B with convenient instructions for CCQ administration. Also, Appendix B includes some illustrative and useful examples of CCQ prototypes. Furthermore, a useful, simplifying "common-language" version of the CCQ suitable for use with nonprofessional sorters is presented (Caspi et al., 1992).

The Child-Rearing Practices Report (CRPR)

The CRPR is a set of Q items developed by Jeanne H. Block, now deceased, for the description of parental socialization attitudes and values (see Appendix C). The initial CRPR-descriptor pool evolved in the course of a number of empirical studies and a thorough review of the socialization literature. It was further enriched by European colleagues from many cultures.

A Q-sort administrative format was used because the procedure is person centered, personally involving, and provides commensurate data thus avoiding response sets that plague many self-descriptive measures, for example, acquiescence, social desirability, other informant idiosyncrasies. In particular, the would-be CRPR user is advised that shifting away from the designated, configurational Q-sort procedure to using the items singly, as so-called Likert items, permits the intrusion of cliché.

The CRPR descriptors characterize both maternal and paternal child-rearing attitudes and values. Two forms of the measure exist: a first-person version appropriate for both mothers and fathers and a third-person version to be completed by young people in describing the child-rearing orientations of their parents. Slight, readily obvious textual changes are required in moving from the first- to the third-person format.

The CRPR has been translated into a number of languages and has proven to be a suitable and sensitive instrument for use in cross-cultural investigations. The Spanish version listed seems especially timely given contemporary South American interest in socialization research.

The parent, when responding to the CRPR items, is advised to focus on a specified child in the family. To encourage closer descriptions of child-rearing attitudes and values, the items are phrased, wherever possible, in the active voice (e.g., "I do," "I ask," "I emphasize," "I believe") and emphasize a behavioral orientation. The test–retest reliability of the CRPR, assessed in two samples, has been impressively high, averaging .7.

Data analysis of the CRPR can proceed as with Q data generally. The use of prototype or criterion CRPR Q-sorts is of special interest because scores on various socialization dimensions are readily derived by correlating a person's CRPR with established CRPR prototypes. As illustration, four prototypes are provided listing Baumrind's (1971) well-known distinctions between *authoritarian–autocratic parenting, authoritative–responsive parenting, indulgent–permissive parenting*, and *indifferent–uninvolved parenting*. Other studies, for which appropriate prototypes have been developed, ask whether the mothers of activist college students are more *autonomy inducing* than the mothers of nonactivist college students. Or, do Scandinavian parents foster *communal values*, as opposed to *agentic values*, more than do American parents? The procedure for developing prototypes is described earlier.

To date, the CRPR has been administered to more than 9,000 persons of different ages (ages 16–50), different socioeconomic levels (unskilled workers to professionals), different educational levels (sixth grade to advanced degrees), and different nationalities. For references to the large body of CRPR studies, one can readily search the psychological literature. The CRPR has an extensive bibliography extending over the last 40 years.

The California Environmental Q-Set (CEQ)

A CAQ description of an individual is *contemporaneous*, intended to characterize a person as understood at the time of evaluation and is expressed without regard for the particular circumstances or history of how the person evolved. However, the antecedents and environmental or situational surround of an individual are no less important in understanding the individual. By the same logic advanced for the CAQ- or CCQ-sets, a carefully selected, comprehensive set of descriptors in terms of which a subject's environmental context and personal past may be described provides a most useful way of registering the *developmental* understanding of an individual.

To this end, a set of 100 Q descriptors was carefully created and amplified to express an appraiser's view of a person's developmental history. The resulting set of descriptors has been designated the CEQ (see Appendix D).

The task for the respondent is to order environmentally relevant descriptors in terms of their conjectured salience in regard to the developmental history of the particular person. The CEQ may be responded to by the person involved or by a knowledgeable appraiser of that person. It is not sufficient simply to list the influences on a person's life; they must be configured and the Q-sorting procedure more closely realizes this person-centered aim. Thus, for example, the CEQ descriptor, "I experienced some form of discrimination due to race, religion, nationality or social class as I was growing up," is perhaps not so salient in 21st century America for a person of Jewish origin as it had been in the earlier 20th century. The CEQ descriptor, "As a child, I was disciplined in psychological ways—by my parents withholding love or making me feel guilty," is probably more contextually salient for someone who has lived in a university town than in a mining community. The CEQ procedure endeavors to permit expression of just how the life-history evaluator intertwines the multitudinous familial and cultural factors contributing toward character.

The CEQ-set has not received the extensive use of the CAQ- or CCQ-sets, but in various prior studies whether responded to by the person involved or a culturally sophisticated assessor it has proven of great value. Given a developmental complement for the CAQ or CCQ, the independently evaluated historical context of a person when later conjoined with contemporaneous assessments of that person may open to study a number of fruitful ways to evaluate large questions of how individuals happen to evolve toward different character structures.

The uniform distribution suggested for the CEQ—9 categories with 11 descriptors in each category except for 12 in the middle category—is advocated because it simplifies communication of instructions to the Q-sorter.

An Adjective Q-Set for Nonprofessional Sorters (AJQ)

Although the primary purpose of this volume has been to present the CQ procedure as an attractive way of encoding the subjective impressions of intelligent and astute observers in regard to other persons, the Q method by itself has important application as a research procedure through which laypersons can describe themselves or others. For this purpose, Q descriptors should be understandable by the relevant person populations. By virtue of the methodological strengths of the Q procedure, various problems and artifacts typically besetting questionnaire response are avoided. Various Q-sets for use by nonprofessionals have appeared in the literature but none in the field of person research, besides the one here presented, appears to have received more than a modicum of usage. Moreover, for various reasons, many of the Q-sets previously used with lay subjects may be judged deficient—they have been redundant or too narrow, and especially susceptible to response sets. For reasons by now repetitious to recite, it is useful to settle on one reasonably adequate Q-set for use in such research. Therefore, an already frequently used Q-set is brought forward for further research in this domain.

The offered adjective Q-set—the AJQ—for use by nonprofessional sorters has evolved in the course of several studies and has further benefited from the suggestions of a number of assessment psychologists (see Appendix E). It consists of 43 descriptors oriented toward coverage of the entire personality sphere. The descriptors are to be arranged into seven categories with six descriptors in each category (except for seven in the middle category, four). The requirements for the prescribed distribution are easy to communicate, and the seven categories do not strain discrimination capacity. In this form, the adjective Q-set may be used as a self-administering procedure with individuals of high-school educational level. Individuals typically complete a sorting of the AJQ-set in less than 15 minutes. Subsequent sortings, with different sorting orientations (e.g., the "targets" of self, ego ideal, mother, father, love object, etc.) may require less time. The procedure does not appear to be onerous for participating subjects and has produced engrossing relations. For example, the congruence of a person's self-AJQ-sort with that person's AJQ of an ideal self provides an effective conceptual index of self-esteem (Block & Robins, 1993); the congruence of a person's self-AJQ-sort with that person's AJQs of mother and of father provides indexes of identification; and so on.

The Teaching Strategy Q-Set (TSQ)

In many teaching or observational situations, in which a parent or adult is interacting with the child, it is capturing of the context to encode the interaction style, mode, and interactive techniques of the parent or adult. For a number of studies, it proved helpful to construct the TSQ-set to describe the various facets of this interaction (see Appendix F). The TSQ consists of 49 descriptors with a prescribed distribution of seven equal-sized categories.

SOME ALTERNATIVE APPROACHES TO THE USE OF Q SORTING

There have been other extensive uses in the literature on the Q-sort procedure. Five approaches are mentioned in the next section and commented on; others can be found by literature search on the Internet. The remarks here are not ex cathedra but are personal reflections.

The Stephenson Tradition

The orientation and specific procedures of Stephenson historically continue because they lend themselves to many, diverse inquiries.[1] The primary

---

[1] Reference to GOOGLE will locate many citations to and results from his approach.

American protagonist of Stephenson's standpoint has been Steven Brown (e.g., Brown, 1980, 1986, 1993), political scientist at Kent State University. His views exemplify and continue to extend Stephenson's earlier groundings.[2]

Stephenson adherents of what they specifically label as *Q methodology* view the CQ procedure espoused here as deviant from their tradition. The use of a standardized, carefully developed set of Q descriptors for a specified domain, as with the CQ procedure's concern with subjective impressions, continues to be disavowed. Instead, within the Stephenson tradition, after deciding on the particular topic of interest, a set of Q items typically is quickly assembled, structured a priori (often questionably) by the investigator along analysis of variance lines, and is not itself further evaluated as to its sufficiency of meaning. A laissez faire (and therefore importantly incommensurate) distribution of the Q-sort statements is permitted. Only a small sample of respondents is usually involved and ". . . little attention typically attends the correlation matrix, which is simply a phase through which the data pass on their way to revealing the structure among the various perspectives" (Brown, in press). For Stephenson, the primary principle underlying a Q-sorting is the individual's personal, subjective point of view—numerically encoded—on the matter at hand. The consequent subjective data are analyzed subsequently only by means of the method of factor analysis and then reported. Replications or alternative interpretations of factor analysis results are rarely attempted.

The substantive topics in the Stephenson-oriented Q literature are variegated and do not fall within a simple rubric. The approach has been directed toward such topics as, for example, beliefs or values about water, metaphorical understandings of the Internet, sustainable communities, musical performance, grizzly bear conservation, young people's attitude toward downloading songs illegally, attitudes toward 9/11, aspects of decision making, and so on.

Proffered interpretations stem from the factor structure viewed as organizing the expressed "subjective" opinions. This focus on self-attitudes in regard to sundry matters is fundamentally different from the present approach, which emphasizes observer Q-sort expressed subjective impressions of other persons. The Stephenson perspective and the present one differ in that the one expresses personal attitudes or opinions in regard to a specified topic or issue whereas the second expresses an appraiser's personal perceptions or evaluations of another person. However, whatever the target of the Q-sort—whether attitudes toward grizzly bear conservation or evaluative description of a person—whenever the process of Q-sorting is used to capture the impressions, values, attitudes, or judgments of the Q-sorter, the consequent data are undeniably subjective. For both approaches, Q-sorting provides a salience ordering of qualities through many implicit cross-attribute comparisons—resulting in a surprisingly reliable quan-

---

[2]For a contemporary perspective on the Stephenson approach and its current applications, the Internet may be consulted at http://www.qmethod.org

tification. The subsequent processing of these data of subjective origin is quite different, where the Stephensonian Q approach and present Q orientation fundamentally diverge in their concerns.

The Q-Sort Study of Attachment

With integration provided by Everett Waters at the State University of New York, a large body of research has come forward that uses the Waters Attachment Q-sort measure (AQS) in a variety of studies (Waters & Deane, 1985).[3] Much substantive and implicative attachment Q research has accrued, and interested readers may wish to refer to the Internet address in Footnote 3 for references.

The Q-Sort Study of the Psychoanalytic Transaction

The work of the late Enrico Jones (2000), reported in his book *Therapeutic Action: A Guide to Psychoanalytic Therapy*, studies the interaction language structure of a psychoanalytic analytic session, session after session. He used his Psychotherapy Process Q-sort (PQS), which has elicited strong interest among fellow psychoanalysts for the aptness of its characterization of the psychoanalytic process.

The Q-Sort Study of Social Behavior

The Riverside Behavioral Q-sort (Funder, Furr, & Colvin, 2000) gathers a wide-ranging description of the behaviors of individuals within dyadic social interaction. It appears to reliably reflect the social behavioral effects of context manipulations and manifests meaningful correlations with personality characteristics alternatively measured. Further use of this procedure seems warranted.

The Shedler–Westen Assessment Procedure–200 (SWAP-200)

More recently, another Q-sort procedure intended for person description—the SWAP-200—has been brought forward (e.g., Shedler & Westen, 1998; Westen & Shedler, 1999a, 1999b, 2006). The SWAP contains 200 descriptors and focuses primarily on characterizing what the *Diagnostic and Statistical Manual of Mental Disorders* (DSM) labels as *personality disorders*. Although offered as "a new language for psychoanalytic diagnosis" (Shedler, 2002), it is questionable whether the language instrument will be viewed as particularly apt for the special psychoanalytic context; it is perhaps better

---

[3]To see Waters's Web site, please visit http://www.psychology.sunysb.edu/attachment/

understandable as a descriptive procedure applicable by mental health practitioners for describing patients.

Similar to the earlier CAQ procedure half its length, the SWAP-200 seeks to augment psychiatric usage of the Q-sort method. Because of these corresponding intentions, a close comparison of the similarity and also the differences between the SWAP and the CAQ seems especially warranted.

In substantial ways, the SWAP is similar to the earlier presented CAQ procedure (Block, 1961, reprinted 1978), other early studies (Block, 1956, 1957a, 1971), and accumulated empirical CQ demonstrations over the years. Shedler had briefly participated during 1989 and 1990 in a previously ongoing Block and Block longitudinal study (e.g., Block & Block, 2006b) heavily dependent on CQ logic and procedures, and had become impressed by the empirical generativity of the method.

Thus, as with the CQ procedure earlier, the SWAP-200 also (a) adopts a standard language, (b) uses a "prescribed" Q distribution to achieve commensurateness, (c) relies also on aggregating similarly targeted Q-sorts to enhance the reliability of composites, (d) leans heavily on the conceptual idea that underlies Q prototypes, and (e) uses Q-sort intercorrelations in taxonomic factor analysis. Furthermore, the SWAP-200 uses Q descriptors reminiscent of many, earlier CAQ descriptors: for example, SWAP Descriptor 1 ("Tends to feel guilty") versus CAQ Descriptor 47 ("Has a readiness to feel guilty"); SWAP Descriptor 2 ("Is able to use his/her talents, abilities, and energy effectively and productively") versus CAQ Descriptor 26 ("Is productive, gets things done"), SWAP Descriptor 3 ("Takes advantage of others, has little investment in moral values, puts own needs first, uses or exploits people with little regard for their feelings or welfare") versus CAQ Descriptor 7 ("Is guileful, deceitful, manipulative, opportunistic, takes advantage of others").

Conceptually and technically, however, when evaluated closely the SWAP-200 seems to offer several unrecognized and fundamental interpretive and practical problems.

1. Newly introduced are a number of SWAP descriptors that require deep, obscurely based psychological conjecture rather than more accessible clinical inference. For example, consider SWAP Descriptor 41 ("Appears unable to describe important others in a way that conveys a sense of who they are as people; descriptions of others come across as two-dimensional and lacking in richness") or SWAP Descriptor 10 ("Feels some important other has a special, almost magical ability to understand his/her innermost thoughts and feelings, for example, may imagine rapport is so perfect that ordinary efforts at communication are superfluous"). It is nowhere indicated how well the salience judgments of clinicians agree among themselves about

the same person or client in regard to such adumbrated descriptors. Given the well-known diversity among credentialed "clinical experts," there is reason to question the presence or attainability of sufficient interappraiser agreement with regard to such Q descriptors. Therefore, it would be reassuring—even necessary—to have empirical support in regard to the agreement among clinical experts who are independently characterizing the same person with respect to such highly inferential SWAP descriptors.

2. The SWAP uses an unprecedented prescribed distribution, described as a flattened right tail of a normal distribution. The 200 SWAP descriptors are to be placed by the sorter into eight decreasingly salient categories, labeled from 7 to zero, according to the designated frequencies of 8, 10, 12, 14, 16, 18, 22, and 100. This lopsided descriptor distribution is asserted, a priori and without empirical support, as being clinically most relevant.

For each patient or diagnostic concept being SWAP characterized, the procedure requires the appraiser to fill the seven highest categories with SWAP descriptors evaluated by the appraiser as psychologically germane, according to their perceived decreasing salience. The remaining 100 SWAP descriptors—50% of the 200—are swept into the lowest category, named *zero*, and described as having no substantive import. That is, relative to the positively assigned descriptors, the 100 remaining descriptors are conceived in the SWAP as "irrelevant" or "inapplicable" or "concerning matters on which the sorter has no information."

The possibility is ignored that many of the 100 necessarily lumped-together, construed as zero or inapplicable SWAP descriptors, may have important differential information in describing what the patient is not. A person can be described not only affirmatively but also, often more trenchantly, by negative information as with the CAQ. The unusual SWAP-prescribed distribution neglects the important information that would be available by further discriminating among the numerically preponderant zero or inapplicable descriptors.

3. Not analytically considered are the statistical consequences of the choices the SWAP sorter is required to make in selecting 100 zero or inapplicable descriptors from the 200 available. Necessarily, given SWAP procedural constraints, the 100 zero or inapplicable descriptors selected by one SWAP Q-sorter must appreciably overlap with the 100 zero or inapplicable descriptors selected by another SWAP Q-sorter. However, although the

SWAP declares 100 of its Q descriptors to have the nominal value of zero, in fact this large group of inapplicable descriptors possesses appreciable psychometric weight. The assigned numbering of the eight SWAP categories, ranging from 7 through 0, it is important to note, is misleading. The designated category numbers are entirely arbitrary. Instead of ranging from 7 to zero, they could as well have been between 8 and 1, 48 and 41, or 672 and 665; the computed correlations between different SWAP-200 Q-sorts would remain unchanged.

Whatever the assigned numbering, the numerous "inapplicable" descriptors lie heavily at one extreme of the eight-category ordering continuum. Because of the unusual L-shaped SWAP-200 distribution prescribed, this preponderance of extreme (i.e., inapplicable) descriptors at one end of the ordering continuum has inordinate product–moment weighting. All SWAP intercorrelations are appreciably heightened because of the inevitable and appreciable overlap of heavily weighted inapplicable descriptors.

At the limit of overlap—when the 100 irrelevant SWAP descriptors are identical for all sorters, but the remaining descriptors are randomly allotted to the other seven categories—the randomly selected correlation between any two SWAP assessors averages .61, is as high as .78, and 5% of the time is more than .67, as revealed by Monte Carlo empirical computer resampling procedures. Although SWAP sorters vary among themselves in the descriptors they leave in the zero or inapplicable category, a substantial degree of overlap between SWAP sorts inevitably is compelled. However, the SWAP manual and other SWAP discussions provide no recognition whatsoever of this built-in correlational artifact. Additionally, by conjecture, SWAP-sorter overlap in the inapplicable category is likely to be further increased when sorters confront and then choose to escape use of the SWAP's highly abstruse descriptors.

The unknown inescapable but appreciable overlap among assessors in regard to the descriptors within the so-called irrelevant category means the chance correlation between SWAP Q-sorts begins at a surprising, unwittingly high level. This heightening effect fundamentally disrupts the subsequent interpretation of all SWAP intercorrelations both directly and when the SWAP data are used in subsequent analyses.

It is quite impossible to nonempirically estimate how this correlation heightening artifact functions in actual SWAP research, but its underlying presence is indubitable. Especially to be noted is that when patients who are presenting different configurations of symptoms are SWAP described, the similarity of their descriptors in the inapplicable category may suggest the existence of a greater comorbidity than is warranted. More extensive and independent studies are required in regard to this troublesome, distorting problem.

4. To demonstrate the "reliability" and "validity" of their instrument, Shedler and Westen (2004) had a large number of seasoned mental health professionals each SWAP describe their conceptual or prototypical understandings of the meaning and implication of one of the various *DSM*-established personality disorder categories. By arithmetically aggregating the individually offered SWAP Q-sort conceptualizations offered for each given diagnosis, they found—as had the earlier aggregate-based CAQ prototypes—that each resulting SWAP-prototype composite was highly reliable (reliabilities of >.90).

They also had other psychiatrists and psychologists SWAP describe a patient already diagnosed as representing a particular *DSM* personality disorder. Again, by arithmetically aggregating the individual SWAP Q-sorts of the various patients already given a specific *DSM* personality disorder diagnosis, the resulting SWAP Q composites were again found to be highly reliable (reliabilities of >.90).

These vaunted high reliabilities of composites are less impressive when viewed within a psychometric perspective. By formula, the reliability of a composite is a function of the number of contributors to that composite and the average degree of agreement among the contributors. Increasing the number of contributors always enhances the reliability of the composite as long as there is at least a beginning of contributor agreement. Thus, for example, although contributors may correlate only a minuscule .10 with each other, given enough contributors— say, 100—the reliability of the aggregate becomes a noble .92! A small correspondence among a large number of contributors always generates a high reliability of the aggregate. The force of aggregation has long been understood in psychometrics but widely underappreciated elsewhere.

It is further instructive to calculate the reverse implications of high-composite reliabilities. In regard to the SWAP reliabilities of composites, knowing the number of contributors to these aggregates, it is readily possible to backward calculate the average degree of agreement among the SWAP contributors. Shedler and Westen (2004, p. 1352) in their Table 1 indicate the number of clinicians that contribute to each kind of SWAP composite. This information is sobering. In describing a hypothetical prototypic patient, from 15 to 20 clinicians were invoked for the aggregate description to achieve a reliability of >.90; in describing patients, each different but all carrying identical *DSM* diagnoses, from 26 to 43 clinicians were called on to create an "empirical" prototype with a reliability of >.90.

Working the Spearman–Brown formula backward, the average SWAP intercorrelation among clinicians SWAP describing their conception of a personality disorder ranged from .38 to .30, rather low figures compared with CAQ equivalents in earlier prototype construction and low for what is supposed to be professionally a common concept understanding. When clinicians SWAP described actual patients, each different but each earlier given the identical *DSM* personality disorder diagnosis, their average intercorrelation ranged from .17 to .25, again rather low figures considering that all of the patients carried the same formal diagnosis. Perhaps these mediocre figures—especially considering the built-in overlap in the preponderant "inapplicable" category—suggest the SWAP has descriptive insufficiencies; perhaps they indicate diverse clinicians have surprisingly diverse diagnostic views.

It would be context providing and clarifying if SWAP information existed somewhere on the correlations between multiple (at least two) clinicians who independently described the same person, across a range of persons or patients. Such information would provide a useful perspective. Nowhere, apparently, have such data been presented; therefore, there is no knowledge currently available on the extent to which a pair of clinicians independently will SWAP-agree with respect to the same person.

5. The SWAP composites derived empirically from the characteristics of patients who were already awarded that *DSM* diagnosis proved to relate to the corresponding SWAP composites on the basis of conceptual *DSM* diagnostic prototypes. This relation has been offered as evidence of the validity of the SWAP. That is, the SWAP Q procedure demonstrated that the aggregate based on compositing SWAPs of patients already labeled as with a particular *DSM* personality disorder proved to correlate with the composite based on the SWAPs through which mental health practitioners separately conceived of this *DSM* disorder. The finding seems tautological, circular rather than revelatory.

6. The final issue with the SWAP is that it is unusually lengthy and has been described by practitioners as onerous in ordinary

clinical practice. In implicit acknowledgement of the taxing nature of the SWAP, the procedure's manual advises the clinician to use only 5-point overall ratings—unspecified as to their distribution—in regard to how well it is thought a patient fits a provided SWAP prototype description. Such idiosyncratic 5-point ratings would inevitably be incommensurate, both within and between clinicians. It would abandon the stable frame of reference provided by the prescribed Q distribution, crucial for comparison, coalescence, and other calculations.

From a larger and longer perspective, a pragmatic and a conceptual problem each warrant consideration. Pragmatically, the highly inferential nature of certain SWAP descriptors requires that the evaluating clinician have especially close knowledge and understanding of the patient or person before a professionally satisfying SWAP Q portrayal can be projected. SWAP instructions advise the clinician to first have 5 or 6 patient or client contact hours. Most busy mental health practitioners are likely to find this recommendation difficult to implement. Alternatively, a SWAP-oriented semistructured interview of the patient is proposed if the interviewer has received prior training in the SWAP and has demonstrated interview reliability. This too is likely to prove practically unfeasible.

Conceptually, the SWAP structuring in terms of currently existing DSM categories may be shortsighted and limiting. Currently, the SWAP-200 expressly targets coverage of the "personality disorders" (Axis II of the *Diagnostic and Statistical Manual of Mental Disorders, Fourth Edition* [DSM–IV]; American Psychiatric Association, 1994)—diagnoses of borderline, schizotypal, schizoid, antisocial, paranoid, histrionic, narcissistic, avoidant, dependent, and obsessive–compulsive. It scarcely mentions *DSM–IV* Axis I disorders— diagnoses of depression, anxiety, bipolar disorder, attention deficit, impulse control, schizophrenia, adjustment problems. However, Axis I is long and widely recognized as importantly coexistent and conflated with Axis II (Frances, 1980), the axes are not truly appreciated as distinctive. It remains an open question whether the SWAP-200 is descriptively sufficient to characterize those psychiatric features typically subsumed under Axis I.

Additionally, in the improved, perhaps restructured, forthcoming fifth edition of the *DSM*, besides necessarily and primarily focusing on psychopathology, it may be important to acknowledge those positive aspects of adjustment-tempering maladaptive person attributes. However, currently the SWAP-200 descriptors have a negative cast. Together with its particular, L-shaped descriptor distribution, the SWAP-200 may not be able to properly portray this enlarged, more positive coverage. In what may be an acknowledgment and attempted rectification of this concern, a SWAP prototype of "high functioning" has been generated, approximating the criterial beacon of the long-established CAQ prototype on "optimal adjustment."

AN APPRECIATION OF STEPHENSON

In conclusion, an appreciation—even homage—is due to William Stephenson. As perspectives have accumulated out of experience, the multiple implications of Q have begun to be better appreciated. In any evaluation, the splendid contribution of Stephenson, the ingenious and vigorous proponent of Q technique 75 years ago, cannot be underestimated.

Stephenson, of course, innovated a fruitful methodology. His more important service, though, was to insist stubbornly on the possibilities and fruitfulness of quantifying the individual person. By recognizing the different kinds of lawfulness available from variable-centered and from person-centered data, he was able to come forward with an analytical orientation that meshes excitingly with multiple, contemporary research needs.

The preceding pages on Q rationale, Q method, and Q applications have chosen to move in certain ways beyond certain early stances of Stephenson. In part, these changes have stemmed from divergence in respective goals; in larger part, these differences stem from later accumulated recognitions and experience. In any event, the very genuine debt the present effort owes to him must be acknowledged. It is hoped that the present work may encourage further evaluation and application of the techniques and principles Stephenson generated.

APPENDIX A

THE CALIFORNIA ADULT Q-SET (CAQ)

PURPOSE

The California Adult Q-set (CAQ; and the important correspondent California Child Q-set [CCQ]) is a language instrument designed to permit comprehensive personality descriptions of adults (or preadolescent children) in a form suitable for subsequent quantitative comparison and analysis. It consists of a standard set of 100 person descriptors, together with instructions for commensurately ordering these descriptors to describe a specifically designated person.

Person characterizations are formulated by knowledgeable psychologically oriented appraisers: teachers, psychiatrists, therapists, personality assessors, parents, college students, or other persons who know the individual being assessed.

THE CAQ DESCRIPTORS: CAQ FORM III–R
(SPECIFIED 9-POINT DISTRIBUTION:
5, 8, 12, 16, 18, 16, 12, 8, 5; $N = 100$)

CAQ Descriptors

1. Is critical, skeptical, not easily impressed.
2. Is dependable and responsible (low placement implies undependable and irresponsible).
3. Has a wide range of interests (regardless of how deep or superficial the interests are).
4. Is a talkative person.
5. Is giving, generous toward others (regardless of the motivation).
6. Is fastidious, meticulous, careful and precise.
7. Favors conservative values in a variety of areas; emphasizes traditional values and beliefs (low placement implies rejection of traditional values).
8. Appears to have a high degree of intellectual capacity (whether or not this capacity translates into actual accomplishments).
9. Is uncomfortable with uncertainty and complexity; is more comfortable with things that are straightforward and uncomplicated.
10. Anxiety and stress find outlet in bodily symptoms (develops physical symptoms in reaction to stress and anxiety, e.g., sweating, racing heart, headaches, stomach aches, rashes, asthma, etc.).
11. Is protective of those close to him/her (placement of this item reflects behavior ranging from overprotectiveness through appropriate caring through underprotectiveness and lack of concern).
12. Tends to be self-defensive; unable to acknowledge personal shortcomings or failures; quick to defend self from criticism.
13. Is thin-skinned; sensitive to anything that can be construed as a criticism or slight or insult; takes offense easily.
14. Genuinely submissive; accepts domination comfortably; gives in easily.
15. Is skilled in social techniques of imaginative play, pretending, and humor.
16. Is introspective; thinks about self; examines own thoughts and feelings (introspectiveness per se does not necessarily imply self-insight, or that person understands himself/herself well).

17. Behaves in a sympathetic and considerate manner (low placement implies unsympathetic and inconsiderate behavior).
18. Initiates humor; makes spontaneous funny remarks.
19. Seeks reassurance from others (high placement implies lack of self-confidence).
20. Has a rapid personal tempo; behaves and acts quickly; is fast paced.
21. Arouses nurturant feelings in others; behaves in ways that lead others to feel caring and protective toward him/her.
22. Feels a lack of meaning in life.
23. Tends to blame others for own mistakes, failures, and shortcomings.
24. Prides self on being rational, logical, and objective (high placement implies a person who is more comfortable with abstractions and intellectual concepts than with feelings).
25. Overcontrols needs and impulses; binds tension excessively; delays gratification unnecessarily (has excessive self-control; keeps a tight rein on feelings; postpones pleasures unnecessarily).
26. Is productive, gets things done.
27. Is condescending toward others; acts superior to others (low placement implies only that the person does not act superior, not necessarily that he/she acts inferior or believes all people are equal in status).
28. Tends to arouse liking and acceptance in people (low placement implies tendency to arouse dislike).
29. Is turned to or sought out for advice and reassurance.
30. Gives up and withdraws when possible in the face of frustration and adversity (high placement implies person gives up easily; low placement implies person does not know when, realistically, it is time to give up).
31. Regards self as physically attractive (low placement implies person sees self as unattractive; Item 81 refers to actual physical attractiveness; this item refers to how person sees himself/herself, whether accurate or not).
32. Seems to be aware of the impression he/she makes on others (low placement implies person is unaware of the impression he/she makes).
33. Is calm, relaxed in manner.
34. Is irritable; overreacts to minor frustrations.
35. Has warmth; has the capacity for close relationships; compassionate.

36. Is subtly negativistic; tends to undermine, obstruct, or sabotage other people.
37. Is guileful, deceitful, manipulative, opportunistic; takes advantage of others.
38. Has hostility toward others (whether or not the hostile feelings are actually expressed; Item 94 reflects manner of expression).
39. Thinks and associates to ideas in unusual ways; has unconventional thought processes.
40. Is generally fearful; is vulnerable to real or imagined threat.
41. Makes moral judgments; judges self and others in terms of right and wrong (regardless of the nature of the moral code, whether traditional or liberal; high placement implies being moralistic and self-righteous; low placement implies an unwillingness to make value judgments).
42. Reluctant to commit self to any definite course of action; tends to delay or avoid making decisions or taking action.
43. Is facially and/or gesturally expressive.
44. Evaluates the motives of others; tries to figure out the intentions underlying people's actions (accuracy of evaluation is not assumed; high placement implies preoccupation with the motives of others; low placement implies being psychologically naive and not considering other people's motives).
45. Has a brittle ego defense system; has a small reserve of integration; would be disorganized or maladaptive under stress or trauma (is psychologically frail, vulnerable; has poor ability to cope with stress).
46. Tends to fantasize, daydream, engage in fictional speculations.
47. Has a readiness to feel guilty (high placement implies a tendency to feel guilt even when he/she is not at fault).
48. Keeps people at a distance; avoids close relationships.
49. Is basically distrustful of people in general; questions their motivations.
50. Is unpredictable and changeable in attitudes and behavior (high placement implies a person whose attitudes toward self and others can undergo marked and erratic changes, depending on life situation, current relationships, the emotions of the moment, etc.).
51. Places high value on intellectual and cognitive matters (does not necessarily imply intellectual achievement or intellectual ability).
52. Behaves in an assertive fashion; not afraid to express opinions; speaks up to get what he/she wants.

53. Needs and impulses tend toward relatively direct and uncontrolled expression; unable to delay gratification (is impulsive, has little self-control; unable to postpone pleasure).

54. Is sociable, gregarious; emphasizes being with others.

55. Is self-defeating; acts in ways that frustrate, hurt, or undermine own chances to get what he/she wants.

56. Responds to and appreciates humor.

57. Is an interesting, colorful person.

58. Appears to enjoy sensuous experiences (e.g., touch, taste, smell, bodily contact).

59. Is concerned about own body, its health and adequacy of functioning (high placement generally implies hypochondriasis; low placement implies insufficient concern for one's body).

60. Has insight into and understands own needs, motives, behavior; knows self well (low placement implies little insight into own motives and behavior).

61. Likes others to be dependent on him/her; actively fosters dependency in people regardless of means used to accomplish this, likes to be thought needed by others (low placement implies encouraging and respecting the individuality and independence of others).

62. Tends to be rebellious and nonconforming.

63. Judges self and others in conventional terms such as "popularity," "the right thing to do," and so forth; is influenced by social pressures.

64. Is socially perceptive of a wide range of interpersonal cues (is alert to cues from other people that reveal what they are thinking and feeling).

65. Characteristically pushes and tries to stretch limits and rules; sees what he/she can get away with.

66. Enjoys aesthetic impressions; is aesthetically sensitive (appreciates and is moved by art, music, drama, etc.).

67. Is self-indulgent; tends to "spoil" or pamper himself or herself.

68. Is basically anxious.

69. Is sensitive to anything that can be construed as a demand or request for favors; is quick to feel imposed on.

70. Behaves ethically; has a personal value system and is faithful to it.

71. Has high aspiration level for self; is ambitious; sets high personal goals.

72. Has doubts about own adequacy as a person; appears to have feelings of inadequacy, either consciously or unconsciously (This item is intended to reflect underlying feelings; it may

be placed high even if person is consciously self-satisfied. Item 74 reflects conscious satisfaction with self).

73. Tends to see sexual overtones in many situations; eroticizes situations (high placement implies that person reads sexual meanings into situations in which none exist; low placement implies inability to recognize sexual signals).

74. Feels satisfied with self; is consciously happy with person he/she believes self to be; is unaware of self-concern (This item is intended to reflect conscious, i.e., subjectively experienced, feelings; it may be placed high even when there is evidence of underlying or unconscious feelings of inadequacy. Item 72 reflects unconscious feelings of inadequacy).

75. Has a clear-cut, internally consistent personality; is relatively easy to understand and describe (low placement implies someone who is relatively difficult to understand and describe).

76. Tends to project own feelings and motivations onto others; imagines that other's needs, wishes, and feelings are the same as his/her own.

77. Appears straightforward, candid, frank in dealing with others.

78. Feels cheated and victimized by life; self-pitying; feels sorry for self.

79. Tends to ruminate and have persistent, preoccupying thoughts.

80. Interested in members of the opposite sex (low placement implies an absence of sexual interest for whatever reason; not necessarily dislike of the opposite sex or having homosexual interest).

81. Is physically attractive; is good-looking (as defined by our culture; low placement implies person is physically unattractive).

82. Has fluctuating moods; moods go up and down.

83. Able to see to the heart of important problems; does not get caught up or sidetracked by irrelevant details.

84. Is cheerful, happy (low placement implies depression).

85. Tends to communicate through actions, deeds, and non-verbal behavior, rather than through words.

86. Handles anxiety and conflicts by, in effect, refusing to recognize their presence; repressive or dissociative tendencies (tends to convince himself/herself that unpleasant thoughts and feelings do not exist; fools self into thinking all is well, when all is not well).

87. Tends to interpret clear-cut, simple situations in complicated ways.

88. Is personally charming.

89. Compares self with others; is alert to real or imagined differences between self and others in status, appearance, achievement, abilities, and so forth.
90. Is concerned with philosophical problems, for example, religions, values, free will, the meaning of life, and so forth.
91. Is power oriented; values power in self and others.
92. Has social poise and presence; appears socially at ease.
93a. Behaves in a masculine style or manner.
93b. Behaves in a feminine style or manner (If person is male, rate 93a; if person is female, rate 93b. The cultural definitions of masculinity and femininity are intended here).
94. Expresses hostility, angry feelings directly (low placement implies someone who is unable to express hostility, who holds angry feelings in).
95. Gives advice; concerns self with other people's business.
96. Values own independence and autonomy; emphasizes his/her freedom to think and act without interference or help from others.
97. Is an unemotional person; is emotionally bland; tends not to experience strong emotions (low placement implies an emotional person).
98. Is verbally fluent; can express ideas well in words.
99. Is self-dramatizing; histrionic (theatrical; prone to exaggerate feelings; behaves in attention-getting ways).
100. Does not vary roles; relates to everyone in the same way (low placement implies role variability, a person who acts differently with different people).

ORIENTATION AND INSTRUCTIONS (APPLICABLE TO BOTH THE CAQ AND CCQ)

The CAQ—or the CCQ—uses a procedure for describing persons, known as Q-sorting, different from ordinary rating methods. The general procedure, described in detail next, is to distribute Q cards, each of which contains one of the 100 descriptors comprising the Q-set, into nine categories that range from those most descriptive or salient for a particular adult or preadolescent to those least descriptive or negatively salient for that person. The guiding question in completing a Q-sort is, "Which cards are most characteristic or salient with respect to the person and which cards are most uncharacteristic or negatively salient with reference to the person?" The Q-sort method is oriented toward the individual, describing the distinguishing characteristics of the particular person. It does not judge a person in comparison with other persons. Instead, in Q-sorting, the assessor is asked to think only of the person to be described and to make observations or evaluations important for others to know to understand that person. The observations or evaluations are expressed by the ordering of the descriptors, the CAQ items (or CCQ items). The descriptors judged most distinguishing, as most important to know about a person—whether positively salient or negatively salient—move toward the extremes of the underlying salience continuum.

The personality descriptors in the Q-set permit a comprehensive and configured portrait of the person. The Q descriptors are written in a behavioral format wherever possible (e.g., the person acts . . . , does . . . , behaves . . .) Some descriptors, however, require one to make a best guess or inference about the person. In interpreting the Q descriptors, the Q-sorter should not search deeply for hidden meanings in the child's behavior; instead the more observable qualities of the person should be the focus.

Especially with the CCQ, some Q descriptors refer to person qualities often not yet developed or ascertainable because of his or her age. For example, descriptors concerned with empathy, moral issues, guilt, and differentiation of emotional response are all attributes expected to be placed generally low for 3- or 4-year-old children but may be expected to rise in salience with age. Because of different individual rates of maturity, some children will show some of these emerging behaviors earlier than other children, and the extent of such development should be noted by descriptor placement in the Q-sort of the particular child.

Specific Instructions for Q-Sorting

In the Q-sort procedure, a specified number of Q descriptors must be placed in each of nine categories, ranging from Category 9 (*most descriptive*) to Category 1 (*least descriptive*). In placing the descriptors, the assessor should be aware that the use of either the extremely high or extremely low categories (i.e., Categories 9 or 8 and 1 or 2) is tantamount to making a very strong statement about the characteristics of the person. The "degree" of a personality quality is expressed in a Q-sort by the extremeness of a descriptor's position rather than by the use of modifying adverbs. For example, if the item, "Is neat and orderly," is placed in Category 9 as a *most descriptive* statement, the assessor is implying that the person is overly fussy and excessively fastidious. If, however, the same descriptor is placed in Category 1 as a *least descriptive* item, the assessor is implying that the person is perceived as extremely sloppy and messy. Or as another example, if the Q descriptor "Is curious and exploring, eager to learn, open to new experiences," is placed in Category 9, it indicates the person is perceived as extremely curious and seeking of new experiences. Conversely, if the descriptor is placed in Category 1, the person is being described as without curiosity, unmotivated by new situations and uninterested in new experiences. Extremely placed descriptors, at either extreme, are the most salient and most informative in conveying understanding of the person being described.

Descriptors placed in the middle categories (Categories 4, 5, and 6) can be of three kinds:

1. Some middle-positioned descriptors are so placed because the particular characteristic is of little salience for understanding the person.
2. Some middle-positioned descriptors are so placed because they are sometimes true and sometimes not so true. In such cases, placing a descriptor in a middle category expresses its average importance.
3. Some middle-positioned descriptors are so placed because the person assessor has little or no information or is uncertain about the behaviors or qualities involved. In describing a person, there may be some aspects of the person uncertain to evaluate. Such descriptors should be placed in the middle where, by virtue of the statistical procedures subsequently used, they will carry the least quantitative weight.

A psychologically complex picture of a person is conveyed by the *constellation* of Q descriptors. Often it is the larger context in which a descriptor is placed that will influence the interpretive meaning of that descriptor. By considering the different attributes surrounding a common item, very different impressions may emerge. A dynamically implicative picture of the person is created by the constellation of items.

Procedure for Q-Sorting

You have been given nine envelopes, labeled as follows:

Category 9. These descriptors are *most descriptive or salient*.
Category 8. These descriptors are *very descriptive or salient*.
Category 7. These descriptors are *quite descriptive or salient*.
Category 6. These descriptors are *somewhat descriptive or salient*.
Category 5. These descriptors are *neither descriptively salient nor undescriptively salient*.
Category 4. These descriptors are *somewhat undescriptive or unsalient*.
Category 3. These descriptors are *quite undescriptive or unsalient*.
Category 2. These descriptors are *very undescriptive or unsalient*.
Category 1. These descriptors are *most undescriptive or unsalient*.

The 100 cards are to be arranged into nine categories, corresponding to these labeled envelopes. How to proceed:

1. Lay the nine envelopes out across a table in numerical order so that you can keep the two ends of the distribution and the

meanings of the categories clearly in mind as you sort the cards.

2. Take the deck of Q cards and shuffle them a bit first.

3. Go through all of the Q cards and arrange them first into three piles: one pile for the statements that impress you as descriptive of the particular person being evaluated, one pile for those that impress you as not descriptive of the person, and a middle pile for those items in between these two extremes. It does not make any difference at this point how many cards are put into each of these three piles, but it will be a bit more convenient subsequently if each pile contains about the same number of cards.

4. Now, take the pile containing the cards that describe the person and from this pile pick out the five cards that are the most descriptive of him/her. Place these cards on top of envelope Number 9. Do not put them inside yet, as later you may wish to switch some of your selections.

5. Next, from the same pile, pick the eight cards you think are very descriptive of the person and place these on top of envelope Number 8.

6. Next, pick the 12 cards you consider as quite descriptive of the person and put these on top of envelope Number 7. If you do not have enough cards in your "descriptive" pile to complete Category 7, you may have to borrow some descriptors from your middle pile that, comparatively, are more descriptive than the remainder.

7. Now, shift to the opposite end of the continuum. Take the pile containing cards categorized as not descriptive and pick out those five cards that are least descriptive of the person. Put these on top of envelope Number 1.

8. Then pick out the eight cards that are very undescriptive and put them on envelope Number 2.

9. Now, pick out the 12 cards that are quite undescriptive and put them on envelope Number 3. As needed, you may have to borrow some Q descriptors from your middle pile that, comparatively, are less salient than the remainder.

10. In all, you should now have 50 cards left over. These are now to be sorted into three piles: 16 cards that are somewhat descriptive of the person (to be placed on envelope Number 6), 16 cards that are somewhat undescriptive of the person (to be placed on envelope Number 4), leaving 18 cards that are neither descriptive nor undescriptive of the person (to be placed on envelope Number 5).

11. Most important! Now you should check the Q descriptors in each of the nine piles to see if the correct number of cards is in each category. Review the cards and consider whether you feel satisfied with your psychological portrait of the designated person. If you now wish to revise the position of any card, do so by exchanging it for another in an adjacent pile, but be sure that you wind up with the right number of descriptors in each pile. When you have adjusted or "tuned" your description of the person to your satisfaction, put the cards into their particular envelope.

12. Put the nine envelopes containing the Q-sort into the large envelope carrying the person's name or code number. Check the identification to ensure that your Q description will be registered as applying to the person described.

Experience over several years indicates that the time taken to complete a Q-sort is from 20 to 40 minutes. The first Q-sorts by an assessor take longer, but with practice the time required drops appreciably. A list of the Q descriptors accompanies the instructions so that the list can be scanned and the sorter can become familiar with the range of psychological characteristics tapped by the descriptors. The sorter is given a separate set of cards and envelopes for each individual to be described.

CAQ PROTOTYPES

Given the CAQ description of an individual, it becomes of interest to evaluate the extent to which this configured person description is congruent with various interesting-person concepts or criteria or *prototypes* already expressed configurationally through CAQ descriptors. The *degree of congruence* between the CAQ-sort of an individual and a CAQ prototype is readily evaluated by simply correlating the person's CAQ description with the conceptual prototype. The correlation values indicate the degree of similarity of the individual with respect to particular configured concepts or constructs. Such correlations, treated as *scores*, have multiple uses in clinical and research analyses.

Prototypes are easily and dependably constructed, as described in chapter 9. Five illustrative and useful prototypes immediately follow, each with reproducibility (reliability) above .9, derived from the prototype definitions of multiple clinicians. Others, as desired, may be readily formulated. In presenting the conceptual prototypes, to first provide a psychological sense of each one, the 13 most positively related descriptors of the prototype and the 13 most negatively related descriptors are indicated, followed by a full listing of the category values for each of the 100 Q descriptors.

THE CAQ OPTIMAL ADJUSTMENT PROTOTYPE

CAQ Items Positively Related to the Optimal Adjustment Prototype

35	Has warmth; capacity for close relationships.	9
2	Is a genuinely dependable and responsible person.	9
60	Has insight into own motives and behavior.	9
26	Is productive; gets things done.	9
64	Socially perceptive of interpersonal cues.	9
70	Behaves in an ethically consistent manner.	8
96	Values own independence and autonomy.	8
77	Appears straightforward, candid.	8
83	Able to see to the heart of important problems.	8
17	Behaves in a sympathetic or considerate manner.	8
33	Calm, relaxed in manner.	8
51	Genuinely values intellectual and cognitive matters.	8
3	Has a wide range of interests.	8

CAQ Items Negatively Related to the Optimal Adjustment Prototype

55	Is self-defeating.	1
22	Feels a lack of personal meaning in life.	1
86	Denies unpleasant thoughts and experiences.	1
78	Feels cheated and victimized by life.	1
45	Brittle ego defense; maladaptive under stress.	1
76	Projects own feelings and motivations onto others.	2
97	Is emotionally bland.	2
38	Has hostility toward others.	2
36	Is subtly negativistic; undermines and obstructs.	2
37	Is guileful and deceitful; manipulative.	2
48	Keeps people at a distance, avoids relationships.	2
68	Is basically anxious.	2
40	Is vulnerable to real or fancied threat; fearful.	2

THE CAQ MALE PARANOID PROTOTYPE

CAQ Items Positively Related to the Male Paranoia Prototype

49	Is basically distrustful.	9
76	Projects own feelings and motivations onto others.	9
23	Extrapunitive; tends to transfer or project blame.	9
38	Has hostility toward others.	9

TABLE A.1

CAQ Optimal Adjustment Prototype Listing

Descriptor Number	1	2	3	4	5	6	7	8	9	10	11	12	13	14	15	16	17	18	19	20
Prototype Value	6	9	8	5	7	5	5	6	3	3	6	3	3	4	7	6	8	6	9	5
Descriptor Number	21	22	23	24	25	26	27	28	29	30	31	32	33	34	35	36	37	38	39	40
Prototype Value	5	1	3	5	3	9	3	7	6	4	5	7	8	4	9	2	2	2	5	2
Descriptor Number	41	42	43	44	45	46	47	48	49	50	51	52	53	54	55	56	57	58	59	60
Prototype Value	4	3	6	7	1	5	3	2	3	4	8	6	4	5	1	7	7	7	4	9
Descriptor Number	61	62	63	64	65	66	67	68	69	70	71	72	73	74	75	76	77	78	79	80
Prototype Value	3	5	4	9	4	7	5	2	4	8	6	4	4	6	6	2	8	1	3	7
Descriptor Number	81	82	83	84	85	86	87	88	89	90	91	92	93	94	95	96	97	98	99	100
Prototype Value	5	5	8	7	5	1	4	6	4	6	5	7	6	6	5	8	2	6	4	4

48	Keeps people at a distance, avoids relationships.	9
68	Is basically anxious.	8
13	Is thin skinned; sensitive to criticism or insult.	8
41	Is moralistic.	8
24	Prides self on being "objective," rational.	8
72	Concerned with own personal adequacy.	8
79	Tends to ruminate and have preoccupying thoughts.	8
91	Is power oriented.	8
87	Particularizes situations.	8

CAQ Items Negatively Related to the Male Paranoia Prototype

21	Arouses nurturant feelings in others.	1
35	Has warmth; capacity for close relationships.	1
58	Enjoys sensuous experiences.	1
14	Genuinely submissive; accepts domination comfortably.	1
60	Has insight into own motives and behavior.	1
54	Emphasizes being with others; gregarious.	2
77	Appears straightforward, candid.	2
17	Behaves in a sympathetic or considerate manner.	2
18	Initiates humor.	2
33	Calm, relaxed in manner.	2
84	Is cheerful.	2
5	Behaves in a giving way with others.	2
28	Tends to arouse liking and acceptance.	2

THE CAQ FEMALE HYSTERIC PROTOTYPE

CAQ Items Positively Related to the Female Hysteric Prototype

86	Denies unpleasant thoughts and experiences.	9
99	Is self-dramatizing; histrionic.	9
93	Is sex typed (masculine/feminine).	9
12	Tends to be self-defensive.	9
63	Judges self and others in conventional terms.	9
9	Is uncomfortable with uncertainty and complexities.	8
54	Emphasizes being with others; gregarious.	8
68	Is basically anxious.	8
72	Concerned with own personal adequacy.	8
10	Anxiety and tension find outlet in bodily symptoms.	8
19	Seeks reassurance from others.	8
59	Concerned with body and adequacy of its functioning.	8
41	Is moralistic.	8

TABLE A.2

CAQ Male Paranoid Prototype Listing

Descriptor Number	1	2	3	4	5	6	7	8	9	10	11	12	13	14	15	16	17	18	19	20
Prototype Value	7	3	4	5	2	6	6	6	7	4	4	7	8	1	3	5	2	2	3	4
Descriptor Number	21	22	23	24	25	26	27	28	29	30	31	32	33	34	35	36	37	38	39	40
Prototype Value	1	4	9	8	6	5	6	2	3	3	5	4	2	6	1	6	5	9	7	7
Descriptor Number	41	42	43	44	45	46	47	48	49	50	51	52	53	54	55	56	57	58	59	60
Prototype Value	8	4	3	7	7	6	3	9	9	5	5	6	3	2	6	3	5	1	5	1
Descriptor Number	61	62	63	64	65	66	67	68	69	70	71	72	73	74	75	76	77	78	79	80
Prototype Value	5	5	4	5	4	4	3	8	7	4	7	8	6	6	4	9	2	7	8	3
Descriptor Number	81	82	83	84	85	86	87	88	89	90	91	92	93	94	95	96	97	98	99	100
Prototype Value	5	5	4	2	5	6	8	4	7	6	8	4	5	3	6	7	4	5	5	6

CAQ Items Negatively Related to the Female Hysteric Prototype

79	Tends to ruminate and have preoccupying thoughts.	1
94	Expresses hostile feelings directly.	1
1	Is critical, skeptical, not easily impressed.	1
83	Able to see to the heart of important problems.	1
60	Has insight into own motives and behavior.	1
77	Appears straightforward, candid.	2
90	Concerned with philosophical problems.	2
35	Has warmth; capacity for close relationships.	2
16	Is introspective.	2
33	Calm, relaxed in manner.	2
62	Tends to be rebellious and nonconforming.	2
64	Socially perceptive of interpersonal cues.	2
39	Thinks and associates ideas in unusual ways.	2

THE CAQ EGO-RESILIENCY PROTOTYPE

CAQ Items Positively Related to Ego-Resiliency Prototype

60	Has insight into own motives and behavior.	9
35	Has warmth; capacity for close relationships.	9
92	Has social poise and presence.	9
26	Is productive; gets things done.	9
33	Calm, relaxed in manner.	9
15	Is skilled in social techniques of imaginative play.	8
64	Socially perceptive of interpersonal cues.	8
83	Able to see to the heart of important problems.	8
2	Is a genuinely dependable and responsible person.	8
56	Responds to humor.	8
96	Values own independence and autonomy.	8
28	Tends to arouse liking and acceptance.	8
18	Initiates humor.	8

CAQ Items Negatively Related to the Ego-Resiliency Prototype

86	Denies unpleasant thoughts and experiences.	1
34	Overreactive to minor frustrations, irritable.	1
9	Is uncomfortable with uncertainty and complexities.	1
55	Is self-defeating.	1
45	Brittle ego defense; maladaptive under stress.	1
22	Feels a lack of personal meaning in life.	2

TABLE A.3

CAQ Female Hysteric Prototype Listing

	1	2	3	4	5	6	7	8	9	10	11	12	13	14	15	16	17	18	19	20
Descriptor Number	1	2	3	4	5	6	7	8	9	10	11	12	13	14	15	16	17	18	19	20
Prototype Value	1	3	3	7	4	6	7	4	8	8	4	9	6	4	6	2	4	5	8	6
Descriptor Number	21	22	23	24	25	26	27	28	29	30	31	32	33	34	35	36	37	38	39	40
Prototype Value	5	3	6	4	5	3	5	5	3	6	6	3	2	5	2	7	6	7	1	6
Descriptor Number	41	42	43	44	45	46	47	48	49	50	51	52	53	54	55	56	57	58	59	60
Prototype Value	8	4	7	3	6	5	4	5	4	6	3	4	4	8	6	5	4	4	8	1
Descriptor Number	61	62	63	64	65	66	67	68	69	70	71	72	73	74	75	76	77	78	79	80
Prototype Value	6	2	9	2	4	5	6	8	6	3	5	8	7	7	3	6	2	5	2	7
Descriptor Number	81	82	83	84	85	86	87	88	89	90	91	92	93	94	95	96	97	98	99	100
Prototype Value	5	7	1	7	7	9	3	5	7	2	5	5	9	1	5	3	5	4	9	4

78	Feels cheated and victimized by life.	2
79	Tends to ruminate and have preoccupying thoughts.	2
40	Is vulnerable to real or fancied threat; fearful.	2
97	Is emotionally bland.	2
30	Gives up and withdraws from frustration, adversity.	2
68	Is basically anxious.	2
100	Does not vary roles; relates to all in same way.	2

THE CAQ UNDERCONTROL PROTOTYPE

CAQ Items Positively Related to the Undercontrol Prototype

53	Unable to delay gratification.	9
65	Characteristically pushes limits.	9
20	Has a rapid personal tempo; behaves and acts quickly.	9
50	Unpredictable and changeable behavior, attitudes.	9
62	Tends to be rebellious and nonconforming.	9
43	Is facially and/or gesturally expressive.	8
94	Expresses hostile feelings directly.	8
58	Enjoys sensuous experiences.	8
67	Is self-indulgent.	8
82	Has fluctuating moods.	8
3	Has a wide range of interests.	8
39	Thinks and associates ideas in unusual ways.	8
56	Responds to humor.	8

CAQ Items Negatively Related to the Undercontrol Prototype

25	Tends toward overcontrol of needs and impulses.	1
97	Is emotionally bland.	1
6	Is fastidious (perfectionist).	1
2	Is a genuinely dependable and responsible person.	1
42	Delays or avoids action.	1
9	Is uncomfortable with uncertainty and complexities.	2
24	Prides self on being "objective," rational.	2
41	Is moralistic.	2
33	Calm, relaxed in manner.	2
14	Genuinely submissive; accepts domination comfortably.	2
79	Tends to ruminate and have preoccupying thoughts.	2
70	Behaves in an ethically consistent manner.	2
63	Judges self and others in conventional terms.	2

TABLE A.4

CAQ Ego-Resiliency Prototype Listing

	1	2	3	4	5	6	7	8	9	10	11	12	13	14	15	16	17	18	19	20
Descriptor Number	1	2	3	4	5	6	7	8	9	10	11	12	13	14	15	16	17	18	19	20
Prototype Value	6	8	7	5	6	5	5	7	1	3	6	3	3	3	8	6	6	8	4	5
Descriptor Number	21	22	23	24	25	26	27	28	29	30	31	32	33	34	35	36	37	38	39	40
Prototype Value	5	2	3	6	3	9	4	8	7	2	5	7	9	1	9	3	4	4	6	2
Descriptor Number	41	42	43	44	45	46	47	48	49	50	51	52	53	54	55	56	57	58	59	60
Prototype Value	3	3	6	7	1	5	4	3	4	4	6	7	3	5	1	8	7	7	4	9
Descriptor Number	61	62	63	64	65	66	67	68	69	70	71	72	73	74	75	76	77	78	79	80
Prototype Value	4	5	4	8	5	7	4	2	4	7	6	5	4	6	6	4	7	2	2	6
Descriptor Number	81	82	83	84	85	86	87	88	89	90	91	92	93	94	95	96	97	98	99	100
Prototype Value	5	4	8	7	5	1	3	6	5	6	5	9	5	5	5	8	2	6	4	2

TABLE A.5

CAQ Undercontrol Prototype Listing

Descriptor Number	1	2	3	4	5	6	7	8	9	10	11	12	13	14	15	16	17	18	19	20
Prototype Value	3	1	8	7	5	1	3	5	2	5	4	4	6	2	7	3	4	7	4	9
Descriptor Number	21	22	23	24	25	26	27	28	29	30	31	32	33	34	35	36	37	38	39	40
Prototype Value	5	5	6	2	1	3	4	5	3	5	6	4	2	7	6	4	6	6	8	3
Descriptor Number	41	42	43	44	45	46	47	48	49	50	51	52	53	54	55	56	57	58	59	60
Prototype Value	2	1	8	4	5	6	3	3	4	9	4	7	9	7	5	8	7	8	4	4
Descriptor Number	61	62	63	64	65	66	67	68	69	70	71	72	73	74	75	76	77	78	79	80
Prototype Value	4	9	2	6	9	7	8	5	6	2	4	5	7	5	4	6	6	4	2	7
Descriptor Number	81	82	83	84	85	86	87	88	89	90	91	92	93	94	95	96	97	98	99	100
Prototype Value	5	8	5	6	7	3	3	6	5	3	5	6	5	8	5	6	1	6	7	3

APPENDIX B

THE CALIFORNIA CHILD Q-SET (CCQ)

PURPOSE

The California Child Q-set is a language instrument designed to permit comprehensive personality descriptions of a child or preadolescent in a form suitable for subsequent quantitative comparison and analysis. It consists of a standard set of 100 person descriptors, together with instructions for commensurately ordering these descriptors to describe a specifically designated child or preadolescent.

Child and preadolescent characterizations are formulated by knowledgeable psychologically oriented appraisers: teachers, psychiatrists, therapists, personality assessors, parents, college students, or other persons knowing the individual being assessed.

THE CCQ DESCRIPTORS: THE CCQ-SET
(SPECIFIED 9-POINT DISTRIBUTION:
5, 8, 12, 16, 18, 16, 12, 8, 5; N = 100)

CCQ Descriptors

1. Prefers nonverbal methods of communication.
2. Is considerate and thoughtful of other children.
3. Is warm and responsive.
4. Gets along well with other children.
5. Is admired and sought out by other children.
6. Is helpful and cooperative.
7. Seeks physical contact with others (touching, hugging, holding, or being held).
8. Tends to keep thoughts, feelings, or products to self.
9. Develops genuine and close relationships.
10. Has transient interpersonal relationships; is fickle.
11. Attempts to transfer blame to others.
12. Reverts to more immature behavior when under stress (e.g., whines, sucks thumb, has tantrums, etc.; when placed very low, implies pseudomature behavior under stress).
13. Characteristically pushes and tries to stretch limits; sees what he/she can get away with.
14. Is eager to please.
15. Shows concern for moral issues, for example, reciprocity, fairness, and the welfare of others. (N.B. For children, this item shows developmental trends. At early ages this item would be placed low for most children; it would be expected to rise in salience over time.)
16. Tends to be pleased with and proud of his/her products and accomplishments.
17. Girls: Behaves in a feminine style and manner.
Boys: Behaves in a masculine style and manner. (N.B. The cultural and subcultural standard should be applied.)
18. Expresses negative feelings toward peers directly and openly. (N.B. Frequency or amount of negative feeling is not at issue; this item is concerned with directness of expression.)
19. Is open and straightforward (when placed low, implies sneakiness or deceit).
20. Tries to take advantage of others.
21. Tries to be the center of attention (e.g., by showing off, demonstrating accomplishments, volunteering, etc.).
22. Tries to manipulate others by ingratiation (e.g., by charm, coyness, or seductiveness).

23. Is fearful and anxious.
24. Tends to brood and ruminate or worry.
25. Uses and responds to reason.
26. Is physically active.
27. Is visibly deviant from peers in appearance, size, or physical condition (e.g., markedly tall or short, under- or overweight, physically handicapped).
28. Is vital, energetic, lively.
29. Is protective of others.
30. Tends to arouse liking and acceptance in adults.
31. Shows a recognition of the feelings of others; is empathic. (N.B. For children this item shows developmental trends. At early ages this item would be placed low for most children; it would be expected to rise in salience over time.)
32. Tends to give, lend, and share (when placed very low, implies retentiveness).
33. Cries easily.
34. Is restless and fidgety.
35. Is inhibited and constricted.
36. Is resourceful in initiating activities.
37. Likes to compete; tests and compares self against others.
38. Has unusual thought processes; thinks and perceives in uncommon ways. (N.B. Quality of thinking is not evaluated; see item 96 for quality rating.)
39. Tends to become rigidly repetitive or immobilized when under stress.
40. Is curious and exploring, eager to learn, open to new experiences.
41. Is persistent in activities; does not give up easily (when placed very high, implies perseveration).
42. Is an interesting, arresting child.
43. Can recoup or recover after stressful experiences.
44. When in conflict or disagreement with others; tends to yield and give in.
45. Tends to withdraw and disengage when under stress.
46. Tends to go to pieces under stress, becomes rattled and disorganized.
47. Has high standards of performance for self.
48. Seeks reassurance from others about his/her worth or adequacy.
49. Shows specific mannerisms or behavioral rituals (e.g., taps fingers, has tics, bites nails, bites lips, thumb sucks, stutters, etc.).
50. Has bodily symptoms as a function of tension and conflict (e.g., headaches, stomach aches, nausea, etc.).

51. Is agile and well coordinated.
52. Is physically cautious.
53. Tends to be indecisive and vacillating.
54. Has rapid shifts in mood; is emotionally labile.
55. Is afraid of being deprived; is concerned about getting enough (e.g., with respect to affection, food, toys, etc.).
56. Is jealous and envious of others.
57. Tends to dramatize or exaggerate mishaps.
58. Is emotionally expressive (facially, gesturally, or verbally).
59. Is neat and orderly in dress and behavior (when placed very high, implies fussiness and overconcern).
60. Becomes anxious when the environment is unpredictable or poorly structured.
61. Tends to be judgmental of the behavior of others.
62. Is obedient and compliant.
63. Has a rapid personal tempo; reacts and moves quickly. (N.B. Brightness is not necessarily implied; only speed of response is at issue.)
64. Is calm and relaxed; easygoing.
65. Is unable to delay gratification; cannot wait for satisfactions (when placed low, implies needless or excessive delay).
66. Is attentive and able to concentrate.
67. Is planful; thinks ahead.
68. Appears to have high-intellectual capacity (whether or not expressed in achievement).
69. Is verbally fluent; can express ideas well in language.
70. Daydreams; tends to get lost in reverie.
71. Looks to adults for help and direction.
72. Has a readiness to feel guilty; puts blame on self (whether verbalized or not; this item would be placed low for most children; it would be expected to rise in salience over time).
73. Responds to humor.
74. Becomes strongly involved in what he/she does.
75. Is cheerful (when placed low, implies unhappiness, despondency).
76. Can be trusted; is dependable.
77. Appears to feel unworthy; thinks of self as "bad."
78. Is easily offended; sensitive to ridicule or criticism.
79. Tends to be suspicious and distrustful of others.
80. Teases other children (including siblings).
81. Can acknowledge unpleasant experiences and admit to own negative feelings. (N.B. For children this item shows developmental trends. At early ages this item would be placed low

for most children; it would be expected to rise in salience over time.)

82. Is self-assertive.
83. Seeks to be independent and autonomous.
84. Is a talkative child. (N.B. No reference to verbal quality or fluency is intended; only the amount of talk is at issue.)
85. Is aggressive (physically or verbally).
86. Likes to be by himself/herself, enjoys solitary activities.
87. Tends to imitate and take over the characteristic manners and behaviors of those admired.
88. Is self-reliant, confident; trusts own judgment.
89. Is competent, skillful.
90. Is stubborn.
91. Is inappropriate in emotive behavior (reactions are excessive, insufficient, or out of context).
92. Is physically attractive, good looking.
93. Behaves in a dominating manner with others.
94. Tends to be sulky or whiny.
95. Overreacts to minor frustrations; is easily irritated and/or angered.
96. Is creative in perception, thought, work, or play (a judgment of creative quality, rather than intelligence per se, is intended).
97. Has an active fantasy life.
98. Is shy and reserved; makes social contacts slowly.
99. Is reflective; thinks and deliberates before speaking or acting.
100. Is easily victimized by other children; tends to be treated as a scapegoat.

ORIENTATION AND INSTRUCTIONS

The orientation and instructions provided for the California Adult Q-set (CAQ) largely apply as well to the CCQ and should be followed.

The Q descriptors permit a comprehensive and configured portrait of the child or preadolescent. The Q descriptors are written in a behavioral format wherever possible (e.g., the person acts . . . , does . . . , behaves . . .). Some descriptors, however, require making a best guess or inference about the person. In interpreting the Q descriptors, the appraiser should not search deeply for hidden meanings in the child's or preadolescent's behavior; instead, the more observable qualities of the person should be the focus.

Especially with the CCQ, some Q descriptors refer to person qualities often not yet developed or ascertainable because of his or her age. For example, descriptors concerned with empathy, concern with moral issues, guilt, and differentiation of emotional response are all attributes expected to be placed generally low for 3- or 4-year-old children but may be expected to rise in salience with age. Because of different individual rates of maturity, some children will show some of these emerging behaviors earlier than other children, and the extent of such development should be noted by descriptor placement in the Q-sort of the particular child.

CCQ PROTOTYPES

As with the CAQ, given the CCQ description of a child, it becomes of interest to evaluate the extent to which this configured child description is congruent with various interesting child concepts or criteria or *prototypes* already expressed configurationally through CCQ descriptors. The *degree of congruence* is readily evaluated by simply correlating the child's CCQ description with the conceptual prototype, also expressed configurationally through CCQ descriptors. The correlation values indicate the relative similarity of the child with respect to particular configured concepts or constructs. Such scores have multiple uses in clinical and research analyses.

Prototypes are easily and dependably constructed, as described in chapter 9. To illustrate, the list that follows contains useful CCQ prototypes, each with substantial reproducibility, derived from multiple clinicians. Others, as needed, may be readily formulated. The correlation of actual CCQ descriptions with such CCQ prototypes can provide diagnoses or numerical scores on various dimensions of interest.

In presenting the conceptual prototypes, to first provide a psychological sense of each one, the several most positively related descriptors of the prototype and the several most negatively related descriptors are indicated, followed by a complete listing of the category values for each Q descriptor.

THE CCQ PROSOCIAL PROTOTYPE

CCQ Items Positively Related to the Prosocial Prototype

2	Is considerate and thoughtful of other children.	9
4	Gets along well with other children.	9
15	Shows concern for moral issues (fairness, reciprocity).	9
31	Recognizes the feelings of others; is empathic.	9
32	Tends to give, lend, and share.	9
6	Is helpful and cooperative.	8
9	Develops genuine and close relationships.	8
29	Is protective of others.	8
3	Is warm and responsive.	8

76	Can be trusted; is dependable.	8
5	Is admired and sought out by other children.	8
30	Tends to arouse liking and acceptance in adults.	8
14	Is eager to please.	8

CCQ Items Negatively Related to the Prosocial Prototype

56	Is jealous and envious of others.	1
85	Is aggressive (physically or verbally).	1
10	Has transient interpersonal relationships; is fickle.	1
20	Tries to take advantage of others.	1
79	Tends to be suspicious and distrustful of others.	1
13	Characteristically pushes and tries to stretch limits.	2
77	Appears to feel unworthy; thinks of self as "bad."	2
94	Tends to be sulky or whiny.	2
98	Is shy and reserved; makes social contacts slowly.	2
91	Is inappropriate in emotive behavior.	2
80	Teases other children (including siblings).	2
95	Overreacts to minor frustrations; is easily irritated.	2
11	Attempts to transfer blame to others.	2

THE CCQ ATTENTION-DEFICIT/HYPERACTIVITY DISORDER (ADHD) PROTOTYPE

CCQ Items Positively Related to the ADHD Prototype

13	Characteristically pushes and tries to stretch limits.	9
26	Is physically active.	9
34	Is restless and fidgety.	9
63	Has a rapid personal tempo; reacts and moves quickly.	9
65	Is unable to delay gratification.	9
84	Is a talkative child.	8
95	Overreacts to minor frustrations; is easily irritated.	8
54	Has rapid shifts in mood; is emotionally labile.	8
28	Is vital, energetic, lively.	8
70	Daydreams; tends to get lost in reverie.	8
80	Teases other children (including siblings).	8
85	Is aggressive (physically or verbally).	8
11	Attempts to transfer blame to others.	8

CCQ Items Negatively Related to the ADHD Prototype

| 30 | Tends to arouse liking and acceptance in adults. | 1 |
| 62 | Is obedient and compliant. | 1 |

TABLE B.1

CCQ Prosocial Prototype Listing

	1	2	3	4	5	6	7	8	9	10	11	12	13	14	15	16	17	18	19	20
Descriptor No.	1	2	3	4	5	6	7	8	9	10	11	12	13	14	15	16	17	18	19	20
Prototype Value	4	9	8	9	8	8	7	3	8	1	2	4	2	8	9	7	5	3	7	1
Descriptor No.	21	22	23	24	25	26	27	28	29	30	31	32	33	34	35	36	37	38	39	40
Prototype Value	5	4	3	3	7	5	4	6	8	8	9	9	4	4	3	7	5	4	4	7
Descriptor No.	41	42	43	44	45	46	47	48	49	50	51	52	53	54	55	56	57	58	59	60
Prototype Value	5	6	6	7	3	3	6	6	4	4	5	5	4	4	4	1	4	6	6	5
Descriptor No.	61	62	63	64	65	66	67	68	69	70	71	72	73	74	75	76	77	78	79	80
Prototype Value	5	6	5	7	3	7	5	5	6	4	6	6	7	5	7	8	2	4	1	2
Descriptor No.	81	82	83	84	85	86	87	88	89	90	91	92	93	94	95	96	97	98	99	100
Prototype Value	6	5	5	7	1	4	5	6	6	3	2	5	3	2	2	6	5	2	6	3

66	Is attentive and able to concentrate.	1
67	Is planful; thinks ahead.	1
99	Is reflective; deliberates before speaking or acting.	1
25	Uses and responds to reason.	2
35	Is inhibited and constricted.	2
64	Is calm and relaxed, easygoing.	2
4	Gets along well with other children.	2
5	Is admired and sought out by other children.	2
31	Recognizes the feelings of others; is empathic.	2
52	Is physically cautious.	2
59	Is neat and orderly in dress and behavior.	2

THE CCQ INTERNALIZING PROTOTYPE

CCQ Items Positively Related to the Internalizing Prototype

98	Is shy and reserved; makes social contacts slowly.	9
72	Has a readiness to feel guilty; puts blame on self.	9
35	Is inhibited and constricted.	9
45	Tends to withdraw and disengage when under stress.	9
50	Has bodily symptoms as a function of stress.	9
78	Is easily offended; sensitive to ridicule or criticism.	8
24	Tends to brood and ruminate or worry.	8
77	Appears to feel unworthy; thinks of self as "bad."	8
48	Seeks reassurance about his/her worth or adequacy.	8
70	Daydreams; tends to get lost in reverie.	8
86	Likes to be by himself/herself, enjoys solitary activities.	8
23	Is fearful and anxious.	8
47	Has high standards of performance for self.	8

CCQ Items Negatively Related to the Internalizing Prototype

82	Is self-assertive.	1
63	Has a rapid personal tempo; reacts and moves quickly.	1
88	Is self-reliant, confident; trusts own judgment.	1
93	Behaves in a dominating manner with others.	1
85	Is aggressive (physically or verbally).	1
37	Likes to compete, tests and compares self with others.	2
18	Expresses negative feelings directly and openly.	2
21	Tries to be the center of attention.	2
75	Is cheerful (low placement implies unhappiness).	2
26	Is physically active.	2
13	Characteristically pushes and tries to stretch limits.	2

TABLE B.2

CCQ ADHD Prototype Listing

Descriptor No.	1	2	3	4	5	6	7	8	9	10	11	12	13	14	15	16	17	18	19	20
Prototype Value	5	3	4	2	2	3	6	5	3	7	8	7	9	5	3	5	6	6	5	6
Descriptor No.	21	22	23	24	25	26	27	28	29	30	31	32	33	34	35	36	37	38	39	40
Prototype Value	7	6	4	5	2	9	5	8	4	1	2	4	7	9	2	5	4	6	4	6
Descriptor No.	41	42	43	44	45	46	47	48	49	50	51	52	53	54	55	56	57	58	59	60
Prototype Value	3	6	4	3	5	7	4	5	4	6	3	2	4	8	6	4	6	6	2	7
Descriptor No.	61	62	63	64	65	66	67	68	69	70	71	72	73	74	75	76	77	78	79	80
Prototype Value	7	1	9	2	9	1	1	4	4	8	3	4	5	5	4	3	6	7	5	8
Descriptor No.	81	82	83	84	85	86	87	88	89	90	91	92	93	94	95	96	97	98	99	100
Prototype Value	4	6	4	8	8	5	5	3	3	7	6	5	7	7	8	5	5	3	1	7

| 28 | Is vital, energetic, lively. | 2 |
| 65 | Is unable to delay gratification. | 2 |

THE CCQ EGO-RESILIENCY PROTOTYPE

CCQ Items Positively Related to the Ego-Resiliency Prototype

28	Is vital, energetic, lively.	9
36	Is resourceful in initiating activities.	9
40	Is curious eager to learn, open to new experiences.	9
88	Is self-reliant, confident; trusts own judgment.	9
43	Can recoup or recover after stressful experience.	9
96	Is creative in perception, thought, work, or play.	8
25	Uses and responds to reason.	8
66	Is attentive and able to concentrate.	8
73	Responds to humor.	8
89	Is competent, skillful.	8
9	Develops genuine and close relationships.	8
19	Is open and straightforward.	8
69	Is verbally fluent; can express ideas well.	8

CCQ Items Negatively Related to the Ego-Resiliency Prototype

35	Is inhibited and constricted.	1
77	Appears to feel unworthy; thinks of self as "bad."	1
39	Becomes rigidly repetitive or immobilized under stress.	1
46	Tends to go to pieces under stress.	1
91	Is inappropriate in emotive behavior.	1
100	Is easily victimized or scapegoated by other children.	2
11	Attempts to transfer blame to others.	2
23	Is fearful and anxious.	2
45	Tends to withdraw and disengage when under stress.	2
50	Has bodily symptoms as a function of stress.	2
60	Becomes anxious in unpredictable environment.	2
94	Tends to be sulky or whiny.	2
95	Overreacts to minor frustrations; is easily irritated.	2

THE CCQ UNDERCONTROL PROTOTYPE

CCQ Items Positively Related to the Undercontrol Prototype

| 10 | Has transient interpersonal relationships; is fickle. | 9 |
| 54 | Has rapid shifts in mood; is emotionally labile. | 9 |

TABLE B.3

CCQ Internalizing Prototype Listing

Descriptor No.	1	2	3	4	5	6	7	8	9	10	11	12	13	14	15	16	17	18	19	20
Prototype Value	4	6	4	3	3	6	5	7	4	4	3	6	2	6	6	4	4	2	4	3
Descriptor No.	21	22	23	24	25	26	27	28	29	30	31	32	33	34	35	36	37	38	39	40
Prototype Value	2	4	8	8	6	2	5	2	4	5	6	4	7	4	9	3	2	7	7	3
Descriptor No.	41	42	43	44	45	46	47	48	49	50	51	52	53	54	55	56	57	58	59	60
Prototype Value	4	4	4	7	9	7	8	8	7	9	3	7	6	5	6	5	5	4	6	7
Descriptor No.	61	62	63	64	65	66	67	68	69	70	71	72	73	74	75	76	77	78	79	80
Prototype Value	5	6	1	3	2	6	6	5	5	8	7	9	3	5	2	5	8	8	5	3
Descriptor No.	81	82	83	84	85	86	87	88	89	90	91	92	93	94	95	96	97	98	99	100
Prototype Value	5	1	3	3	1	8	6	1	4	5	5	5	1	6	5	5	7	9	6	7

TABLE B.4

CCQ Ego-Resiliency Prototype Listing

Descriptor No.	1	2	3	4	5	6	7	8	9	10	11	12	13	14	15	16	17	18	19	20
Prototype Value	3	6	7	6	6	6	4	3	8	3	2	3	3	4	6	7	5	6	8	3
Descriptor No.	21	22	23	24	25	26	27	28	29	30	31	32	33	34	35	36	37	38	39	40
Prototype Value	5	3	2	3	8	6	3	9	5	7	7	6	4	3	1	9	5	6	8	9
Descriptor No.	41	42	43	44	45	46	47	48	49	50	51	52	53	54	55	56	57	58	59	60
Prototype Value	6	7	9	3	2	1	6	3	3	2	6	4	3	3	3	3	3	7	5	2
Descriptor No.	61	62	63	64	65	66	67	68	69	70	71	72	73	74	75	76	77	78	79	80
Prototype Value	3	5	5	5	3	8	7	6	8	4	4	4	8	6	6	7	1	3	3	3
Descriptor No.	81	82	83	84	85	86	87	88	89	90	91	92	93	94	95	96	97	98	99	100
Prototype Value	7	6	7	5	4	4	4	9	8	5	1	5	5	2	2	8	7	4	7	2

58	Is emotionally expressive.	9
63	Has a rapid personal tempo; reacts and moves quickly.	9
65	Is unable to delay gratification.	9
95	Overreacts to minor frustrations; is easily irritated.	8
13	Characteristically pushes and tries to stretch limits.	8
21	Tries to be the center of attention.	8
26	Is physically active.	8
34	Is restless and fidgety.	8
82	Is self-assertive.	8
84	Is a talkative child.	8
12	Reverts to more immature behavior when under stress.	8

CAQ Items Negatively Related to the Undercontrol Prototype

35	Is inhibited and constricted.	1
41	Is persistent in activities; does not give up easily.	1
52	Is physically cautious.	1
86	Likes to be by himself/herself; enjoys solitary activities.	1
99	Is reflective; deliberates before speaking or acting.	1
72	Has a readiness to feel guilty; puts blame on self.	2
39	Becomes rigidly repetitive or immobilized under stress.	2
24	Tends to brood and ruminate or worry.	2
62	Is obedient and compliant.	2
66	Is attentive and able to concentrate.	2
67	Is planful; thinks ahead.	2
98	Is shy and reserved; makes social contacts slowly.	2
8	Tends to keep thoughts, feelings, or products to self.	2

A COMMON LANGUAGE CCQ VERSION

Developed by Caspi et al. (1992), the following CCQ version was created for lay, nonprofessional respondents. The text requires obvious, slight gender changes as appropriate.

Common Language CCQ Descriptors

1. She shows her thoughts and feelings in the way she looks and acts, but she does not talk much about what she thinks and about how she feels.
2. She is considerate and thoughtful of other people.
3. She is a warm person and responds with kindness to other people.

TABLE B.5

CCQ Undercontrol Prototype Listing

Descriptor No.	1	2	3	4	5	6	7	8	9	10	11	12	13	14	15	16	17	18	19	20
Prototype Value	5	4	6	4	3	3	7	2	3	9	5	8	8	4	3	6	5	5	5	5
Descriptor No.	**21**	**22**	**23**	**24**	**25**	**26**	**27**	**28**	**29**	**30**	**31**	**32**	**33**	**34**	**35**	**36**	**37**	**38**	**39**	**40**
Prototype Value	8	7	5	2	3	8	4	7	3	4	4	5	7	8	1	6	5	7	2	8
Descriptor No.	**41**	**42**	**43**	**44**	**45**	**46**	**47**	**48**	**49**	**50**	**51**	**52**	**53**	**54**	**55**	**56**	**57**	**58**	**59**	**60**
Prototype Value	1	7	5	4	3	6	4	4	3	3	5	1	3	9	4	5	7	9	3	3
Descriptor No.	**61**	**62**	**63**	**64**	**65**	**66**	**67**	**68**	**69**	**70**	**71**	**72**	**73**	**74**	**75**	**76**	**77**	**78**	**79**	**80**
Prototype Value	3	2	9	3	9	2	2	4	5	4	3	2	7	4	7	3	4	5	4	5
Descriptor No.	**81**	**82**	**83**	**84**	**85**	**86**	**87**	**88**	**89**	**90**	**91**	**92**	**93**	**94**	**95**	**96**	**97**	**98**	**99**	**100**
Prototype Value	5	8	7	8	8	1	5	4	4	4	4	4	5	4	8	7	7	2	1	3

4. She gets along well with other people.
5. Other kids look up to her and seek her out.
6. She is helpful and cooperates with other people.
7. She likes physical affection. For example, she likes to hug; she likes to be held.
8. She likes to keep her thoughts and feelings to herself.
9. She makes good and close friendships with other people.
10. Her friendships don't last long; changes friends a lot.
11. She tries to blame other people for things she has done.
12. She starts to act immature when she faces difficult problems or when she is under stress (e.g., she whines or has tantrums).
13. She tries to see what and how much she can get away with. She usually pushes limits and tries to stretch the rules.
14. She tries hard to please other people.
15. She shows concern about what's right and what's wrong. For example, she tries to be fair.
16. She is proud of the things she's done and made.
17. She acts very masculine.
18. She lets other kids know it when she's upset or angry. She doesn't hold back her feelings.
19. She is open and straightforward.
20. She tries to take advantage of other people.
21. She tries to be the center of attention. For example, by showing off, or by offering to do things.
22. She tries to get others to do what she wants by playing up to them. She acts charming to get her way.
23. She is nervous and fearful.
24. She worries about things for a long time.
25. She thinks things out and you can explain things to her as you can explain to a grown-up.
26. She is physically active. She enjoys running, playing, and exercise.
27. She looks different from other kids her own age. For example, she is much taller or shorter, under- or overweight, or physically handicapped (if she doesn't look different, put this card in the middle pile).
28. She is energetic and full of life.
29. She is protective of others. She protects people who are close to her.
30. Most adults seem to like her.
31. She is able to feel how others feel; she put herself in their place.
32. She gives, lends, and shares things.

33. She cries easily.
34. She is restless and fidgety; she has a hard time sitting still.
35. She holds things in. She has a hard time expressing herself; she's a little bit uptight.
36. She finds ways to make things happen and get things done.
37. She likes to compete; she's always testing and comparing herself to other people.
38. She has an unusual way of thinking about things. For better or for worse, she puts things together in her head in a different way than other people would.
39. She freezes up when things are stressful, or else she keeps doing the same thing over and over.
40. She is curious and exploring; she likes to learn and experience new things.
41. She is determined in what she does; she does not give up easily.
42. She is an interesting child; people notice her and remember her.
43. She can bounce back or recover after a stressful or bad experience.
44. She gives in or backs up when she has conflict or disagreement with others.
45. When she is under stress, she gives up and backs off.
46. She tends to go to pieces under stress; she gets rattled when things are tough.
47. She has high standards for herself. She needs to do very well in the things she does.
48. She needs to have people tell her what she's doing well or okay. She is not very sure of herself.
49. She has specific habits or patterns of behavior. For example, she taps her fingers on table, bites fingernails, stutters, bites lips (if she doesn't do this, then put this card in the middle pile).
50. She tends to get sick when things go wrong or when there is a lot of stress. For example, she gets headaches, stomach aches, throws up (if she doesn't do any of this, then put the card in the middle pile).
51. She is well-coordinated. For example, she does well in sports.
52. She is careful not to get hurt physically.
53. She has a hard time making up her mind; she changes her mind a lot.
54. Her moods are unpredictable; they change often and quickly.
55. She worries about not getting her shares of toys, food, or love. She seems afraid she won't get enough.

56. She is jealous and envious; she wants what other people have.
57. She exaggerates about things that happen to her; she blows things out of proportion.
58. She openly shows the way she feels, whether good or bad. She shows her emotions openly.
59. She is neat and orderly in the way she dresses and acts.
60. She gets nervous if she's not sure what is going to happen or when it is not clear what she's supposed to do.
61. She judges other people; she has very strong opinions about the things other people do.
62. She is obedient and does what she is told.
63. She is fast paced; she moves and reacts to things quickly.
64. She is calm and relaxed; easygoing.
65. When she wants something, she wants it right away. She has a hard time waiting for things she wants and likes.
66. She pays attention well and concentrates on things.
67. She plans things ahead; she thinks before she does something. She "looks before she leaps."
68. She is a very smart kid even though her grades in school might not show this.
69. She has a way with words; she can express herself well with words.
70. She daydreams; she often gets lost in thoughts or a fantasy world.
71. She often asks grown-ups for help and advice.
72. She often feels guilty; she is quick to blame herself, even though she might not talk about it.
73. She has a sense of humor; she likes to laugh at funny things.
74. She usually gets wrapped up in what she is doing.
75. She is cheerful.
76. She can be trusted; she's reliable and dependable.
77. She feels unworthy; she has a low opinion of herself.
78. Her feelings get hurt easily if she is made fun of or criticized.
79. She is suspicious, she doesn't really trust other people.
80. She teases and picks on other kids (including her own brothers and sisters).
81. She can talk about unpleasant things that have happened to her.
82. She speaks up and sticks up for herself; she goes after what she wants.
83. She tries to be independent and do things without the help of other people, she tries not to rely on other people.
84. She is a talkative child; she talks a lot.

85. She is aggressive. For example, she picks fights or starts arguments.
86. She likes to be by herself; she enjoys doing things alone.
87. She tries to copy and act like the people she admires and looks up to.
88. She is self-confident and sure of herself; she makes up her own mind on her own.
89. She's able to do many things well; skillful.
90. She is stubborn.
91. Her emotions don't seem to fit the situation. For example, she either overreacts, doesn't seem to care, or sometimes her reactions just don't make sense.
92. She is attractive, good looking.
93. She's bossy and likes to dominate other people.
94. She whines or pouts often.
95. She lets little problems get to her and she is easily upset. It doesn't take much to get her irritated or mad.
96. She is creative in the way she looks at things; the way she thinks, works, or plays is creative.
97. She likes to dream up fantasies; she has a good imagination.
98. She is shy; she has a hard time getting to know people.
99. She thinks about her actions and behavior; she uses her head before doing or saying something.
100. Other kids often pick on her; she's also often blamed for things she didn't do.

APPENDIX C

THE CHILD-REARING PRACTICES REPORT (CRPR)

PURPOSE

The CRPR is a language instrument designed to permit comprehensive descriptions by parents of their child-rearing attitudes and behaviors or reports by adult children of the parenting they experienced. The information provided is in a form suitable for subsequent quantitative comparison and analysis. The CRPR consists of a standard set of 91 attitudinal or behavioral descriptors, together with instructions for commensurately ordering these descriptors to describe a parenting context. Characterizations of parenting contexts are formulated by the parents involved or an adult child, and in their quantitative form provide information generative of various analyses.

THE CRPR DESCRIPTORS: CHILD-REARING PRACTICES REPORT BY PARENT (SPECIFIED 7-STEP DISTRIBUTION: 13, 13, 13, 13, 13, 13, 13)

CRPR Descriptors

1. I respect my child's opinions and encourage him or her to express them.
2. I encourage my child always to do his/her best.
3. I put the wishes of my mate before the wishes of my child.
4. I help my child when he/she is being teased by friends.
5. I often feel angry with my child.
6. If my child gets into trouble, I expect him/her to handle the problem mostly by himself/herself.
7. I punish my child by putting him/her off somewhere by himself/herself for a while.
8. I watch closely what my child eats and when he/she eats.
9. I don't think young children of different sexes should be allowed to see each other naked.
10. I wish my spouse were more interested in our children.
11. I feel a child should be given comfort and understanding when he/she is scared or upset.
12. I try to keep my child away from children of families who have different ideas or values from our own.
13. I try to stop my child from playing rough games or doing things wherein he/she might get hurt.
14. I believe physical punishment to be the best way of disciplining.
15. I believe that a child should be seen and not heard.
16. I sometimes forget the promises I have made to my child.
17. I think it is good practice for a child to perform in front of others.
18. I express affection by hugging, kissing, and holding my child.
19. I find some of my greatest satisfactions in my child.
20. I prefer that my child not try things if there is a chance he/she will fail.
21. I encourage my child to wonder and think about life.
22. I usually take into account my preferences in making plans for the family.
23. I wish my child did not have to grow up so fast.
24. I feel a child should have time to think, daydream, and even loaf sometimes.
25. I find it difficult to punish my child.
26. I let my child make many decisions for himself/herself.

27. I do not allow my child to say bad things about his/her teachers.
28. I worry about the bad and sad things that can happen to a child as he/she grows up.
30. I teach my child that in one way or another punishment will find him/her when he/she is bad.
31. I do not blame my child for whatever happens if others ask for trouble.
32. I do not allow my child to get angry with me.
33. I feel my child is a bit of a disappointment to me.
34. I expect a great deal of my child.
35. I am easy going and relaxed with my child.
36. I give up some of my own interests because of my child.
37. I tend to spoil my child.
38. I have never caught my child lying.
39. I talk it over and reason with my child when he/she misbehaves.
40. I trust my child to behave as he/she should, even when I am not with him/her.
41. I joke and play with my child.
42. I give my child a good many duties and family responsibilities.
43. My child and I have warm, intimate times together.
44. I have strict, well-established rules for my child.
45. I think one has to let a child take many chances as he/she grows up and tries new things.
46. I encourage my child to be curious, to explore and question things.
47. I sometimes talk about supernatural forces and beings in explaining things to my child.
48. I expect my child to be grateful and appreciate all the advantages he/she has.
49. I sometimes feel that I am too involved with my child.
50. I believe in toilet training a child as soon as possible.
51. I threaten punishment more often that I actually give it.
52. I believe in praising a child when he/she is good and think it gets better results than punishing him/her when he/she is bad.
53. I make sure my child knows that I appreciate what he/she tries or accomplishes.
54. I encourage my child to talk about his/her troubles.
55. I believe children should not have secrets from their parents.
56. I teach my child to keep control of his/her feelings at all times.
57. I try to keep my child from fighting.
58. I dread answering my child's questions about sex.
59. When I am angry with my child, I let him/her know it.

60. I think a child should be encouraged to do things better than others.
61. I punish my child by taking away a privilege he/she otherwise would have had.
62. I give my child extra privileges when he/she behaves well.
63. I enjoy having the house full of children.
64. I believe that too much affection and tenderness can harm or weaken a child.
65. I believe that scolding and criticism makes my child improve.
66. I believe my child should be aware of how much I sacrifice for him/her.
67. I sometimes tease and make fun of my child.
68. I teach my child that he/she is responsible for what happens to him/her.
69. I worry about the health of my child.
70. There is a good deal of conflict between my child and me.
71. I do not allow my child to question my decisions.
72. I feel that it is good for a child to play competitive games.
73. I like to have some time for myself, away from my child.
74. I let my child know how ashamed and disappointed I am when he/she misbehaves.
75. I want my child to make a good impression on others.
76. I want my child to be independent of me.
77. I make sure I know where my child is and what he/she is doing.
78. I find it interesting and educational to be with my child for long periods.
79. I think a child should be weaned from the breast or bottle as soon as possible.
80. I instruct my child not to get dirty while he/she is playing.
81. I don't go out if I have to leave my child with a stranger.
82. I think jealousy and quarreling between brothers and sisters should be punished.
83. I think children must learn early not to cry.
84. I control my child by warning him/her about the bad things that can happen to him/her.
85. I think it is best if the mother, rather than the father, is the one with the most authority over the children.
86. I don't want my child to be looked upon as different from others.
87. I don't think children should be given sexual information before they can understand everything.
88. I believe it is very important for a child to play outside and get plenty of fresh air.

89. I get pleasure from seeing my child eating well and enjoying his/her food.
90. I don't allow my child to tease or play tricks on others.
91. I think it is wrong to insist that young boys and girls have different kinds of toys and play different sorts of games.
92. I believe it is unwise to let children play a lot by themselves without supervision from grown-ups.

PARENTAL PRACTICES REPORT (CRPR) BY CHILD (SPECIFIED 7-STEP DISTRIBUTION: 13, 13, 13, 13, 13, 13, 13)

CRPR Descriptors

These descriptors are used by the child and are provided in third person, Mother form. For use with Fathers, the items are changed to read "My father . . ."

1. My mother respected my opinions and encouraged me to express them.
2. My mother encouraged me always to do my best.
3. My mother placed my father's wishes ahead of those of her children.
4. My mother helped me when I was being teased by my friends.
5. My mother often felt angry with me.
6. When I got into trouble, I was expected to handle the problem mostly by myself.
7. My mother used to punish me by putting me off somewhere by myself for a while.
8. My mother watched closely what I ate and when I ate.
9. My mother did not believe young children of different sexes should be allowed to see each other naked.
10. My mother wished my father had been more involved in his children.
11. My mother gave me comfort and understanding when I was scared or upset.
12. My mother tried to keep me away from children of families who had different ideas or values from hers.
13. My mother did not want me to play rough games or do things wherein I might get hurt.
14. My mother believed physical punishment was the best method of discipline.
15. My mother thought a child should be seen and not heard.
16. My mother sometimes forgot the promises she made to me.

17. My mother thought it was good practice for me to perform in front of others.
18. My mother expressed affection physically, by hugging, kissing, holding me.
19. Some of my mother's greatest satisfactions were gotten from her children.
20. My mother did not want me to try things if she thought I might fail.
21. My mother encouraged me to wonder and think about life.
22. My preferences were usually taken into account in making plans for the family.
23. My mother was reluctant to see me grow up.
24. My mother felt I should have time to think, daydream, and to loaf sometimes.
25. My mother found it difficult to punish me.
26. My mother let me make many decisions for myself.
27. My mother did not allow me to say bad things about my teachers.
28. My mother worried about the bad and sad things that could happen to me as I grew up.
29. My mother taught me that in one way or another, punishment would find me when I was bad.
30. My mother did not blame me for whatever happened if others asked for trouble.
31. My mother did not allow me to get angry with her.
32. My mother felt I was a bit of a disappointment to her.
33. My mother expected a great deal of me.
34. My mother was easy going and relaxed with me.
35. My mother gave up some of her own interests because of her children.
36. My mother tended to spoil me.
37. My mother believed that I always told the truth.
38. My mother talked it over and reasoned with me when I misbehaved.
39. My mother trusted me to behave as I should, even when she was not around.
40. My mother joked and played with me.
41. My mother gave me a good many family duties and responsibilities.
42. My mother and I shared many warm, intimate times together.
43. My mother had strict, well-established rules for me.
44. My mother realized she had to let me take some chances as I grew up and tried new things.

45. My mother encouraged me to be curious, to explore and question things.
46. My mother sometimes explained things to me by talking about supernatural forces and beings.
47. My mother expected me to be grateful and appreciate all the advantages I had.
48. My mother was too wrapped up in her children.
49. My mother believed in starting toilet training as early as possible.
50. My mother threatened punishment more often than she actually gave it.
51. My mother emphasized praising me when I was good more than punishing me when I was bad.
52. My mother let me know she appreciated what I tried or accomplished.
53. My mother encouraged me to talk about my troubles.
54. My mother did not believe children should have secrets from their parents.
55. My mother encouraged me to keep control of my feelings at all times.
56. My mother discouraged me from fighting.
57. My mother dreaded answering my questions about sex.
58. My mother let me know she was angry.
59. My mother encouraged me to do things better than others.
60. My mother deprived me of privileges to punish me.
61. My mother gave me extra privileges when I was good.
62. My mother enjoyed having the house full of children.
63. My mother felt that too much affection and tenderness can harm or weaken a child.
64. My mother thought scolding and criticism would make me improve.
65. My mother let me know how much she sacrificed for me.
66. My mother sometimes used to tease and make fun of me.
67. My mother taught me that I was responsible for what happened to me.
68. My mother worried about the state of my health.
69. There was a good deal of conflict between my mother and me.
70. My mother did not allow me to question her decisions.
71. My mother believed it was good for me to play competitive games.
72. My mother liked to have time for herself—away from her children.

73. My mother used to tell me how ashamed and disappointed she felt when I misbehaved.
74. My mother wanted me to make a good impression on others.
75. My mother encouraged me to be independent of her.
76. My mother always made sure she knew where I was and what I was doing.
77. My mother found being with her children interesting and educational—even for long periods of time.
78. My mother believed a child should be weaned from the breast or bottle as soon as possible.
79. My mother expected me not to get dirty while I was playing.
80. My mother preferred to stay home when I was young rather than leave me with a stranger.
81. My mother punished me if I expressed jealousy or resentment toward my brothers or sisters.
82. My mother taught me at an early age not to cry.
83. My mother used to control what I did by warning me of all the bad things that could happen to me.
84. My mother was the one with the most authority over the children.
85. My mother did not want me looked upon as different from others.
86. My mother did not believe I should be given sexual information until I could understand everything.
87. My mother felt it was very important for me to play outdoors and get lots of fresh air.
88. My mother enjoyed seeing me eat well and enjoying my food.
89. My mother did not allow me to tease or play tricks on others.
90. My mother did not insist that young boys and girls have different kinds of toys and play different sorts of games.
91. My mother thought it unwise to let children play a lot by themselves without supervision from grown-ups.

ORIENTATION AND INSTRUCTIONS

In trying to gain more understanding of children and their development, it is important for us to know of you as a parent and what kinds of methods you use in raising your child (or how your parents responded to you as a child). You can indicate your opinions and understandings by sorting a special set of cards containing statements about bringing up children.

Procedure

In all cases when appropriate or possible, both mother and father complete the task. However, each parent does the task separately, without discussion with the other parent. Mothers and father use differently colored sets of CRPR cards. After completing the task, some parents find it interesting to discuss their CRPR-sorts, but should not change the placement of any card after this discussion. It is very important to find out the real differences, as well as similarities between mothers and fathers in their child-rearing attitudes and behavior.

The Cards and Envelopes

Each set or deck contains 91 cards. Each card contains a sentence having to do with child rearing. Some of these sentences will be true or descriptive of your attitudes and behavior in relation to your child. Some sentences will be untrue or undescriptive of your feelings and behavior toward this child. By sorting these cards according to the instructions that follow, you will be able to show how descriptive or undescriptive each sentence is for you.

Together with the cards, you have received seven envelopes, with the following labels:

7. These cards are most descriptive.
6. These cards are quite descriptive.
5. These cards are fairly descriptive.
4. These cards are neither descriptive nor undescriptive.
3. These cards are fairly undescriptive.
2. These cards are quite undescriptive.
1. These cards are most undescriptive.

Your task is to choose 13 cards that fit into each category and to put them into their proper envelopes.

How to Sort the Cards (You May Wish to Check Off Each Step as Completed)

1. Find a large cleared surface, such as a kitchen table or desk, and spread out the envelopes in a row, going from Number 7 to Number 1 (*most descriptive* to *most undescriptive*)
2. Now take the shuffled deck of cards, and read each sentence carefully. Make three piles of cards: one pile containing cards that are generally true or descriptive, one pile about which you are not certain, and one pile of cards that are generally not true or descriptive. It does not make any difference how many cards

are put in each of the three piles at this time, because there will probably be some switching around later. But it may be helpful if each pile contains about the same number of cards.

Now your cards and envelopes look like this:

| 7 | 6 | 5 | 4 | 3 | 2 | 1 envelopes |

Descriptive   Not Sure   Undescriptive
Cards   Cards   Cards

3. Now, take the pile of *descriptive* cards and pick out the 13 cards that are most descriptive of your behavior with your child. Put these cards on top of envelope Number 7. Don't put them inside yet, because you might want to shift some of them later.
4. Next, from the remaining cards in that pile, pick out 13 cards that are quite descriptive of your behavior and put these on top of envelope Number 6. (If you run out of cards from your *descriptive* pile, you'll have to add some of the more descriptive cards from your *not sure* pile).
5. Now, begin at the other end. Take the pile of *undescriptive* cards and pick out the 13 cards that are *most undescriptive* of you. Put these on top of envelope Number 1.
6. Then pick out the 13 cards which are *quite undescriptive* and put them on envelope Number 2. (Again, you may have to borrow from your *not sure* pile to get the necessary 13 cards for envelope Number 2).
7. You should now have 39 cards left over. These are to be sorted into three new piles with 13 cards in each: 13 cards that are *fairly descriptive* of you (and are to be put on envelope Number 5) and 13 cards that are *fairly undescriptive* (and are to be put on envelope Number 3). You will then have 13 cards that are neither descriptive nor undescriptive (to be put on envelope Number 4).

   You may find it hard, as others have, to put the same number of cards in each pile but you are asked to follow these directions exactly, even if you feel limited by them.
8. Now, as a final step, look over your card arrangement to see if you wish to make any changes. When the cards seem to belong where you have put them, double check to be sure there are 13 cards in each pile. Then put each pile in the proper envelope, tucking in the flaps. The small envelopes go into the larger envelope for return.

CRPR PROTOTYPES: AUTHORITARIAN–AUTOCRATIC PROTOTYPE (See Table C.1)

CRPR Items Positively Related to the Authoritarian–Autocratic Prototype

15	Believes C should be seen and not heard.	7
31	Doesn't allow C to get angry with me.	7
43	Has strict, well-established rules for C.	7
70	Doesn't allow C to question parental decisions.	7
54	Believes C should not have secrets from parents.	7
29	Teaches C punishment will find him/her when he/she is bad.	7
33	Expects a great deal of C.	7
58	When angry with C, lets him/her know it.	7
63	Too much affection/tenderness can harm/weaken C.	7
76	Know where C is and what he/she is up to.	7
82	Thinks C must learn early not to cry.	7
27	Doesn't allow C to say bad things about teacher.	7
55	Teaches C to keep control of feelings at all times.	7
64	Believes scolding and criticism makes C improve.	6
12	Insulates C from different ideas or values.	6
14	Believes physical punishment best form of discipline.	6
41	Gives C many duties and family responsibilities.	6
47	Expects C to be grateful, appreciative of advantages.	6
91	Unwise to let C play alone without grown-up supervision.	6
49	Believes in toilet training C as soon as possible.	6
74	Wants C to make good impression on others.	6
83	Controls C by warning about bad that can occur.	6
60	Punishes C by withdrawing privileges.	6
65	C should be aware of how much sacrificed for him/her.	6
78	Earliest possible weaning for C.	6
79	Instructs C not to get dirty while playing.	6

CRPR Items Negatively Related to the Authoritarian–Autocratic Prototype

40	Jokes and plays with C.	1
45	Encourages C to be curious/explore/question things.	1
77	Finds long periods with C interesting, educational.	1
22	Future plans include C's preferences.	1
32	Feels C is a bit of a disappointment to me.	1
34	Is easy going and relaxed with C.	1
1	Respects C opinions, encourages expression.	1
24	Feels C should have time to think/daydream/loaf.	1
25	Finds it difficult to punish C.	1

26	Lets C make many decisions for himself.	1
36	Tends to spoil C.	1
38	Talks it over, reasons with C when he/she misbehaves.	1
53	Encourages C to talk about his/her troubles.	1
75	Encourages C to be independent of parent.	2
88	Gets pleasure watching C eat well and enjoying food.	2
11	C should be comforted when scared.	2
52	Lets C knows attempts/accomplishments appreciated.	2
90	Sex-typed games, toys wrong for C.	2
18	Expresses affection by hugging, kissing, holding C.	2
23	Wishes C did not have to grow up fast.	2
48	Sometimes feels too involved with C.	2
4	Helps C when being teased by friends.	2
21	Encourages C to wonder and think about life.	2
42	Parent and C have warm/intimate times together.	2
51	Believes praising good better than punishing bad.	2
62	Enjoys having the house full of children	2

AUTHORITARIAN–RESPONSIVE PROTOTYPE (See Table C.2)

CRPR Items Positively Related to the Authoritarian–Responsive Prototype

1	Respects C opinions, encourages expression.	7
38	Talks it over, reasons with C when he/she misbehaves.	7
2	Encourages C to always do his/her best.	7
22	Future plans include C's preferences.	7
39	Trusts C to behave properly even when not with him.	7
45	Encourages C to be curious/explore/question things.	7
51	Believes praising good better than punishing bad.	7
52	Lets C knows attempts/accomplishments appreciated.	7
19	Finds some of greatest satisfactions in C.	7
53	Encourages C to talk about his/her troubles.	7
21	Encourages C to wonder and think about life.	7
61	Gives C extra privileges for good behavior.	7
11	C should be comforted when scared.	7
72	Likes to have some time away from C.	6
26	Lets C make many decisions for himself/herself.	6
41	Gives C many duties and family responsibilities.	6
42	Parent and C have warm/intimate times together.	6
60	Punishes C by withdrawing privileges.	6
18	Expresses affection by hugging, kissing, holding C.	6
33	Expects a great deal of C.	6
24	Feels C should have time to think/daydream/loaf.	6

TABLE C.1

Authoritarian–Autocratic Prototype Listing

1	2	3	4	5	6	7	8	9	10	11	12	13	14	15	16	17	18	19	20
10	46	46	20	46	40	44	54	54	36	24	60	32	60	70	38	42	22	26	32
21	**22**	**23**	**24**	**25**	**26**	**27**	**28**	**29**	**30**	**31**	**32**	**33**	**34**	**35**	**36**	**37**	**38**	**39**	**40**
20	14	22	10	10	10	62	32	66	34	40	14	64	12	34	10	26	10	26	18
41	**42**	**43**	**44**	**45**	**46**	**47**	**48**	**49**	**50**	**51**	**52**	**53**	**54**	**55**	**56**	**57**	**58**	**59**	**60**
60	20	70	26	18	38	60	22	58	34	20	24	10	68	62	46	40	64	48	56
61	**62**	**63**	**64**	**65**	**66**	**67**	**68**	**69**	**70**	**71**	**72**	**73**	**74**	**75**	**76**	**77**	**78**	**79**	**80**
32	20	64	62	56	38	50	34	34	70	44	42	48	58	26	64	18	56	56	36
81	**82**	**83**	**84**	**85**	**86**	**87**	**88**	**89**	**90**	**91**									
54	64	58	30	44	52	34	26	44	24	60									

35	Gives up some of own interests because of C.	6
44	Thinks C must take chances while growing.	6
58	When angry with C, lets him/her know it.	6
75	Encourages C to be independent of parent.	6
76	Know where C is and what he/she is up to.	6

CRPR Items Negatively Related to the Authoritarian–Responsive Prototype

12	Insulates C from different ideas or values.	1
27	Doesn't allow C to say bad things about teacher.	1
16	Sometimes forgets promises made to C.	1
14	Believes physical punishment best form of discipline.	1
20	Prefers C not try things chancing failure.	1
63	Too much affection/tenderness can harm/weaken C.	1
66	Sometimes teases and makes fun of C.	1
31	Doesn't allow C to get angry with me.	1
70	Doesn't allow C to question parental decisions.	1
32	Feels C is a bit of a disappointment to me.	1
55	Teaches C to keep control of feelings at all times.	1
82	Thinks C must learn early not to cry.	1
15	Believes C should be seen and not heard.	1
25	Finds it difficult to punish C.	2
49	Believes in toilet training C as soon as possible.	2
50	Threatens punishment more often than administers it.	2
64	Believes scolding and criticism makes C improve.	2
86	C given sex information only when able to understand.	2
29	Teaches C punishment will find him/her when he/she is bad.	2
57	Dreads answering C questions about sex.	2
78	Earliest possible weaning for C.	2
5	Often feels angry with C.	2
36	Tends to spoil C.	2
65	C should be aware of how much sacrificed for him/her.	2
69	Good deal of conflict between parent and C.	2
10	Wishes spouse were more interested in C.	2

INDULGENT–PERMISSIVE PROTOTYPE (See Table C.3)

CRPR Items Positively Related to the Indulgent–Permissive Prototype

24	Feels C should have time to think/daydream/loaf.	7
26	Lets C make many decisions for himself/herself.	7

TABLE C.2

Authoritarian–Responsive Prototype Listing

1	2	3	4	5	6	7	8	9	10	11	12	13	14	15	16	17	18	19	20
1	**2**	**3**	**4**	**5**	**6**	**7**	**8**	**9**	**10**	**11**	**12**	**13**	**14**	**15**	**16**	**17**	**18**	**19**	**20**
70	68	42	44	22	26	50	42	30	20	62	20	36	16	10	18	40	58	66	16
21	**22**	**23**	**24**	**25**	**26**	**27**	**28**	**29**	**30**	**31**	**32**	**33**	**34**	**35**	**36**	**37**	**38**	**39**	**40**
64	68	28	56	26	60	20	30	24	36	14	12	58	48	56	22	30	70	68	52
41	**42**	**43**	**44**	**45**	**46**	**47**	**48**	**49**	**50**	**51**	**52**	**53**	**54**	**55**	**56**	**57**	**58**	**59**	**60**
60	60	52	56	68	28	40	28	26	26	68	68	66	28	12	44	24	56	44	60
61	**62**	**63**	**64**	**65**	**66**	**67**	**68**	**69**	**70**	**71**	**72**	**73**	**74**	**75**	**76**	**77**	**78**	**79**	**80**
64	44	16	26	22	16	52	36	22	14	44	62	36	52	56	54	52	24	30	34
81	**82**	**83**	**84**	**85**	**86**	**87**	**88**	**89**	**90**	**91**									
32	12	32	30	28	26	42	36	48	48	38									

1	Respects C opinions, encourages expression.	7
11	C should be comforted when scared.	7
22	Future plans include C's preferences.	7
25	Finds it difficult to punish C.	7
36	Tends to spoil C.	7
44	Thinks C must take chances while growing.	7
34	Is easy going and relaxed with C.	7
40	Jokes and plays with C.	7
45	Encourages C to be curious/explore/question things.	7
53	Encourages C to talk about his/her troubles.	7
18	Expresses affection by hugging, kissing, holding C.	7
51	Believes praising good better than punishing bad.	6
75	Encourages C to be independent of parent.	6
21	Encourages C to wonder and think about life.	6
38	Talks it over, reasons with C when he/she misbehaves.	6
42	Parent and C have warm/intimate times together.	6
62	Enjoys having the house full of children.	6
88	Gets pleasure watching C eat well and enjoying food.	6
90	Sex-typed games, toys wrong for C.	6
39	Trusts C to behave properly even when not with him/her.	6
30	C not blamed for others troublemaking.	6
61	Gives C extra privileges for good behavior.	6
77	Finds long periods with C interesting, educational.	6
87	Believes outdoor play/fresh air very important for C.	6

CRPR Items Negatively Related to the Indulgent–Permissive Prototype

63	Too much affection/tenderness can harm/weaken C.	1
76	Know where C is and what he/she is up to.	1
78	Earliest possible weaning for C.	1
79	Instructs C not to get dirty while playing.	1
82	Thinks C must learn early not to cry.	1
91	Unwise to let C play alone without grown-up supervision.	1
43	Has strict, well-established rules for C.	1
49	Believes in toilet training C as soon as possible.	1
15	Believes C should be seen and not heard.	1
64	Believes scolding and criticism makes C improve.	1
70	Doesn't allow C to question parental decisions.	1
14	Believes physical punishment best form of discipline.	1
55	Teaches C to keep control of feelings at all times.	1
89	Doesn't allow C to tease or play tricks on others.	2
5	Often feels angry with C.	2
54	Believes C should not have secrets from parents.	2

13	Prevents rough games, other dangerous acts.	2
56	Tries to keep C from fights and fighting.	2
57	Dreads answering C questions about sex.	2
81	Sibling jealousy/quarreling punished.	2
31	Doesn't allow C to get angry with me.	2
33	Expects a great deal of C.	2
9	C of different sex shouldn't see each other naked.	2
12	Insulates C from different ideas or values.	2
27	Doesn't allow C to say bad things about teacher.	2
41	Gives C many duties and family responsibilities.	2

INDIFFERENT–UNINVOLVED PROTOTYPE (See Table C.4)

CRPR Items Positively Related to the Indifferent–Uninvolved Prototype

6	C expected to handle problems by self.	7
72	Likes to have some time away from C.	7
16	Sometimes forgets promises made to C.	7
26	Lets C make many decisions for himself.	7
75	Encourages C to be independent of parent.	7
3	Puts wishes of mate before those of C.	7
44	Thinks C must take chances while growing.	7
32	Feels C is a bit of a disappointment to me.	7
15	Believes C should be seen and not heard.	7
39	Trusts C to behave properly even when not with him/her.	7
47	Expects C to be grateful, appreciative of advantages.	7
67	Teaches C responsibility for own life.	7
87	Believes outdoor play/fresh air very important for C.	7
7	Punishes C by putting him/her off by self.	6
65	C should be aware of how much sacrificed for him/her.	6
49	Believes in toilet training C as soon as possible.	6
63	Too much affection/tenderness can harm/weaken C.	6
82	Thinks C must learn early not to cry.	6
30	C not blamed for others' troublemaking.	6
10	Wishes spouse were more interested in C.	6
24	Feels C should have time to think/daydream/loaf.	6
50	Threatens punishment more often than administers.	6
58	When angry with C, lets him/her know it.	6
70	Doesn't allow C to question parental decisions.	6
31	Doesn't allow C to get angry with me.	6
74	Wants C to make good impression on others.	6

TABLE C.3

Indulgent–Permissive Prototype Listing

1	**2**	**3**	**4**	**5**	**6**	**7**	**8**	**9**	**10**	**11**	**12**	**13**	**14**	**15**	**16**	**17**	**18**	**19**	**20**
68	42	34	50	26	44	36	30	20	46	68	20	24	10	12	46	44	62	50	40
21	**22**	**23**	**24**	**25**	**26**	**27**	**28**	**29**	**30**	**31**	**32**	**33**	**34**	**35**	**36**	**37**	**38**	**39**	**40**
60	68	52	70	68	70	18	50	28	54	22	36	22	64	52	68	46	60	56	64
41	**42**	**43**	**44**	**45**	**46**	**47**	**48**	**49**	**50**	**51**	**52**	**53**	**54**	**55**	**56**	**57**	**58**	**59**	**60**
18	58	14	68	64	42	34	40	14	38	62	52	64	26	10	24	24	60	38	28
61	**62**	**63**	**64**	**65**	**66**	**67**	**68**	**69**	**70**	**71**	**72**	**73**	**74**	**75**	**76**	**77**	**78**	**79**	**80**
54	58	16	12	36	40	42	38	28	12	44	52	34	44	62	16	54	16	16	32
81	**82**	**83**	**84**	**85**	**86**	**87**	**88**	**89**	**90**	**91**									
24	16	28	34	34	32	54	58	28	58	16									

CRPR Items Negatively Related to the Indifferent–Uninvolved Prototype

53	Encourages C to talk about his/her troubles.	1
62	Enjoys having the house full of children.	1
68	Worries about health of C.	1
13	Prevents rough games, other dangerous acts.	1
23	Wishes C did not have to grow up fast.	1
43	Has strict, well-established rules for C.	1
19	Finds some of greatest satisfactions in C.	1
91	Unwise to let C play alone without grown-up supervision.	1
76	Know where C is and what he/she is up to.	1
22	Future plans include C's preferences.	1
35	Gives up some of own interests because of C.	1
77	Finds long periods with C interesting, educational.	1
80	Doesn't go out if C has to be left with stranger.	1
61	Gives C extra privileges for good behavior.	2
40	Jokes and plays with C.	2
1	Respects C opinions, encourages expression.	2
12	Insulates C from different ideas or values.	2
56	Tries to keep C from fights and fighting.	2
88	Gets pleasure watching C eat well and enjoying food.	2
42	Parent and C have warm/intimate times together.	2
4	Helps C when being teased by friends.	2
28	Worries about bad/sad things happening as C grows up.	2
38	Talks it over, reasons with C when he/she misbehaves.	2
48	Sometimes feels too involved with C.	2
8	Watches closely what and when C eats.	2
36	Tends to spoil C.	2

A SPANISH TRANSLATION OF THE CRPR

Various translations exist. Forms exist for the Scandinavian languages. A pictorial Chinese version also exists. The following is a translation suitable for Spain and Latin America.

CHILD-REARING PRACTICES REPORT, SPANISH TRANSLATION[1]

Spanish CRPR Descriptors

1. Yo respeto las opiniones de mi niño o niña y lo o la animo que las exprese.

---

[1]Translation by Dr. Ana Almeida, aalmeida@iec.uminho.pt and Emily Leonard.

TABLE C.4

Indifferent–Uninvolved Prototype Listing

1	**2**	**3**	**4**	**5**	**6**	**7**	**8**	**9**	**10**	**11**	**12**	**13**	**14**	**15**	**16**	**17**	**18**	**19**	**20**
26	32	66	22	44	70	60	20	34	54	30	26	18	42	62	68	44	30	14	32
21	**22**	**23**	**24**	**25**	**26**	**27**	**28**	**29**	**30**	**31**	**32**	**33**	**34**	**35**	**36**	**37**	**38**	**39**	**40**
32	10	18	54	40	68	42	22	36	56	52	64	34	44	10	20	40	22	62	28
41	**42**	**43**	**44**	**45**	**46**	**47**	**48**	**49**	**50**	**51**	**52**	**53**	**54**	**55**	**56**	**57**	**58**	**59**	**60**
48	24	18	66	30	44	62	22	58	54	40	30	20	32	32	26	48	54	40	42
61	**62**	**63**	**64**	**65**	**66**	**67**	**68**	**69**	**70**	**71**	**72**	**73**	**74**	**75**	**76**	**77**	**78**	**79**	**80**
30	20	58	34	60	46	62	20	38	54	50	70	46	52	68	12	10	52	44	10
81	**82**	**83**	**84**	**85**	**86**	**87**	**88**	**89**	**90**	**91**									
38	58	44	44	50	44	62	26	36	48	14									

2. Animo a mi niño o niña que siempre haga lo mejor que pueda.

3. Los deseos de mi esposo o esposa siempre tienen el primer lugar sobre los de mi niño o niña.

4. Le ayudo a mi niño o niña cuando sus amigos lo o la molestan.

5. A menudo me enojo con mi niño o niña.

6. Cuando mi niño o niña está inquieto o inquieta, espero que por la mayor parte él mismo o ella misma resuelva sus problemas.

7. Castigo a mi niño o niña por medio de apartarlo o apartarla en un lugar solo.

8. Observo atentamente cuando come mi niño o niña y lo que come.

9. No creo que niños de diferentes sexos deben ser permitidos aL verse uno al otro desnudos.

10. Yo quisiera que mi esposo o esposa tomara más interés en nuestros niños.

11. Yo creo que un niño o una niña debe recibir consuelo y entendimiento cuando está asustado o asustada o trastornado o trastornada.

12. Yo trato de apartar a mi niño o niña de niños o familias que tienen ideas o aprecios diferentes a los nuestros.

13. Trato de detener a mi niño o niña que juegue de una manera alborotadora o que haga actividades en las que se pueda lastimar.

14. Yo creo que el castigo corporal es la mejor manera de disciplina.

15. Yo creo que un niño o niña debe ser visto o vista y no escuchado o escuchada.

16. Algunas veces olvido las promesas que le hago a mi niño o niña.

17. Yo creo que es buena práctica que un niño o niña desempeñe en frente de otros.

18. Yo expreso afecto a mi niño o niña cuando lo o la abrazo, beso, y sostengo.

19. Encuentro unas de mis más grandes satisfacciones en mi niño o niña.

20. Prefiero que mi niño o niña no trate de hacer cosas en las cuales hay peligro de fracaso.

21. Yo animo a mi niño o niña que piense y que tenga curiosidad sobre la vida.

22. Cuando hago planes para la familia usualmente tomo en cuenta mis propias preferencias.

23. Quisiera que mi niño o niña no creciera tan pronto.

24. Yo creo que un niño o niña debe de tener tiempo para pensar, hacerse ilusiones, y a veces ser perezoso o perezosa.

25. Se me hace difícil castigar a mi niño o niña.

26. Yo permito que mi niño o niña decida por sí mismo o misma.
27. No permito que mi niño o niña diga cosas malas de su maestro.
28. Yo me preocupo de las cosas malas y tristes que le pueden pasar a mi niño o niña cuando está creciendo.
29. Yo le enseño a mi niño o niña que de una forma u otra será castigado o castigada cuando se porta mal.
30. Yo no culpo a mi niño o niña por lo que pase si otros se buscan problemas con él o ella.
31. Yo no permito que mi niño o niña se enoje conmigo.
32. Yo siento que mi niño o niña me decepciona un poco.
33. Yo tengo grandes esperanzas para mi niño o niña.
34. Yo soy tolerante y tranquilo o tranquila con mi niño o niña.
35. Yo renuncio algunos de mis propios intereses por razón de mi niño o niña.
36. Tengo la tendencia de mimar a mi niño o niña.
37. Nunca he encontrado a mi niño o niña en una mentira.
38. Cuando mi niño o niña es malcriado o malcriada hablo con y trato de razonar con él o ella.
39. Tengo confianza que mi niño o niña se porte como debe, aunque no esté con él o ella.
40. Yo juego y bromeo con mi niño o niña.
41. Le doy a mi niño o niña bastantes tareas y responsabilidades familiales.
42. Mi niño o niña y yo pasamos ratos cariñosos e íntimos.
43. Yo tengo reglas estrictas y bien establecidas para mi niño o niña.
44. Yo creo que uno tiene que dejar que a menudo un niño o niña se arriesgue y que pruebe cosas nuevas mientras crece.
45. Yo animo a mi niño o niña que sea curioso o curiosa, que explore, y que haga preguntas.
46. Algunas veces hablo sobre seres y poderes sobrenaturales cuando le expliqo cosas a mi niño o niña.
47. Yo espero que mi niño o niña agradesca y aprecie todas las ventajas que tiene.
48. Algunas veces siento que estoy demasiado envuelto o envuelta en los asuntos de mi niño o niña.
49. Yo creo que un niño o niña debe ser entrenado a hacer sus necesidades tan pronto como sea posible.
50. Amenazo a mi niño o niña con el castigo más de lo que actualmente lo hago.
51. Yo creo que es mejor ensalzar un niño o niña cuando se porta bien y que eso rinde mejores resultados que castigarlo o castigarla cuando se porta mal.

52. Le doy a conocer a mi niño o niña cuanto aprecio sus pruebas y acontecimientos.
53. Animo a mi niño o niña que hable acerca de sus problemas.
54. No creo que los niños deben tener secretos aparte de sus padres.
55. Yo le enseño a mi niño o niña que siempre controle sus sentimientos.
56. Trato de evitar que mi niño o niña pelée con otros.
57. Temo a contestar las prequntas de mi niño o niña sobre el sexo.
58. Cuando me enojo con mi niño o niña se lo doy a saber.
59. Yo pienso que un niño o niña debe ser animado o animada para hacer las cosas mejor que otras personas.
60. Yo castigo a mi niño o niña evitándole un privilegio que de otra manera él o ella hubiera tenido.
61. Le doy privilegios adicionales a mi niño o niña cuando se porta bien.
62. Me gusta tener la casa llena de niños.
63. Yo creo que mucha ternura y afecto pueden dañar o debilitar a un niño o niña.
64. Yo creo que mi niño o niña se mejora con regaños y crítica.
65. Yo creo que mi niño o niña se debe dar cuenta cuanto me sacrifico por él o ella.
66. Algunas veces le molesto y me burlo de mi niño o niña.
67. Yo le enseño a mi niño o niña que él o ella es responsable por lo que le suceda.
68. Me preocupo por la salud de mi niño o niña.
69. Hay muchos conflictos entre mi niño o niña y yo.
70. No permito que mi niño o niña pregunte el porqué de mis decisiones.
71. Yo pienso que es bueno que mi niño o niña participe en juegos competitivos.
72. Me gusta estar solo o sola algunas veces, lejos de mi niño o niña.
73. Le doy a conocer a mi niño o niña lo que me decepciona y avergüenza cuando se porta mal.
74. Yo quiero que mi niño o niña tenga una buena impresión a cerca de los demás.
75. Animo a mi niño o niña que sea independiente de mí.
76. Me aseguro de donde está mi niño o niña y lo que está haciendo.
77. Lo encuentro interesante y educativo estar con mi niño o niña por largos períodos de tiempo.
78. Yo creo que un niño o niña debe ser desacostumbrado o desacostumbrada de amamantar o tomar el biberón lo más pronto posible.

79. Yo instruyo a mi niño o niña que no se ensucie mientras juega.
80. No salgo si tengo que dejar a mi niño o niña con un extraño.
81. Yo creo que los celos y las peleas entre los hermanos y hermanas deben ser castigados.
82. Yo creo que los niños deben aprender muy pronto a no llorar.
83. Yo controlo a mi niño o niña amenazándole con las cosas malas que le pueden suceder.
84. Yo creo que es mejor que la madre, en vez del padre, tenga más autoridad sobre los niños.
85. Yo no quiero que a mi niño o niña lo o la vean como diferente a otros.
86. Yo no creo que los niños deben recibir información en cuanto al sexo antes de que puedan entenderlo.
87. Yo creo que es muy importante que un niño o niña juegue afuera y que tome bastante aire fresco.
88. Me da gusto ver a mi niño o niña comer bien y gozar mientras come.
89. No permito que mis niños se molesten o que se engañen uno al otro.
90. Yo creo que es malo insistir que los niños y niñas tengan juguetes y juegos diferentes.
91. Creo que es imprudente dejar que los niños jueguen solos por mucho tiempo sin ser supervisados por adultos.

APPENDIX D

THE CALIFORNIA ENVIRONMENTAL Q-SORT (CEQ)

PURPOSE

The CEQ was developed to permit characterization of the context in which the person experientially evolved—his developmental home situation and experienced environmental and cultural surround. It expresses in Q-sort form the subjective impressions and evaluations held by the person him- or herself, or by an assessor deeply knowledgeable of the person's upbringing. Crucially, the CEQ is sorted by an individual or individuals on the basis of subjective understandings and inferences absolutely independent of any, quite separate, California Adult Q-set (CAQ) or California Child Q-set (CCQ) person descriptions that may be developed. Thus, any relation between CEQ descriptors and CAQ or CCQ descriptors represents empirical connection between the domain of psychological development and the domain of contemporary character attributes.

THE CEQ DESCRIPTORS: THE CALIFORNIA ENVIRONMENTAL Q-SET (SPECIFIED 9-POINT DISTRIBUTION: 11, 11, 11, 11, 12, 11, 11, 11, 11; N = 100)

CEQ Self-Descriptors

1. My mother and father generally share similar values and orientations.
2. *My mother is career oriented for herself.
3. I have been physically healthy throughout childhood.
4. *My mother is constructively active outside the home (e.g., employed, engaged in community activities, etc.).
5. My father is knowledgeable and competent in masculine activities and skills (e.g., handy about the house, athletic, mechanical, outdoorsy, etc.).
6. My father emphasizes the life value of physical activity, the outdoors, and nature.
7. *My mother is a respected and admired woman by community standards.
8. I am naturally physically competent.
9. *My parents emphasize manners and being proper.
10. *My family is concerned with social and political problems and causes.
11. *My mother tends to be controlled and restrained.
12. *I was reared in a stable family setting, one with a sense of permanence.
13. My home environment is well-organized, orderly, and predictable. (Note that opposite end implies disorganization, disorder, chaos.)
14. My father tends to be self-controlled and restrained.
15. *My family environment includes a significant and genuine religious element; values, ethics, and meaning are emphasized.
16. *My mother is authoritarian.
17. *My mother is knowledgeable and competent in feminine activities and skills (e.g., a good homemaker, cook, decorator, gardener, dressmaker).
18. As a child, I was disciplined by physical punishment or by threats of physical punishment.
19. My father pressures me to achieve.
20. My father is authoritarian.
21. *My mother pressures me to achieve.
22. *My mother (or mother substitute) has been generally available to me all my life. (Note that placement at opposite end

implies the absence of a motherly presence, for whatever reason.)

23. My father dominates the fundamental family decisions. (Note that opposite end implies mother dominates.)
24. *My mother is an anxious, nervous person.
25. *My mother emphasizes the life value of an intellectual orientation, of rationality in decision and outlook.
26. *My mother emphasizes the life value of status, power, and material possessions.
27. My father emphasizes the life value of an intellectual orientation, of rationality in decision and outlook.
28. My parents are inhibited about sex.
29. My father is career oriented for himself.
30. *My mother is an educated woman.
31. I have had the opportunity to be with and to communicate with my father a great deal.
32. My parents emphasize the life value of fairness, equity, ethics, and responsibility to others.
33. *My mother emphasizes the life value of tenderness, love, and related forms of interpersonal communion.
34. As a child, I was disciplined in psychological ways—by my parents withholding love or making me feel guilty.
35. I was an attractive child.
36. I have had the opportunity to be with and to communicate with my mother a great deal.
37. My father discourages my steps toward personal independence and maturity. (Note that opposite end implies encouragement and support.)
38. *There is an atmosphere of discord, conflict, and recrimination in our family.
39. *My mother discourages my steps toward personal independence and maturity. (Note that opposite end implies encouragement and support.)
40. My father is a respected and successful man by community standards.
41. My parents emphasize "togetherness," doing things as a family unit.
42. *My mother is introverted, keeps things to herself.
43. My father is introverted, keeps things to himself.
44. My father emphasizes the life value of tenderness, love, and not being aggressive.
45. *Our family has experienced many tragedies and misfortunes (e.g., illness, death, accidents).

46. As a child, I was taught what I should and should not do by being given rational explanations of the effects of my behavior.
47. My parents are restrictive of my activities.
48. My father is an anxious, nervous person.
49. I feel rejected by my mother. (Note that opposite end implies feeling favored by mother.)
50. My parents encourage me to discuss problems with them.
51. My father emphasizes the life value of status, power, and material possessions.
52. My father is knowledgeable and competent in regard to culture and the arts (e.g., music, theater, literature, decoration).
53. My father is an educated man.
54. *My mother emphasizes the life value of culture and the arts.
55. *My home environment is sophisticated and interesting.
56. I have been physically disadvantaged during my childhood and adolescence.
57. My siblings and I compete for the attention of our parents.
58. *My mother is a self-sacrificing person who gave up her own interests for the sake of her family.
59. My father is a self-sacrificing person who gave up his own interests for the sake of his family.
60. *My mother emphasizes the life value of physical activity, the outdoors, and nature.
61. *Relatives play a role in the way I am brought up.
62. *My home situation is warm and feeling oriented. (Note that opposite end implies family is cold and undemonstrative.)
63. My father teases me and is playfully contradictory.
64. I feel rejected by my father. (Note that opposite end implies feeling favored by father.)
65. *My mother teases me and is playfully contradictory.
66. My mother is knowledgeable and competent in regard to technology, science, construction, and mechanics (e.g., mechanically inclined).
67. *I experienced some form of discrimination because of race, religion, nationality, or social class as I was growing up.
68. *I experienced cultural conflict or cultural discrepancies in my childhood years.
69. *The financial condition of my family is generally comfortable. (Note that placed high, implies wealth; placed low, implies poverty.)
70. *My home is oriented toward the children and their friends. (Note that opposite end implies an adult-oriented home.)

71. *My home is a center for activities (e.g., parties, meetings, visitors, play, etc.).
72. *Communication in our family is direct and open.
73. *The atmosphere of my home is constricted and cheerless. (Note that opposite end implies family atmosphere is cheerful.)
74. *My mother enjoys her maternal role.
75. My father enjoys his paternal role.
76. *My parents emphasize the life value of conformity, acceptance by peers, popularity, and the like.
77. I am given a number of responsibilities and chores in our home.
78. *I had contact with other children when younger.
79. *My parents tend to be politically and philosophically conservative.
80. My father (or father substitute) has been generally available to me all my life. (Note that opposite end implies the absence of a fatherly presence, for whatever reasons.)
81. *My mother tends to indulge me.
82. My father tends to indulge me.
83. My mother's personal style tends to induce conflict and resentment in the children.
84. My father's personal style tends to induce conflict and resentment in the children.
85. My parents express their physical affection to one another.
86. My mother is restrictive about dating.
87. My father is restrictive about dating.
88. *My mother's limitations, needs, and vulnerabilities are apparent.
89. My father's limitations, needs, and vulnerabilities are apparent.
90. My parents have strongly held principles, opinions, prejudices, and moral convictions.
91. I reached physical maturity before many of my friends. (Note that opposite end implies reaching maturity later than most.)
92. *Our house is generally neat and well-maintained.
93. *Members of our family are generally considerate of one another's needs.
94. *My mother is effective in managing the demands made on her.
95. *Our house is a center for many kinds of activities—people are often engaged in projects, crafts, hobbies.
96. *Our house is nicely furnished.
97. *Our house tends to be crowded and cramped.
98. *I have always had space to play out-of-doors—in the yard, dead-end street, nearby playground or park.

99. *The noise level in our house tends to be high.
100. *The atmosphere of our house is friendly, informal, and inviting.

Note that asterisks denote a subset of the Environmental Q-set items completed by home observers following an interview with the mother.

ORIENTATION AND INSTRUCTIONS

"I would like you to describe the home and environmental situation in which you have grown up, using this set of cards (showing the CEQ-set deck) which contains 100 phrases useful for describing one's life background. Some of the phrases will be descriptive or true of your background and some will not be descriptive or true. Please look at each phrase and decide how well it describes your personal environment over the years.

If you look at the Q-sort board, you will see sets of boxes arranged in nine rows. When you have finished the task, you will have 11 cards in each row, except in the middle row in which you will have 12 cards. The cards will range from those that are *most descriptive* of your personal past life (point to appropriate boxes) to those that are *least descriptive* of your personal past (point to appropriate boxes).

We will start out by making three piles of cards: one pile should contain cards that are generally true or descriptive of your life circumstances; one pile should contain cards that are not true or descriptive of your life circumstances; and, in the middle, should be a pile containing cards that you are not certain about.

It does not make any difference how many cards you put in each pile the first time through, because you will probably want to do some switching around later."

(Examiner gives further instructions only when the subject has completed the initial categorizing.)

> Now, I think you will find it easiest to take the pile of descriptive cards and pick out 11 cards that are *most descriptive* or *applicable* for you. Put these cards in the boxes above Category 9. Then, find the 11 cards that are *very descriptive* or *very applicable* for you and place these in the boxes above Category 8. Next, find the 11 cards for the *quite descriptive* or *quite applicable* category.
>
> Then, it is helpful to begin at the other end. Take the pile of undescriptive cards and pick out 11 cards that are *most undescriptive* or *most inapplicable* for you. Put these cards in the boxes above Category 1. Then, pick out the next 11 cards that are *very undescriptive* or *very inapplicable* for you. Put these cards in the boxes above Category 2. Then pick out the

next 11 cards that are *quite undescriptive* or *quite inapplicable* and put them into Category 3. You will have 12 cards left, which should be placed in the middle category, Category 4.

(Note that the subject may have to borrow from his or her *not sure* pile to obtain the necessary number of cards for the more extreme categories. If the subject runs out of cards in the more extreme categories, the examiner indicates cards can be taken from the *not sure* pile but in a way that seeks to maintain the essential ordering of the cards.)

When the subject indicates the CEQ-sort is finished, the examiner says, "Take a final look at the way you have placed the cards. See if the placement expresses your description well. Now is the time to make final changes or adjustments."

(Pause for any changes the subject may make.)

"If you are finished, I will put the cards for each category in this set of envelopes. Thank you for accomplishing this task."

APPENDIX E

THE ADJECTIVE Q-SET (AJQ) FOR THE NONPROFESSIONAL SORTERS

PURPOSE

The 43-item AJQ is used by a person to describe his or her self, or ideal, or father, or mother, or ideal love object, or whatever. Using a prescribed distribution, the AJQ-sort permits the person to generate a description of his or her "target" person, which can be subsequently compared commensurately with descriptions similarly generated for the person's other "targets" (e.g., self, ideal self, ideal love object, etc).

By itself, the AJQs of different individuals are of interest when referenced to various prototypes. When the AJQs of "target" pairs are correlated (e.g., the AJQ of the person's "perceived self" correlated with the individual's AJQ of an "ideal self" or the AJQ of the "perceived self" correlated with the person's AJQ of "like-sexed parent"), these correlation values may be taken as (personally unacknowledged) expressions of various intriguing concepts (in the present instance, e.g., "self-esteem" and "identification with parent").

THE ADJECTIVE Q-SET DESCRIPTORS: THE ADJECTIVE Q-SORT
(SPECIFIED 7-STEP DISTRIBUTION: 6, 6, 6, 7, 6, 6, 6)

Adjective Q Descriptors

1. energetic, active
2. adventurous
3. affectionate, loving
4. assertive
5. ambitious, likes to do well
6. calm, relaxed
7. playful, fun to be with
8. competitive, likes to win
9. considerate, thoughtful
10. critical, not easily satisfied
11. cheerful
12. curious, questioning
13. self-centered, selfish
14. self-controlled, does not show feelings
15. generous, shares with others
16. helpful
17. creative, imaginative
18. independent
19. planful
20. orderly, neat
21. sociable
22. rebellious
23. reasonable, logical
24. reserved, shy
25. responsible
26. restless, fidgety
27. self-confident
28. show off
29. stubborn
30. sympathetic
31. talkative
32. worrying, fearful
33. feminine, ladylike
34. competent
35. distractible
36. mischievous
37. sensible, wise
38. obedient
39. impulsive

40. needs approval
41. trusting
42. gets upset easily
43. masculine, manly

ORIENTATION AND INSTRUCTIONS

"In this task, I would like you to describe your 'target person' (e.g., yourself, mother, father, love object, boss, etc.) through this set of Q cards. This adjective Q deck contains 43 adjectives or phrases that can be used to describe a person. Some of the adjectives will be descriptive or true of your target person and some will not be descriptive or true. Please look at each adjective and decide how well it describes your target person.

If you look at the Q-sort board, you will see sets of boxes arranged in seven rows. When you have finished the task, you will have six cards in each row, except the middle one in which you will have seven cards. The cards will range from those that are most descriptive of your target person (point to appropriate boxes) to those that are least descriptive of your target person (point to appropriate boxes).

Start out by making three piles of cards: One pile should contain cards that are generally true or descriptive of your target person; one pile should contain cards that are generally not true or descriptive of your target person; and, in the middle, should be a pile containing cards that you are not certain about.

It does not make any difference how many cards you put in each of the three piles the first time through, because you will probably want to do some switching around later."

(Examiner gives further instructions only when the subject has completed the initial categorizing.)

> Now, I think you will find it easiest to take the pile of descriptive cards and pick out the six cards that are *most descriptive* of your target person. Put these cards in the boxes above Category 7. Then, find the six cards for the *quite descriptive* category. Then, it is helpful to begin at the other end. Take the pile of undescriptive cards and pick out six cards that are *least descriptive* of your target person. Put these cards in the boxes above Category 1 and then pick out the next six cards that are *quite undescriptive* and put them in Category 2. The leftover cards are further arranged into the remaining three middle categories of six, seven, and six cards, following the same principles of ordering.

(Note that the subject may have to "borrow" from his or her *not sure* pile to obtain the necessary number of cards for more extreme categories. If the subject runs out of cards in the more extreme categories, the examiner indicates cards can be taken from the *not sure* pile but in a way that seeks to maintain the essential ordering of the cards.)

When subject indicates the Q-sort is finished, the examiner says, "Take a final look at the way you have placed the cards. See if the placement expresses your description well. Now is the time to make final changes or adjustments."

(Pause for any changes that the subject may wish to make.)

If you are finished, I will put the cards for each category in this set of envelopes. (At this point, the examiner puts the cards in the appropriately labeled envelopes for subsequent encoding. Each adjective is given a numerical value, depending on the category to which it was assigned by the responding person, e.g., an item placed in the *least descriptive* category receives a 1; the same item placed in the *most descriptive* category receives a 7.) This will yield 43 variables with scores ranging from Number 1 to Number 7 across all subjects. An AJQ usually requires no more than 15 minutes.

APPENDIX F

THE TEACHING STRATEGY
Q-SET (TSQ)

PURPOSE

In certain contexts, it may be important and psychologically instructive to quantitatively describe the parent when operating within a child-teaching situation. For such circumstances, a set of suitable TSQ descriptors was developed and found empirically useful in codifying adult–child interactions.

THE TEACHING STRATEGY DESCRIPTORS
(SPECIFIED 7-POINT DISTRIBUTION: 7, 7, 7, 7, 7, 7, 7; $N = 49$)

TSQ Descriptors

1. Adult is hostile.
2. Allows child to engage in nontask-oriented play.
3. Adult becomes involved in the situation.
4. Adult attends to the cognitive elements in the situation.
5. Is spontaneous with child.
6. Is straightforward and direct with child.

7. Is responsive to child's needs from moment to moment.
8. Adult's pacing of session is faster.
9. Tends toward overcontrol of own needs and impulses.
10. Expresses needs in relatively direct or undercontrolled way.
11. Adult and child express disagreements openly.
12. Handles child with kid gloves; avoids confrontation with child.
13. Adult and child engage in conversation with each other.
14. Adult is anxious about imposing authority in situation.
15. Surrenders control of situation to child.
16. Gets into power struggle with child; adult and child compete.
17. Is critical of child; rejects child's ideas and suggestions.
18. Appears ashamed of child; lacks pride in child.
19. Enjoys his or her role as teacher.
20. Appears frustrated in inability to find adequate strategies.
21. Encourages child to proceed independently.
22. Conducts session in unusual or atypical ways.
23. Seems confused about what is expected in the situation.
24. Has high standards for child.
25. Values child's originality.
26. Seems easy and relaxed in situation.
27. Gives up and retreats from difficulties; fails to cope.
28. Is supportive and encouraging of child in situation.
29. Praises child.
30. Is reserved and unexpressive.
31. Is able to establish good working relationship with child.
32. Dramatizes teaching.
33. Makes the situation fun (vs. grim or distasteful).
34. Has a clear and coherent teaching style.
35. Pressures child to work at tasks.
36. Gives the child reasons and explanations.
37. Uses physical means to communicate with child.
38. Is protective of child.
39. Is overly interested in child's performance, in child doing well.
40. Is impatient with child.
41. Adult is talkative in situation.
42. Is resourceful in helping child accomplish assigned tasks.
43. Appears to elicit child's best performance.
44. Child appears to enjoy situation.
45. Adult structures tasks at outset.
46. Adult derives pleasure from being with child.
47. Adult exploits incidental opportunities for teaching.

48. Adult intrudes physically in tasks.
49. Adult emphasizes principles and strategies involved in completing tasks (as opposed to focusing on specific solutions).

ORIENTATION AND INSTRUCTIONS

The TSQ is intended for an observer or observers of the parent who are interacting in a teaching situation with the parent's child. Conventional Q-sorting instructions apply.

APPENDIX G

CREATING A Q-SORT DECK USING MICROSOFT WORD

The **Mail Merge** feature of Microsoft Word 2003 makes it relatively easy and inexpensive to create nicely formatted Q-sort card decks. Although the general process is unfamiliar to most Word users, and involves an alternative interpretation of Microsoft computerese, the following steps should provide enough background and detail to guide one through the process.

BACKGROUND INFORMATION

Mail Merge allows merging (a) a **data file** containing the data to be printed with (b) a **template** file containing "placeholders" to be filled in by information from that **data file**. Examples of **Mail Merge** are familiar to anyone who has ever received a personalized piece of junk mail such as:

```
┌─────────────────────────────────────────────────────┐
│                                                       │
│              A C M E   M O R T G A G E                │
│                    Anytown, USA                       │
│                                                       │
│                                         Jan 6, 2007   │
│                                                       │
│   Dear David,                                         │
│                                                       │
│   According to our records, we can save you money     │
│   on your mortgage payment of $2,157 on your house    │
│   in Berkeley, CA . . .                               │
│                                                       │
└─────────────────────────────────────────────────────┘
```

ACME Mortgage started with a **template** file that might have looked something like this:

```
┌─────────────────────────────────────────────────────┐
│                                                       │
│              A C M E   M O R T G A G E                │
│                                                       │
│                    Anytown, USA                       │
│                                                       │
│                                         Jan 6, 2007   │
│                                                       │
│   Dear <<First Name>>,                                │
│                                                       │
│   According to our records, we can save you money     │
│   on your mortgage payment of $<<Amount>> on your     │
│   house in <<City>>, <<State>> . . .                  │
│                                                       │
└─────────────────────────────────────────────────────┘
```

They then used a **data file** consisting of a list of names, addresses and mortgage amounts, to "**merge**" or combine this information for each prospect with a prepared **template**, resulting in now personalized copies of their standardized letter.

This same feature can be used to create Q-sort decks with relative ease. Although Microsoft Word 2003 has been used in this example, similar steps exist for earlier versions of MS Word and will exist as well for later versions of Word. The instructions below must be followed **precisely.** If puzzlement ensues, consult a local computer sophisticate.

For creating a Q-set, the **data file** will be the list of Q descriptors for the particular Q deck; the **template** will be appropriately formatted sheets of die-cut cards on which the various Q descriptors will be printed by your computer printer. Die-cut card sheet stock is readily commercially available from such firms as Avery Office Products and can generate multiple different Q cards per die-cut card sheet. The ultimate result will be a set of die-cut card sheets on which have been printed all the Q-descriptor statements, numbered and formatted, that constitute an entire Q deck. Later, when these printed-upon die-cut sheets are easily separated, the result will be a complete set of Q-descriptor cards for that Q-set.

CREATING THE LIST OF Q DESCRIPTORS

The first step in creating the Q-sort cards is to create the **data file**, the list of Q descriptors. To create the **data file**:

1. Create a New, Blank document in Microsoft Word.
2. Enter "Q-Descriptor List" as the first line of text.
3. Enter all of the Q descriptors, one after another, starting with Line 2, numbering each one sequentially (i.e., 1, 2, 3 . . .). Although long Q descriptors may take up multiple lines, they will automatically "wrap." It is crucial that you not break up the lines yourself—let Word do it. Each Q descriptor should be separated from the next with the Enter key.
4. Save the file using a name and location that will allow you to find it again, remembering where you saved it.

You should now have something that looks like:

Q-Descriptor List

1. Is critical, skeptical, not easily impressed.
2. Is a genuinely dependable and responsible person.
3. Has a wide range of interests.
4. Is a talkative individual.
5. Behaves in a giving way toward others
   (and so forth).
6. Is thin-skinned; sensitive to anything that can be construed as criticism or an interpersonal slight.
7. Favors conservative values in a variety of areas. . . .

CREATING THE Q-SORT DECK TEMPLATE

Before you can create the **template**, you will need to choose a readily available card stock that is supported by Microsoft Word. For instance, the Avery Office Products Company makes a variety of possibilities. The Avery #3612 business card sheets consist of 8.5″ by 11″ sheets of 10 2″ by 3.5″ die-cut cards that can be easily separated into individual Q-descriptor cards after printing on your laser or inkjet printer. For larger, 3″ by 5″ index-card sized Q-descriptor cards, the Avery #5388 die-cut card stock can be chosen. Of course, 8.5″ by 11″ sheets of a nice thick paper stock and a paper cutter may be chosen instead—just print as if using an Avery card stock, and then cut the cards out manually.

After choosing the card stock to print on, you are ready to begin:

1. Start Microsoft Word 2003. You should see a new, blank document. Make sure that this is the only file that is open in Word.

2. From the Tools menu, choose **Letters and Mailings** and then select the **Mail Merge** . . . Option 3. The Mail Merge "Wizard" will be displayed along the right edge of the document.

3. In the Wizard, choose the option, **Labels,** and click **Next: Starting Document.**

4. Select the option, **Change document layout,** and click on **Label options** . . . the Label Options Dialog box will appear.

5. Choose the Avery Standard product list, and from it choose an appropriate die-cut sheet type, as discussed above. Click **OK.** The document will change to show a grid of cards of the selected size.

6. If you are satisfied with the chosen size, click **Next: Select recipients.** Otherwise, click on the **Label options** . . . selection to choose a different size.

7. After clicking **Next: Select recipients,** click on **Browse** to select the Q-descriptor **data file** you created and saved earlier, make sure it is the relevant one, and click the **Open** button to open it. The **Header Records Delimiters** dialog will appear, and you should see a preview which starts with "Q-descriptor List," and includes the first few Q descriptors underneath. Click on **OK.** The **Mail Merge Recipients** dialog will appear showing the list of Q descriptors. Click **OK** to close the dialog. The Heading Records Delimiter dialog box will then appear once again. Click **OK** once more to close it again and you will notice that the document will have been updated to show «Next Record» in all but the first card shown. Click

Next: Arrange your labels (as Word calls them) to move on to the next step.

8. Since Word does not know anything about Q descriptors, you yourself need to add the Q descriptors to the labels. To do this, choose **More Items** to display the **Insert Merge Field** dialog. You will see the dialog box, with a single item called **QDescriptor_List_** (note that Word specifically generates this particular phrase by itself).

   Now, make sure that this QDescriptor_List_ item is selected, and click **Insert.** The document will be updated to show «QDescriptor_List_» in the first cell (i.e., card position) as a placeholder for the first Q descriptor to be printed. Also, a **Close** button will appear. Click **Close** to close the **Insert Merge Field** dialog box.

9. You may now select this newly added «QDescriptor_List_» item in the first cell and format this text (i.e. Q Card) as you want all the Q cards to appear, For example, you may wish to set a bold, larger, 14-point font.

10. When the first cell is formatted as wished, click the **Update all Labels** button that appears **below** the **Replicate labels** heading in the Wizard in order to duplicate this same layout and appearance for all the cards.

11. Click on **Next: Preview your labels** below the **Replicate labels** button to see a preview of the first page of labels. If this appears OK, click **Next: Complete the merge** to complete the merge. You can click **Previous: Arrange your labels** if you wish to go back and make changes.

12. After completing the merge, you can Print from your printer already loaded with die-cut sheets, or save the resulting document for editing or printing later. In some printers, it may be necessary to insert the blank die-cut sheets to be printed in the manual feed tray.

13. For additional Q decks, simply repeat this process as often as needed.

QED!

REFERENCES

Adorno, T. W., Frenkel-Brunswik, E., Levinson, D. J., & Sanford, R. N. (1950). *The authoritarian personality*. New York: Harpers.

Ægisdottir, S., White, M. J., Spengler, P. M., Maugherman, A. S., Anderson, L. A., Cook, R. S., et al. (2006). The meta-analysis of clinical judgment project: Fifty-six years of accumulated research on clinical versus statistical prediction. *The Counseling Psychologist, 34*, 341–382.

Akse, J., Hale, W. W., III, Engels, R. C. M. E., Raaijmakers, Q. A. W., & Meeus, W. H. J. (2004). Personality, perceived parental rejection and problem behavior in adolescence. *Social Psychiatry and Psychiatric Epidemiology, 39*, 980–988.

American Psychiatric Association. (1994). *Diagnostic and statistical manual of mental disorders* (4th ed.). Washington, DC: Author.

American Psychiatric Association. (2000). *Diagnostic and statistical manual of mental disorders* (4th ed., text revision). Washington, DC: Author.

Armstrong, J. S. (2001). Combining forecasts. In J. S. Armstrong (Ed.), *Principles of forecasting: A handbook for researchers and practitioners*. (pp. 417–439). Norwell, MA: Kluwer Academic.

Asendorpf, J. B., & van Aken, M. A. (1999). Resilient, overcontrolled, and under-controlled personality prototypes in childhood: Replicability, predictive power, and the trait-type issue. *Journal of Personality and Social Psychology, 77*, 815–832.

Attneave, F. (1959). *Application of information theory to psychology*. New York: Holt-Dryden.

Baumrind, D. (1971). Current patterns of parental authority. *Developmental Psychology, 4*, 1–103.

Block, J. (1955). The difference between Q and R. *Psychological Review, 62*, 356–358.

Block, J. (1956). A comparison of the forced and unforced Q-sorting procedures. *Educational and Psychological Measurement, 16*, 481–493.

Block, J. (1957a). A comparison between ipsative and normative ratings of personality. *Journal of Abnormal and Social Psychology, 54*, 50–54.

Block, J. (1957b). A study of affective responsiveness in a lie-detection situation. *Journal of Abnormal and Social Psychology, 55*, 11–15.

Block, J. (1960). On the number of significant findings to be expected by chance. *Psychometrika, 25*, 369–380.

Block, J. (1961). *The Q-sort method in personality assessment and psychiatric research*. Springfield, IL: Charles C Thomas.

Block, J. (1965). *The challenge of response sets: Unconfounding meaning, acquiescence, and social desirability in the MMPI*. New York: Appleton-Century-Crofts.

Block, J. (1971). *Lives through time*. Berkeley, CA: Bancroft Books.

Block, J. (2004). The Stroop effect: Its relation to personality. *Personality and Individual Differences, 38*, 735–746.

Block, J., & Baker, B. O. (1957). Accuracy of interpersonal prediction as a function of judge and object characteristics. *Journal of Abnormal and Social Psychology, 54*, 37–43.

Block, J., & Bennett, L. (1955). The assessment of communication. III. Perceptions and transmission as a function of the social situation. *Human Relations, 8*, 317–325.

Block, J., & Block, J. H. (2006a). Nursery school personality and political orientation two decades later. *Journal of Research in Personality, 40*, 35–55.

Block, J., & Block, J. H. (2006b). Venturing a 30-year longitudinal study. *American Psychologist, 61*, 318–327.

Block, J., Block, J. H., & Harrington, D. M. (1974). Some misgivings about the Matching Familiar Figures Test as a measure of reflection-impulsivity. *Developmental Psychology, 10*, 611–632.

Block, J., Block, J. H., & Keyes, S. (1988). Longitudinally foretelling drug usage in adolescence: Early childhood personality and environmental factors. *Child Development, 59*, 336–355.

Block, J., & Gjerde, P. F. (1986a). Continuity and transformation in the psychological meaning of category breadth. *Developmental Psychology, 22*, 832–840.

Block, J., & Gjerde, P. F. (1986b). Distinguishing between antisocial behavior and undercontrol. In D. Olweus, J. Block, & M. Radke-Yarrow (Eds.), *Development of antisocial and prosocial behavior: Research, theories, and issues* (pp. 177–206). New York: Academic Press.

Block, J., Gjerde, P. F., & Block, J. H. (1991). Personality antecedents of depressive tendencies in 18-year-olds. *Journal of Personality and Social Psychology, 60*, 726–738.

Block, J., & Kremen, A. M. (1996). IQ and ego-resiliency: Conceptual and empirical connections and separateness. *Journal of Personality and Social Psychology, 70*, 349–361.

Block, J., & Petersen, P. (1955). Some personality correlates of confidence, caution and speed in a decision situation. *Journal of Abnormal and Social Psychology, 51*, 34–41.

Block, J., & Robins, R. W. (1993). A longitudinal study of consistency and change in self-esteem from early adolescence to early adulthood. *Child Development, 94*, 909–923.

Brown, S. R. (1980). *Political subjectivity: Applications of Q methodology in political science*. New Haven, CT: Yale University Press.

Brown, S. R. (1986). Q technique and method: Principles and procedures. In W. D. Berry & M. S. L. Beck (Eds.), *New tools for social scientists: Advances and applications in research methods* (pp. 57–76). Beverly Hills, CA: Sage.

Brown, S. R. (1993). A primer on Q methodology. *Operant Subjectivity, 16*, 91–138.

Brown, S. R. (in press). Q methodology. In L. M. Given (Ed.), *The SAGE Encyclopedia of Qualitative Research Methods*. Thousand Oaks, CA: Sage.

Burt, C. (1937). Correlation between persons. *British Journal of Psychology, 28*, 59–96.

Burt, C., & Stephenson, W. (1939). Alternative views on correlation between persons. *Psychometrika, 4*, 269–281.

Carroll, J. B. (1961). The nature of the data, or how to choose a correlation coefficient. *Psychometrika, 26*, 347–372.

Caspi, A., Block, J., Block, J. H., Klopp, B., Lynam, D., Moffitt, T. E., et al. (1992). A "common-language" version of the California Child Q-Set for personality assessment. *Psychological Assessment, 4*, 512–523.

Cattell, R. B. (1944). Psychological measurement: Ipsative, normative, and interactive. *Psychological Review, 51*, 292–303.

Cattell, R. B. (1952). The three basic factor-analytic research designs—their interrelations and derivatives. *Psychological Bulletin, 49*, 499–520.

Comrey, A. L., & Lee, H. B. (1992). *A first course in factor analysis* (2nd ed.). Hillsdale, NJ: Erlbaum.

Cronbach, L. J. (1953a). *A consideration of information theory and utility theory as tools for psychometric problems*. Urbana, IL: College of Education, University of Illinois.

Cronbach, L. J. (1953b). Correlations between persons as a research tool. In O. H. Mowrer (Ed.), *Psychotherapy and research* (pp. 376–388). New York: Ronald Press.

Cronbach, L. J., & Gleser, G. (1954). Book review of Stephenson, W. *The study of behavior. Psychometrika, 19*, 327–331.

Cronbach, L. J., & Meehl, P. E. (1955). Construct validity in psychological tests. *Psychological Bulletin, 52*, 281–302.

Dana, J., & Dawes, R. M. (2004). The superiority of simple alternatives to regression for social science prediction. *Journal of Educational and Behavioral Statistics, 29,* 317–331.

Dawes, R. M. (1977). Suppose we measured height with rating scales instead of rulers. *Applied Psychological Measurement, 1,* 267–273.

Dawes, R. M. (1989). Experience and validity of clinical judgment: The illusory correlation. *Behavioral Science and the Law, 7,* 457–467.

Dawes, R. M., Faust, D., & Meehl, P. E. (1989, March 31). Clinical versus actuarial judgment. *Science, 243,* 1668–1674.

Donahue, E. M., Robins, R. W., Roberts, B. W., & John, O. P. (1993). The divided self: Concurrent and longitudinal effects of psychological adjustment and social roles on self-concept differences. *Journal of Personality and Social Psychology, 64,* 834–846.

Efron, B. (1979). Bootstrap method: Another look at the jackknife. *Annals of Statistics, 7,* 1–26.

Efron, B., & Tibshirani, R. (1986). Bootstrap methods for standard errors, confidence intervals, and other measures of statistical accuracy. *Statistical Science, 1,* 54–77.

Epstein, S. (1993). Implications of cognitive–experiential self-theory for personality and developmental psychology. In D. C. Funder, R. D. Parke, C. Tomlinson-Keasey, & K. Widaman (Eds.), *Studying lives through time: Personality and development* (pp. 399–438). Washington, DC: American Psychological Association.

Epstein, S. (1994). An integration of the cognitive and the psychodynamic unconscious. *American Psychologist, 49,* 709–724.

Epstein, S. (2007). *Demystifying intuition: What it is, what it does, and how it does it.* Unpublished manuscript, University of Massachusetts at Amherst.

Eysenck, H. J. (1954). The science of personality: Nomothetic! *Psychological Review, 61,* 339–342.

Fabrigar, L. R., Wegener, D. T., MacCallum, R. C., & Strahan, E. (1999). Evaluating the use of exploratory factor analysis in psychological research. *Psychological Methods, 4,* 272–299.

Ferguson, G. A. (1949). On the theory of test discrimination. *Psychometrika, 14,* 61–68.

Finch, J. F., & West, S. G. (1997). The investigation of personality structure: Statistical models. *Journal of Research in Personality, 31,* 439–485.

Frances, A. (1980). The *DSM–III* personality disorders section: A commentary. *American Journal of Psychiatry, 137,* 1050–1054.

Funder, D. C. (1995). On the accuracy of personality judgment: A realistic approach. *Psychological Review, 102,* 652–670.

Funder, D. C., & Block, J. (1989). The role of ego-control, ego-resiliency, and IQ in delay of gratification in adolescence. *Journal of Personality and Social Psychology, 57,* 1041–1050.

Funder, D. C., Furr, R. M., & Colvin, C. R. (2000). The Riverside Behavioral Q-sort: A tool for the description of social behavior. *Journal of Personality, 68,* 451–489.

Garb, H. N. (1989). Clinical judgment, clinical training, and professional experience. *Psychological Bulletin, 105,* 387–396.

Garb, H. N. (1998). *Studying the clinician: Judgment research and psychological assessment*. Washington, DC: American Psychological Association.

Goldberg, L. R. (1970). Man vs. model of man: A rationale, plus some evidence, for a method of improving on clinical inferences. *Psychological Bulletin, 73*, 422–432.

Goldberg, L. R. (1991). Human mind versus regression equation: Five contrasts. In D. Cicchetti & W. M. Grove (Eds.), *Thinking clearly about psychology: Essays in honor of Paul E. Meehl: Vol. 1. Matters of public interest* (pp. 173–184). Minneapolis: University of Minnesota Press.

Goldberg, L. R. (2006). Doing it all bass-ackwards: The development of hierarchical factor structures from the top down. *Journal of Research in Personality, 40*, 347–358.

Goldberg, L. R., & Velicer, W. F. (2006). Principles of exploratory factor analysis. In S. Strack (Ed.), *Differentiating normal and abnormal personalities* (2nd ed., pp. 209–237). New York: Springer Publishing Company.

Gorsuch, R. L. (1983). *Factor analysis* (2nd ed.). Hillsdale, NJ: Erlbaum.

Grove, W. M., & Meehl, P. E. (1996). Comparative efficiency of informal (subjective, impressionistic) and formal (mechanical, algorithmic) prediction procedures: The clinical–statistical controversy. *Psychology, Public Policy, and Law, 2*, 293–323.

Grove, W. M., Zald, D. H., Lebow, B. S., Snitz, B. E., & Nelson, C. (2000). Clinical versus mechanical prediction: A meta-analysis. *Psychological Assessment, 12*, 19–30.

Guilford, J. P. (1954). *Psychometric methods*. New York: McGraw-Hill.

Haggard, E. A. (1958). *Intaclass correlation and the analysis of variance*. New York: Dryden.

Haig, B. D. (2005). Exploratory factor analysis, theory generation, and scientific method. *Multivariate Behavioral Research, 40*, 303–330.

Harman, H. H. (1976). *Modern factor analysis* (3rd ed.). Chicago: University of Chicago Press.

Hart, D., Burock, D., London, B., Atkins, R., & Bonilla-Santiago, G. (2005). The relation of personality types to physiological, behavioural, and cognitive processes. *European Journal of Personality, 19*, 391–407.

Hart, D., Hofman, V., Edelstein, W., & Keller, M. (1997). The relation of childhood personality types to adolescent behavior and development: A longitudinal study of Icelandic children. *Developmental Psychology, 33*, 195–205.

Haviland, M. G., & Reise, S. R. (1996). A California Q-set alexithymia prototype and its relationship to ego-control and ego resilience. *Journal of Psychosomatic Research, 41*, 597–608.

Helson, R. (1971). Women mathematicians and the creative personality. *Journal of Consulting and Clinical Psychology, 36*, 210–220.

Helson, R., & Srivastava, S. (2002). Creative and wise people: Similarities, differences, and how they develop. *Personality and Social Psychology Bulletin, 28*, 1430–1440.

Hofstee, W. K. B. (1994). Who should own the definition of personality? *European Journal of Personality, 8*, 149–162.

Horn, J. L. (1965). A rationale and test for the number of factors in factor analysis. *Psychometrika, 30*, 179–185.

Horowitz, L. M., Inouye, D., & Siegelman, E. Y. (1979). On averaging judge's ratings to increase their correlations with an external criterion. *Journal of Consulting and Clinical Psychology, 47*, 453–458.

John, O. P., Cheek, J. M., & Klohnen, E. C. (1996). On the nature of self-monitoring: Construct explication with Q-sort ratings. *Journal of Personality and Social Psychology, 71*, 763–776.

Jones, E. (2000). *Therapeutic action: A guide to psychoanalytic therapy.* Northvale, NJ: Jason Aronson.

Kelley, E. L., & Fiske, D. W. (1951). *The prediction of performance in clinical psychology.* Ann Arbor: University of Michigan Press.

Kirk, S. A. (2004). Are children's DSM diagnoses accurate? *Brief Treatment and Crisis Intervention, 4*, 255–270.

Klohnen, E. C. (1996). Conceptual analysis and measurement of the construct of ego-resiliency. *Journal of Personality and Social Psychology, 70*, 1067–1079.

Kobak, R., Cole, H. E., Ferenz-Gillies, R., & Fleming, W. S. (1993). Attachment and emotion regulation during mother–teen problem solving: A control theory analysis. *Child Development, 64*, 231–245.

Kremen, A. M., & Block, J. (1998). The roots of ego control in young adulthood: Links with parenting in early childhood. *Journal of Personality and Social Psychology, 75*, 1062–1075.

Kremen, A. M., & Block, J. (2002). Absorption: Construct explication by Q-sort assessments of personality. *Journal of Research in Personality, 36*, 252–259.

Kutchins, H., & Kirk, S. A. (1997). *Making us crazy. DSM: The psychiatric bible and the creation of mental disorders.* New York: Free Press.

Little, K. B. (1961). Confidence and reliability. *Educational and Psychological Measurement, 21*, 95–101.

MacLeod, C. M. (1991). Half a century of research on the Stroop effect: An integrative review. *Psychological Bulletin, 109*, 163–203.

McKeown, B., & Thomas, D. (1988). *Q methodology.* Newbury Park, CA: Sage.

McNiel, D. E., Sandberg, D. A., & Binder, R. L. (1998). The relationship between confidence and accuracy in clinical assessment of psychiatric patients' potential for violence. *Law and Human Behavior, 22*, 655–669.

Meehl, P. E. (1954). *Clinical vs. actuarial prediction: A theoretical analysis and a review of the evidence.* Minneapolis: University of Minnesota Press.

Meehl, P. E. (1956). Wanted—a good cookbook. *American Psychologist, 11*, 263–272.

Meehl, P. E. (1959). Some ruminations on the validation of clinical procedures. *Canadian Journal of Psychology, 13*, 106–128.

Meehl, P. E. (1960). The cognitive activity of the clinician. *American Psychologist, 15*, 19–27.

Meehl, P. E. (1962). Schizotaxia, schizotypy, schizophrenia. *American Psychologist, 17*, 827–838.

Meehl, P. (1992). Factors and taxa, traits and types, differences of degree and differences in kind. *Journal of Personality, 60*, 117–174.

Mischel, W., Shoda, Y., & Peake, P. K. (1988). The nature of adolescent competencies predicted by preschool delay of gratification. *Journal of Personality and Social Psychology, 54*, 687–696.

Mowrer, O. H. (1953). "Q-technique"—description, history, and critique. In O. H. Mowrer (Ed.), *Psychotherapy theory and research* (pp. 316–375). New York: Ronald Press.

Mulaik, S. A. (1972). *The foundations of factor analysis*. New York: McGraw-Hill.

Murray, H. A. (1938). *Explorations in personality*. New York: Oxford University Press.

Nunnally, J. C., & Bernstein, I. H. (1994). *Psychometric theory* (3rd ed.). New York: McGraw-Hill.

Peevers, B. H., & Secord, P. (1973). Developmental changes in attribution of descriptive concepts to persons. *Journal of Personality and Social Psychology, 27*, 120–128.

Pitman, E. J. G. (1937). Significance tests which may be applied to samples from any population. *Journal of the Royal Statistical Society Supplement, 4*, 119–130.

Reichenbach, H. (1951). *The rise of scientific philosophy*. Berkeley: University of California Press.

Robins, R. W., John, O. P., Caspi, A., Moffitt, T. E., & Stouthamer-Loeber, M. (1996). Resilient, overcontrolled, and undercontrolled boys: Three replicabled personality types. *Journal of Personality and Social Psychology, 70*, 157–171.

Sawyer, J. (1966). Measurement *and* prediction. *Psychological Bulletin, 66*, 178–200.

Scholte, R. H. J., van Lieshout, C. F. M., de Wit, C. A. M., & van Aken, M. A. G. (2005). Adolescent personality types and subtypes and their psychosocial adjustments. *Merrill-Palmer Quarterly, 51*, 258–286.

Schulz, M. S., & Waldinger, R. J. (2005). The value of pooling "naive" expertise. *American Psychologist, 60*, 656–657.

Shedler, J. (2002). A new language for psychoanalytic diagnosis. *Journal of the American Psychoanalytic Association, 50*, 429–456.

Shedler, J., & Westen, D. (1998). Refining the measurement of Axis II: A Q-sort procedure for assessing personality pathology. *Assessment, 5*, 333–353.

Shedler, J., & Westen, D. (2004). Refining personality disorder diagnosis: Integrating science and practice. *American Journal of Psychiatry, 161*, 1350–1365.

Siegelman, E., Block, J., Block, J. H., & von der Lippe, A. (1970). Antecedents of optimal psychological adjustment. *Journal of Consulting and Clinical Psychology, 35*, 283–289.

Simon, J. L. (1974). *Resampling: The new statistics* (1st ed.). Arlington, VA: Resampling Stats.

Simon, J. L. (1999). *Resampling: The new statistics* (2nd ed.). Arlington, VA: Resampling Stats.

Sines, J. O. (1970). Actuarial versus clinical prediction in psychopathology. *British Journal of Psychology, 116*, 129–144.

Stephenson, W. (1935). Correlating persons instead of tests. *Character and Personality, 4*, 17–24.

Stephenson, W. (1936). Introduction to inverted factor analysis, with some applications to studies in orexis. *Journal of Educational Psychology, 27*, 353–367.

Stephenson, W. (1953). *The study of behavior*. Chicago: University of Chicago Press.

Stern, W. (1911). *Die differentielle psychologie in ihren methodischen Grundlagen* [Methodological foundations of differential psychology]. Leipzig, Germany: Barth.

Stroop, J. R. (1935). Studies of interference in serial verbal reactions. *Journal of Experimental Psychology, 18*, 643–662.

Surowiecki, J. (2004). *The wisdom of crowds: Why the many are smarter than the few and how collective wisdom shapes business, economies, and nations*. New York: Doubleday.

Thurstone, L. L. (1944). *A factorial study of perception*. Chicago, IL: University of Chicago Press.

Thurstone, L. L. (1947). *Multiple-factor analysis: A development and expansion of the vectors of the mind*. Chicago: University of Chicago Press.

Tucker, L. R. (1966). Learning theory and multivariate experiment: Illustration by determination of generalized learning curves. In R. B. Cattell (Ed.), *Handbook of multivariate experimental psychology* (pp. 476–501). Chicago: Rand McNally.

van Aken, M. A. G., van Lieshout, C. F. M., Scholte, R. H. J., & Haselager, G. J. T. (2002). Personality types in childhood and adolescence: Main effects and person-relationship transactions. In L. Pulkkinen & A. Caspi (Eds.), *Paths to successful development: Personality in the life course* (pp. 129–156). Cambridge, England: Cambridge University Press.

Wainer, H. (1976). Estimating coefficients in linear models: It don't make no never mind. *Psychological Bulletin, 83*, 213–217.

Waldinger, R. J., Schulz, M. S., Hauser, S. T. P., Allen, J. P., & Crowell, J. A. (2004). Reading others' emotions: The role of intuitive judgments in predicting marital satisfaction, quality, and stability. *Journal of Family Psychology, 18*, 58–71.

Waller, N. (2007). A general method for computing hierarchical component structures by Goldberg's bass-ackwards method. *Journal of Research in Personality, 41*, 745–752.

Waller, N. G., & Meehl, P. E. (1998). *Multivariate taxometric procedures: Distinguishing types from continua*. Thousand Oaks, CA: Sage.

Waters, E., & Deane, K. E. (1985). Defining and assessing individual differences in attachment relationships: Q-methodology and the organization of behavior in infancy and early childhood. *Monographs of the Society for Research in Child Development, 50*, 41–65.

Westen, D., & Shedler, J. (1999a). Revising and assessing Axis II, Part I: Developing a clinically and empirically valid assessment method. *American Journal of Psychiatry, 126,* 258–272.

Westen, D., & Shedler, J. (1999b). Revising and assessing Axis II, Part II: Toward an empirically based and clinically useful classification of personality disorders. *American Journal of Psychiatry, 126,* 273–285.

Westen, D., & Shedler, J. (2006). A prototype approach to personality disorder diagnosis. *American Journal of Orthopsychiatry, 163,* 846–856.

Westen, D., & Weinberger, J. (2004). When clinical description becomes statistical prediction. *American Psychologist, 59,* 595–613.

Widiger, T. A., & Clark, L. A. (2000). Toward *DSM–V* and the classification of psychopathology. *Psychological Bulletin, 126,* 946–963.

Widiger, T. A., & Lowe, J. R. (2007). Five-factor model assessment of personality disorder. *Journal of Personality Assessment, 89,* 16–29.

Widiger, T. A., & Trull, T. J. (2007). Plate tectonics in the classification of personality disorders. *American Psychologist, 62,* 71–83.

AUTHOR INDEX

Edelstein, W., 91
Efron, B., 79
Engels, R. C. M. E., 91
Epstein, S., 104
Eysenck, H. J., 86

Fabrigar, L. R., 88
Faust, D., 93
Ferenz-Gillies, R., 80
Ferguson, G. A., 41, 52
Finch, J. F., 88
Fiske, D. W., 59n1
Fleming, W. S., 80
Frances, A., 117
Frenkel-Brunswik, E., 81
Funder, D. C., 4, 80, 111
Furr, R. M., 111

Gjerde, P. F., 80, 85, 98
Gleser, G., 31n1
Goldberg, L. R., 86, 88, 92, 95
Gorsuch, R. L., 88
Grove, W. M., 93
Guilford, J. P., 14, 51, 77

Haggard, E. A., 77
Haig, B. D., 88
Hale, W. W., III, 91
Harman, H. H., 88
Harrington, D. M., 98
Hart, D., 91
Haselager, G. J. T., 91
Hauser, S. T. P., 101n1
Haviland, M. G., 80
Helson, R., 26, 80, 98, 99
Hofman, V., 91
Horn, J. L., 89
Horowitz, L. M., 101n1

Inouye, D., 101n1

John, O. P., 91, 99
Jones, E., 111

Keller, M., 91
Kelley, E. L., 59n1
Keyes, S., 75

Kirk, S. A., 4, 41, 82
Klohnen, E. C., 80, 99
Kobak, R., 80
Kremen, A. M., 80, 98, 99
Kutchins, H., 4, 82

Lebow, B. S., 93
Lee, H. B., 88
Levinson, D. J., 81
Little, K. B., 44, 46
London, B., 91
Lowe, J. R., 10

MacLeod, C. M., 73
McKeown, B., 45n1
McNiel, D. E., 44, 46
Meehl, P. E., 10, 51, 84, 93, 94, 98, 102
Meeus, W. H. J., 91
Mischel, W., 80
Moffitt, T. E., 91
Mowrer, O. H., 19
Mulaik, S. A., 88

Nelson, C., 93
Nunnally, J. C., 14

Peake, P. K., 80
Peevers, B. H., 56
Petersen, P., 72, 98
Pitman, E. J. G., 78

Raaijmakers, Q. A. W., 91
Reichenbach, H., 62
Reise, S. P., 80
Roberts, B. W., 99
Robins, R. W., 73, 91, 99, 109

Sandberg, D. A., 44, 46
Sanford, R. N., 81
Sawyer, J., 93
Scholte, R. H. J., 14, 91
Schulz, M. S., 101n1, 102
Secord, P., 56
Shedler, J., 80, 111, 115
Shoda, Y., 80
Siegelman, E., 99, 101n1
Simon, J. L., 79

Sines, J. O., 93
Snitz, B. E., 93
Srivastava, S., 80, 99
Stephenson, W., 19, 32, 52, 84, 86
Stern, W., 14
Stouthamer-Loeber, M., 91
Stroop, J. R., 73
Surowiecki, J., 57

Thomas, D., 45n1
Thurstone, L. L., 88, 89
Tibshirani, R., 79
Trull, T. J., 4, 10
Tucker, L. R., 84

Van Aken, M. A., 14, 91
Van Lieshout, C. F. M., 14, 91
Von der Lippe, A., 99

Wainer, H., 59
Waldinger, R. J., 101n1, 102
Waller, N. G., 84, 92
Waters, E., 111
Weinberger, J., 59n1, 102
West, S. G., 88
Westen, D., 59n1, 80, 102, 111, 115
Widiger, T. A., 4, 10, 82

Zald, D. H., 93

SUBJECT INDEX

Adjective Q-set for nonprofessional
    sorters (AJQ), 108–109, 191–194
    (Appendix E)
Aggregation, 97–98, 101, 101n1
Allegations, use of term, 3
Alternative approaches to Q-sort proce-
    dure, 109–117
American Psychiatric Association,
    *Diagnostic and Statistical Manual of
    Mental Disorders*, 41, 91
    fifth edition, forthcoming, 10
    fourth edition, 117
    fourth edition, text revision, 4, 82
Apperceived recognition, and CQ
    prototype, 79–80
Appraiser, use of term, 4
Assessment psychology, 9, 26–28
Assessment research, 81
Assessor, use of term, 4
Attachment Q-sort measure (AQS), 111

Attenuation effects, 95
Attributes, use of term, 3
Average interperson correlation, and
    CQ descriptors, 37–38

Balance between costs and gains, in CQ
    procedure, 26
Baumrind, D., 107
Behavioral indicator, tied to psycholog-
    ical meaning, 12
Behavioral opposites, and CQ descrip-
    tors, 34
Bernstein, I. H., 14
Bias, in CQ descriptors, 39–40
Block, J., 70, 112
Block, J. H., 106, 112
Bootstrapping, 79
Brown, S. R., 110
Burt, C., 86–87

Calibration session, for interpretability problem, 42

California Adult Q-set (CAQ), 5, 19, 106, 119–138 (Appendix A)
criticism, 39–44
development, 31–38
Form I, 35–36
Form II, 36–37
Form III–R, 38, 42

California Child Q-set (CCQ), 5, 19, 38, 106, 139–157 (Appendix B)

California Environmental Q-sort (CEQ), 107–108, 183–189 (Appendix D)

California Q-sort (CQ)
applied illustrations, 20–28
and factor analysis, 86–92
as language for person evaluation, 17–18
methodology, 18–20, 45–53

California Q-sort (CQ) descriptors, 20, 32–35, 37–38, 40–42, 70
bias in, 39–40
development of, 35–36
interdependence among, 77–79
redundancy in, 33–35
sorting of, 19–20

California Q-sort (CQ) prototypes, 79–84
diagnostic, 82–83
illustrative uses, 81–83

Carroll, J. B., 51n2

Case conference, 59n1

Case examples, 20–28

Category placement, of CQ descriptors, 20

Cattell, R. B., 14, 87

Child-Rearing Practices Report (CRPR), 106–107, 159–182 (Appendix C)

Clinical expertise, evaluating, 101–104

Clinical formulations, and person-centered approach, 14

Clinical psychologists, and development of CAQ descriptors, 36

Clinical psychology, 93–95

Cluster analysis, 86

Commensurability, 4–6, 80n2
and fixed distribution, 46–48

Comparison, of evaluations, 20–26, 69–71

Composites, 56–58, 80n2, 98
and individual evaluation, 60–62
and prototype, 79–81

Computer software, 79n1, 84, 88, 199–203 (Appendix G)

Concentering approach, 98

Conceptual–experiential self-theory, 104

Conceptual independence, in CQ descriptors, 33

Confidence issues, 72–73

Consensual utility, 37

Consensus, 56–58
in case conference, 59n1
in development of CAQ descriptors, 35–36
forming, 59–60

Constraints, in CQ descriptors, 40–42

Continuum, in CQ descriptors, 32

Correlation among persons, in factor analysis, 88

Correlation among variables, in factor analysis, 88

Correlation coefficient, and similarity coefficient, 83–84

CQ-sort. See California Q-sort (CQ)

Creativity in women mathematicians, as example of CQ procedure, 26–28

Criterion CQ-sort. See California Q-sort (CQ) prototypes

Cronbach, L. J., 87

Dawes, R. M., 57

Descriptor configurations, 41

Diagnostic and Statistical Manual of Mental Disorders. See American Psychiatric Association, Diagnostic and Statistical Manual of Mental Disorders

Diagnostic council, 59n1

Diagnostic label, and CQ prototype, 79–80

ABOUT THE AUTHOR

Jack Block received his BA from Brooklyn College in Brooklyn, New York; his MA from the University of Wisconsin in Madison; and his PhD from Stanford University in Palo Alto, California, majoring in clinical psychology with minors in sociology and physiology. His subsequent career has been as Professor of psychology at the University of California at Berkeley.

He has published extensively. He is known for the book *Lives Through Time*, on the Berkeley longitudinal study from the 1930s; an ambitious 3-decade longitudinal research study with his late wife, Jeanne Humphrey Block (cf., e.g., "Venturing a 30-Year Longitudinal Study," in *American Psychologist*, 2006); his theoretical writings (e.g., the book *Personality as an Affect-Processing System*, 2002, and the 1982 *Child Development* article "Assimilation, Accommodation, and the Dynamics of Personality Development"); various influential methodological evaluations (e.g., the book *The Challenge of Response Sets* and the 1995 *Psychological Bulletin* critique "A Contrarian View of the Five-Factor Approach to Personality Description"); and diverse empirical contributions regarding the central constructs of resiliency and ego control. He has received the Henry A. Murray Award from the American Psychological Association's Division 8 (Society for Personality and Social Psychology) and the G. Stanley Award from Division 7 (Developmental Psychology). He has also received the award for Distinguished Scientific Contribution from the International Society for the Study of Behavioral Development.